English Essays

English Essays

SELECTED AND WITH AN INTRODUCTION

BY

J. H. LOBBAN

Essay Index Reprint Series

BOOKS FOR LIBRARIES PRESS
FREEPORT, NEW YORK

First Published 1902
Reprinted 1972

" *As we read in these delightful volumes of the* Tatler *and* Spectator *the past age returns, the England of our ancestors is revivified. The Maypole rises in the Strand again in London; the churches are thronged with daily worshippers; the beaux are gathering in the coffee-houses; the gentry are going to the drawing-room; the ladies are thronging to the toy-shops; the chairmen are jostling in the streets; the footmen are running with links before the chariots, or fighting round the theatre doors.*"— THACKERAY: English Humourists.

Library of Congress Cataloging in Publication Data

Lobban, J   H   ed.
    English essays.

    (Essay index reprint series)
    Reprint of the 1902 ed.
    1. English essays.
PR1363.L7 1972   824'.008   72-320
ISBN 0-8369-2800-8

PRINTED IN THE UNITED STATES OF AMERICA
BY
NEW WORLD BOOK MANUFACTURING CO., INC.
HALLANDALE, FLORIDA 33009

CONTENTS.

INTRODUCTION.

"A LOOSE sally of the mind; an irregular, in-
digested piece; not a regular and orderly composition "—such is Johnson's definition of an essay.
The first of these phrases admirably describes the
typical eighteenth-century essay, but the term has
so wide an application, embracing the maxims of
Bacon, the philosophy of Locke, and the loose sallies
of Steele and Addison, that the necessity is at once
obvious of drawing some broad lines of demarcation
among its various significances. The difficulty of
making any such division is probably greater in
the case of the essay than with any other generic
name employed in literature, but three leading
senses may be noted in which the term is used. It
may be modestly applied to an elaborately finished
treatise ; or, with more direct reference to its
primary meaning, it may denote the brief, general
treatment of any topic, an author's preliminary
skirmish with his subject; while again, it may
mean a short discursive article on any literary,
philosophical, or social subject, viewed from a personal or a historical standpoint. It is with essays
of the last kind that this volume deals, and its
scope is still farther limited by the exclusion of
professedly critical papers. Literary criticism is
a subject of so much importance and interest that

it must be regarded as an independent development, and the separation can be justified also on
another ground. It is no violence to literary usage
to think of the English Essayists as those who took
for their special subject-matter the varying phases
of contemporary manners and customs; and in
tracing the course of this particular kind of writing,
one meets with everything that is most characteristic in the periodical essay. The titles employed
by the earlier essayists indicate pretty clearly the
range of the subjects attempted. They hint, also,
that the essayist must possess experience of and
insight into character, a critical taste free from
pedantry, and an easy literary style. The typical
essayist must to some extent be at once a rambler,
a spectator, a tatler, and a connoisseur.

It is a suggestive fact that after the artificial
comedy of manners the next great development in
literature was the essay of contemporary manners.
It began at a time when the stage was in a state
of decline. Artificial comedy, the characteristic
product of the Restoration age, was still reeling
under the onset of Jeremy Collier. Dryden had
made a dignified apology, Congreve had prevari-
cated in vain, Farquhar, and more especially Steele,
had in some degree purified the stage, but the
theatre had no longer a paramount literary importance until Garrick appeared to act and Goldsmith
to write. When the disorderly pulses of Restoration activity had finally resumed a normal beat, a
vast change had taken place in the nature of social
life, and there was need of some new form of literature to gratify the cravings of Queen Anne society.

It was the work of the essay to supply this demand, to judiciously season culture with the requisite spice of scandal, and to exhibit the foibles of the time with a humour that should not be impure.

In tracing the course of any literary development, one is apt to exaggerate the importance of the casual coincidences to be found in the literature of different periods. Passages might be singled out from Elizabethan prose bearing a certain resemblance to the essay proper; but, as Professor Saintsbury has pointed out, importance is to be attached not to "the occasional flash here and flash there of 'modernism', but the general presence of a tendency distinctly different from that of the main body of forerunners". Bacon's essays form a collection of wonderfully shrewd and pithy observations, and have been a veritable mine of suggestions for writers since; but in no real sense can they be said to be prototypes of the eighteenth-century essay. They are, in his own words, but "certain brief notes set down rather significantly than curiously; not vulgar, but of a kind whereof men shall find much in experience and little in books". Between them and the *Tatler* there is nothing more than a nominal connection, and even to Dryden, Cowley, and Temple the *Spectator* owes but little obligation. To Dryden belongs the credit of having given modernism to English prose and of having founded literary criticism. His Prefaces are certainly essays, not dissimilar in kind to the critical papers in the *Spectator*; but then it is not in these latter that the peculiar significance of Addison's work is to be found. It is often difficult to draw a line between literary criticism and gossip about literature, but any essay in which the predominance of the former element is tolerably clear must be relegated to a different current of development from that of the periodical essay. Still, Dryden must be included among the remote pioneers of the latter, from the one fact that he made frequent use of a simple, colloquial style, intended to appeal not to a small circle of critics but to a wider and more popular audience. On the other hand it is sometimes claimed that the essay was the product of French and Italian influence, and Dr. Johnson, in his account of its origin, has singled out for mention the works of Casa, Castiglione, and La Bruyère. It is only misleading, however, to connect the essay with such a book as Casa's *Galateo*, a somewhat rambling and casuistical treatise on polite behaviour which, nearly two centuries later, found a counterpart in Chesterfield's *Letters to his Son*. Nor is it less far-fetched to attach much importance to *The Courtier* of Castiglione. That this work enjoyed a great popularity is evident from the number of its editions and translations, but it would be absurd to say that its diffuse moralizings on the character of the ideal courtier of Urbino had any sensible influence on the English essay. The *Characters* of La Bruyère, avowedly modelled on those of Theophrastus, are in many respects so admirable as to justify their mention by Johnson. They were known to both Steele and Addison, to whom they very probably suggested many subjects for treatment; but they are too fragmentary, too much after the style of the seventeenth-century "character", to be seriously included among the antecedents of the *Tatler*, and their importance still further diminishes when it is remembered that Montaigne, Bacon, Dryden, and Cowley had all written prior to them. The truth is that the only obligation the English essay owes to foreign suggestion is to the essays of Montaigne. To what extent he borrowed from Seneca and Plutarch is not worth considering, for it would be as hypercritical to engineer a parentage for Montaigne's happy egotism as to ferret out the antecedents of Pepys' *Diary*. His essays at the time were unique, and Montaigne is the first philosopher in an easy chair. It can scarcely be determined at what point his influence first made itself felt in the progress of the English essay. Bacon owed him nothing, but it is interesting to find as a connecting-link between Montaigne and Dryden that the latter, after declaring that a preface should be "rambling", admits that he learned this "from the practice of honest Montaigne". Cowley's essay, *Of Myself*, implicitly makes the same admission. Once for all the Frenchman had vindicated the essayist's right to be pleasantly discursive, and the spirit of his influence breathes in the lucubrations of Bickerstaff not more than in the essays of Hazlitt, Hunt, and Lamb. Montaigne is, indeed, the prince of tatlers. There is no questioning his right to be called the inventor of the essay form in its most general sense, but it remained for his English successors to limit its scope by prescribing a certain unity of design, and some restraint in the essayist's use of irrelevancy and egotism.

The work of Temple and Dryden is more important in connection with the development of
English prose as a whole than with respect to the
particular little bit of literary evolution here considered. Lamb pointed out the affinity between
Temple and Addison as writers of "genteel"
English, and Addison in his statelier vein clearly
shows that he had profited by Temple's courtly
style. That the aim of Temple was not dissimilar
to that of Steele and Addison may be inferred from
his own statement that he "never wrote anything
for the public without the intention of some public
good". He did not, however, make any striking
anticipation of the *Tatler's* method, and his position in literature is that, improving on Evelyn, he
pointed out the way to Dryden, who made a yet
bolder inroad on the stiffness of Elizabethan prose.
When Dryden's masculine vigour had quite broken
adrift from the influence of Euphuism, the result
was that, for the first time in the seventeenth century, there was a terse, vigorous, and to some extent homely prose. Dryden unquestionably affected
the whole subsequent history of prose literature;
but of him, as of Temple, it must be said that,
leaving criticism out of the question, he did more to
influence the style than the form of the eighteenth-
century essay. He said himself that "he could
write severely with more ease than he could write
gently", and this avowal shows how wide the gulf
really is between him and his less vehement but
sprightlier successors. "When we pass," says Mr.
Craik, "from him to Steele and Addison, we find
that the model he had formed has been adapted to

new purposes for which by its nature it was admirably fitted."

On March 8, 1702, Anne ascended the throne, and three days later the *Daily Courant*, the first regular daily newspaper, appeared, "giving all the Material News as soon as every Post arrives". It is not within the scope of this volume to treat of the growth of the newspaper press, but since at some points the essay and the newspaper come into touch, it must be observed that in one form or another papers were plentiful before the appearance of the *Tatler*. So far back as 1621 Burton complains of the prevalence and popularity of "pamphlets of news", and in Nichols' *Literary Anecdotes* there is a list of more than two hundred pamphlets and sheets of intelligence which were prior to the *Daily Courant*. Of most of these the very names are generally forgotten, though a few are famous as indicating important stages in the development of the press, or are remembered, like the *British Apollo* ridiculed by Thackeray, for the degree of absurdity they succeeded in attaining. None of them, however, influenced the essay in anything like the same degree as Defoe's *Review*; which, in a manner characteristic both of the daring nature of its author and of the feverish state of the time, was begun, in 1704, within the walls of Newgate. *The Review of the Affairs of France* became, in the course of its second volume, a tri-weekly, appearing like the *Tatler* on every Tuesday, Thursday, and Saturday, and in this form it survived until 29th July, 1712, when the Stamp Act imposed a duty of a penny per sheet. " Grub Street has

but ten days to live", wrote Swift on 19th July, and
the collapse of the *Review* was only one of an
enormous number of cases which fulfilled the *Spectator's* punning prophecy of a general "fall of the
leaf". While Defoe's *Review*, with its invention of
the leading article, its splendid versatility, and its
fearless criticism of topics of the day, must be granted
an important place in the history of journalism;
large reservation must be made when it is claimed
that its author anticipated Steele. Few writers
more than Defoe elude classification. He occupies
a tantalizing position at the threshold of two great
developments in prose literature, and it is as difficult
to deny that the *Review* led the way to the *Tatler*
as to maintain that *Pamela* was not influenced by
Crusoe or *Roxana*. Although Defoe's object was
primarily a political one, it had soon occurred to
him that some attention to society scandal would
further recommend his paper, and with this in view
he added to it the "Mercure Scandale; or Advices
from the Scandalous Club". The author of *Roxana*
was clearly the very man to preside over such a club,
but it is not surprising to find that he frequently
allowed politics to invade the society corner of his
journal, and that his gossip is characterized rather
by realistic piquancy than by any endeavour to
elevate his age. The Scandal Club may not unfairly be supposed to have suggested to Steele the
idea of using club life as a suitable framework for
his essays. The project can, indeed, be traced
farther back to the *Athenian Gazette*, but then,
even in regard to the other novel features of the
Review, Defoe humorously complains that he was

charged with being "only a Mimic of Harry Carr,
in his Weekly Packet of Advice from Rome".
"All the Wit of Mankind," he adds, "seems now to
be composed of but Imitations, and there 'is nothing
new under the sun'." Defoe's theory of amusement was better than his practice. He strikingly
anticipates Steele when he declares "and thus we
wheedle them in (if it may be allowed that expression) to the knowledge of the world, who, rather
than take more pains, would be content with their
ignorance, and search into nothing"; but his laudable design of wheedling the ignorant into knowledge took the form generally of what he truly calls
"impertinence and nonsense", of frivolous answers
to fictitious questions, and most frequently of scath-
ing rejoinders to scurrilous attacks from Grub Street
upon himself. It is a matter of some difficulty,
especially at the present time, to say where literature
begins and journalism ends. In Defoe's time the
separation was tolerably broad, and he himself in
his early efforts at essay-writing did not succeed in
deviating into pure literature. With his wonted
clear-sightedness he foresaw the possibilities in
store for such a paper as the *Tatler*, but there were
several obstacles in the way of his undertaking it.
The buffetings of fortune left him no time to indulge
in the learned ease of Addison, and he seems to have
regarded literature only with the eye of a practical
man of business. His extraordinary attention to
realistic detail, and his plain, rugged style are only
the natural literary expressions of the outstanding
traits of his character. M. Taine has said of the
Spectator that it "is only an honest man's manual,

and is often like the Complete Lawyer", and this misapplied phrase would not unfitly describe much of Defoe's literary work. He had not sufficient humour in his nature to enable him to laugh at the follies he was chiding, nor was he, in spite of his endless fertility of resource, possessed in large measure of the literary sense. That an essay ought to be something more than a hastily-written article on a subject of passing interest did not occur to him; he did not, like its greatest exponents, regard it as a thing to be lovingly touched and retouched until it emerged from its author's hands as an artistic whole. It is generally hazardous to appeal against any long-sustained verdict of public literary opinion, but it cannot be admitted that the oblivion into which the *Review* has fallen is a wholly merited one. A rich crop of mushroom periodicals sprang up after the disappearance of the *Spectator*, and their names and histories have frequently been recorded in literature. Most of them exhibit no ability comparable to that of the *Review*, so that some other cause must be sought for its failure than want of literary merit. Two reasons are readily found. There is no doubt that the main one is the *Review's* interference with politics, and the conjecture is supported by the subsequent fate of Addison's *Freeholder*. Again, the fact must be reckoned with that Defoe was never admitted into the inner circle of wits and gentlemen who presided at that time over the destinies of authors. His works, accordingly, never went forth to the public stamped with the imprimatur of coffee-house applause. He was known in

the highest literary circles only as an old hosier
and a seditious brawler. Pope chained him in the
Dunciad along with some notorious scribblers, and
Swift could allude to him only as an illiterate
fellow who had stood in the pillory. However
obvious his deficiencies as an essayist, it is impossible to withhold admiration for his single-handed
achievement, begun, as he says, "*in tenebris*", and
carried out with indomitable courage. Yet, if the
Review be called the prototype of the *Tatler*, it
must be kept in mind that all it could have done
was to suggest the possibility of holding up the
follies of society in a periodical paper. Defoe's
best essays must be looked for among the numerous
articles discovered by Mr. Lee, which were subsequently contributed to *Mist's* and *Applebee's*
Journals. It is not, however, by them but by his
earlier work that the question of his priority to
Steele must be judged, and it is certainly not of
a kind to entitle him to be called the first English
essayist. Of any attempt to give a literary finish
to his style, or to laugh his age into virtue by
means of coherent, neatly-rounded essays, there is
no sign in the earlier essays of Defoe; and that he
had himself no thought of having been the pioneer
of Steele is evident from the fact that, long after
the *Tatler* and the *Spectator* had begun to meet
with the neglect generally paid to established
classics, he appeared in the preface of the *Universal
Spectator* as a professed imitator of the Addisonian
essay. It remained for some one to follow up
Defoe's suggestion by employing as a literary
medium a prose style which should have both the

propriety of that of Temple and Dryden, and the
ease and gaiety of ordinary conversation. The
credit of making this combination, and of thereby
inaugurating a new development in literature, belongs entirely to Sir Richard Steele.

In Hatton's *New View of London*, published six
years after the accession of Queen Anne, it is
seriously asked, with reference to the existence of
coffee-houses, "who would have thought London
would ever have had near 3000 such Nusances,
and that Coffee should have been (as now) so much
Drank by the best of Quality and Physicians?"
This question at once brings one face to face with
the most characteristic feature of Queen Anne
society, and it is not devoid of literary significance
inasmuch as the periodical essay is closely connected with the history of clubs and coffee-houses.
It was eminently natural for the early essayists,
when they were on the outlook for a simple device
by which to give some degree of unity to their loose
sallies, to avail themselves of this predominating
social feature. The atmosphere of the coffee-house
pervaded the whole of the literature of the reign,
and affected it in many obvious ways. Both Defoe
and Swift conceived the idea of an English academy,
and the coffee-house to a certain extent realized the
conception. In the later days of Johnson this becomes more apparent, but even in Queen Anne's
time the literary taste of the town was almost entirely directed by the judgments of the chief coffee-
house dictators. The first half of the eighteenth
century witnessed a vast improvement in the manners and customs of society, a reformation in effect-

ing which the essay was not the least powerful factor; but at the same time it is indubitable that the coffee-house and not the home was the centre of social life, and that the former was regarded as a sort of happy compromise between Restoration profligacy and Puritan domesticity. Most of Steele's letters to his wife are more or less ingenious apologies for his "dining abroad", but the practice which Lady Steele resented was really a not unimportant element in her husband's education as an essayist. What was written of the earliest coffee-houses is equally descriptive of those in 1709:—

> " You may see there what fashions are,
> How periwigs are curled,
> And for a penny you may hear
> All novels in the world ".

Nor does the doggerel enumerate all the aspects of coffee-house entertainment ; at Button's literature was eagerly canvassed, while again at Will's

> " The gentle beau, too, joins in wise debate,
> Adjusts his cravat, and reforms the state ".

Surely in no other school could Steele so well have learned, like Will Honeycomb, "the history of every mode ". In May, 1707, he had been appointed Gazetteer, and there can be little doubt that it was during the performance of this duty that the conception of the *Tatler* dawned upon him. His work in Lord Sunderland's office could not have been very congenial; Steele was more a beau than a politician, and it is easy to conjecture with what pleasure he determined to vary official drudgery by becoming the voluntary gazetteer of the coffee-house. In the dedication of the first collected volume of the *Tatler* to Arthur Maynwaring, he throws some light on the history of his brilliant project. He resolved, he says, " to publish a paper which should observe upon the manners of the pleasurable, as well as the busy part of mankind ". From this it is not rash to infer that Steele claimed to have made a distinct advance on any former periodical, and to have been the first to make the essay an instrument for exhibiting contemporary manners. Had he had any previous paper in his mind, had he in any degree considered himself an imitator, one may be sure that he would have admitted the fact, for he was always unjust to himself in his acknowledgment of debt to others. He also points out that "it seemed the most proper method to form it by way of a letter of intelligence"—and here it is Steele, the Gazetteer, who speaks, while his proposal to include "the ordinary occurrences of common journals of news " indicates his connection with preceding journalists. Indeed, the *Tatler* contains within itself many signs of the transition from journalism to essay-writing, and may fairly be regarded as standing midway between the *Review* and the *Spectator*. It is very noticeable that the journalistic element in the *Tatler* diminishes as the work proceeds. How much of the change was due to Addison cannot be determined, but probably he was the first to realize the full possibilities of Steele's design, and by the gradual exclusion of communications dated from St. James's coffee-house to make the *Tatler* ultimately approximate to the form of the *Spectator*. Usually, in comparisons between them, great emphasis is laid on the superior unity of the *Spectator*. Such superiority was inevitable, and only points out, in an indirect way, that the *Tatler* was the beginning of a new development, and was therefore bound to betray some signs of its journalistic origin.

When two authors collaborate, there is an irresistible tendency for critics to set about apportioning their respective claims, and there is always considerable danger of transferring interest from their actual works to rival theories concerning them. Only irrational optimism can hope that there will ever be a time when disputes will have ceased about Beaumont and Fletcher, or Addison and Steele; and even in the most honest attempts at forming a reconciliation, there is always the necessity of reviewing the history of the antagonism, and the liability of thereby reopening the controversy. In the case of writers like Steele and Addison, where interest in the authors' personalities is a factor in any critical estimate too strong to be wholly eliminated, this danger is especially obvious, so that it is not surprising to find that many writers who deprecate any antagonism are apt to proceed on the tacit assumption that Addison's was the more important share in the partnership. Such an assumption is, to say the least, highly questionable. Phrases such as "Addison's *Spectator*" or "Addison's *Sir Roger*" are entirely question-begging phrases, and do a manifest injustice to the originality of Steele. If Addison be allowed to have been the more brilliant contributor, yet to Steele must be given all the credit of having been the projector and editor; and,

whatever his literary deficiencies, it is his name that
must rank the higher, if regard be had merely to the
development of the English essay. In Steele there
was a strange blending of acute enterprise and
boyish thoughtlessness, and it is the fate of all
authors who have a special place in their readers'
affections that the latter side of their character
should be unduly emphasized. A claim to pity, even
if it be a loving pity, is a dangerous attribute for
an author to possess, and it has militated against
Steele's purely literary reputation that he is thought
of as being, like his friend Gay, "in wit a man,
simplicity a child". So enamoured of Addison's
"elegance" were his earlier editors that they rather
grudged Steele any share of his fame, and it is
unfortunate that some of the absurdities of Hurd
should have been endorsed by the eloquence of
Macaulay. Nor are some of Steele's sincerest admirers free from blame. Perhaps there is no more
stimulating introduction to the literature of last
century than Thackeray's lectures—or *Esmond*;
but it is well in approaching Steele's writings to
recognize that Thackeray's lovable Dick Steele is
not altogether the same man as the founder of the
English Essay. De Quincey pointed out several
necessary qualifications in the exaggerated opinions
current as to Addison's extensive learning. It may
be admitted that he was better versed in classics
than his friend, but it has to be set against this that
Steele possessed many qualities even more essential
to an essayist than extensive learning. His was an
exceptionally strong emotional temperament; he
could sympathize with every side of character, and

temporarily identify himself with the feelings of another, and it was this that gave him so wide a knowledge of men and enabled him to sketch the outline of the Spectator Club. Steele rather than Addison was the true *Spectator*; he mixed freely in every kind of society, and it frequently happened that the general impressions he drew were afterwards improved and amplified by Addison. It is precisely what one would expect from the characters of the two men, that Steele should have taken the chief part in inventing the *dramatis personae* of the essays, and that Addison should appear to most advantage in handling mental abstractions of his own creation, and in critical and allegorical writing.

The *Tatler* ran from 12th April, 1709, to 2nd January, 1711, and consisted in all of 271 numbers, of which Steele contributed four to his coadjutor's one. At first somewhat of a medley, it was not till it had run about a third of its course that it attained to anything like the unity of its successors, and for this change, as has been said, probably Addison was responsible. That it was thrown off in a hurry is a boast sometimes made by the author of a laboured composition, but of most of his work Steele could have said so with the utmost sincerity. Indeed, if capacity for taking pains be an indispensable part of the connotation of genius, Steele possessed but a slender stock. His talent lay not in elaboration, but in striking out disconnected happy thoughts, and for this purpose the earlier and looser form of the *Tatler* was best adapted. Of his sustained pieces of humour there is none better than the description of the Trumpet Club, whose president Sir Jeoffery Notch, with his story of the game-cock, Gantlett, is of the same family as Squire Hardcastle, Sir Roger, and Sir Peter Teazle. Of four papers which might justly be described as the best of his pathetic writing, three are in the *Tatler*. The scene of domestic felicity, with its sequel, is no less remarkable for its delicate word-painting than for the careful delineation which makes it rank as an anticipation of *Pamela*, while the description of his father's death is not only a masterpiece but is undoubtedly Steele's most characteristic effusion. Overcharged emotion can go no farther; the collapse is inevitable, and with unconscious imitation Steele has relieved the scene by the Shakespearian device of a knocking at the door. His pathos is singularly pure, and free from that maudlin self-consciousness which offends in Sterne, and is often repellent in the Man of Feeling. At such times, too, his writing reaches its highest water-mark; sincerity of feeling breaks through the affectations of fine writing and demands an equal simplicity of expression. Addison's contributions to the *Tatler* are completely overshadowed by his subsequent work, and it is on it that his reputation must be based. The paper in his most typical vein is the bantering sketch of Ned Softly, an admirably sustained bit of farcical writing. Steele would have probably compressed the subject into a paragraph, at any rate he had not the knack of drawing the humour out to such extreme tenuity. That he could do so without having recourse to commonplace interludes is one of Addison's most distinctive characteristics as a

humorist. **Steele** has described four of Addison's
Tatlers as being the "greatest embellishments" of
the whole work, but this is only the three-piled
hyperbole of a biassed critic. It is remarkable that
it is in the same place that he refers to himself
as a distressed prince undone by his auxiliary.
This statement has often been unfairly quoted
against him, and has been used with reference to
his works as a whole. Steele meant it to apply
only to the *Tatler*, and when it is remembered
that he did four times the work of his brilliant
auxiliary, one may be pardoned for refusing to
accept literally his generous condemnation of himself. It is impossible to believe that the *Tatler*
came to an end because the editor was gravelled
for lack of matter. Swift ill-naturedly expressed
no surprise, charged Steele with laziness, and declared that the last *Tatlers* had been "cruel dull and
dry". There is little doubt that the real cause of
the termination was that suggested by Gay, that
Mr. Bickerstaff "had a mind to vary his shape, and
appear again in some new light". Steele had decided that it was impossible to graft a new project
on the old design, and that the time had come for
gratifying the public with a new series of characters.
Its success justified the resolution, but the *Tatler*
has merits apart from its historical interest. As a
faithful picture of the time it excels the *Spectator*,
and if it contains less literature, it contains more
agreeable reading. It had completely realized its
object; from the first it was hailed with unqualified
approval by a public surfeited with third-rate plays
and sombre divinity; it overthrew by ridicule

not a few of the follies of fashion, and it fought chivalrously and successfully for the dignity of woman.

When the *Spectator* appeared after an interval of two months its success was assured. Its audience was ready to believe that the new paper would excel the old, and no writer had as yet appeared who could seriously rival the felicitous combination of Addison and Steele. Their contributions were of nearly equal extent; out of five hundred and ten papers Addison wrote thirty-eight more than Steele, while forty-five were done by occasional correspondents. The lead was taken by Addison with his description of the Spectator, and Steele followed with his six portraits of the members of the Spectator Club. Of these most interest attaches to Sir Roger de Coverley, for both authors bestowed special attention on the delineation of his character. They were not invariably successful in regarding the character from the same point of view, but after making due allowance for slight discrepancies, it must be admitted that they achieved a hitherto unequalled triumph in character-drawing. In the original sketch Steele described the knight as having formerly been a " fine gentleman ", a man about town, and none of his subsequent papers are incongruous with this outline. Addison, on the contrary, laid hold on the eccentric side of the character, and his Sir Roger is only an unusually simple country squire, who visits the play-house, the Abbey, and Vauxhall with the bewilderment of a rustic. But while Steele had an important share in the series of papers, there is no doubt about the literary

blemishes which are apparent in his contributions.
His sketches are replete with good-humour and with
the results of an observant study of character, but
they show scarcely anything of Addison's artistic
skill in developing a picture. Sir Roger at the assizes, or at the play-house, may be taken as supreme
instances of Addison's craftsmanship. The humour,
tinged with irony, is never boisterous; indeed, it has
nearly always a certain solemnity which makes it
the more admirably in keeping with the character
of the squire, and the archaic turn of expression,
which often appears strained in Addison's essays,
serves only to heighten the effect of Sir Roger's
whimsical foibles. It is possible that Addison had
a political motive for so treating the character, but
it is unnecessary to read too much into his playful
irony; and, judging the result merely as literature,
one is forced to admit the delicacy of the portraiture
and the artist's admirable lightness of touch. The
essays on Nicolini, on Fans, and on Grinning are
other typical specimens of Addison's wit, and after
all has been said in praise of his criticisms and
allegories, the humorous papers in the *Spectator* are
unquestionably the best. A comparison of any one
of these three essays with the account of the Ugly
Club reveals the striking difference between the
humour of Addison and of Steele. The latter
laughs joyously without the suspicion of a sneer,
and so heartily appreciates the spectacle of his
distorted heroes that he pokes fun at the shortcomings of his own face. Addison's sympathy
stopped short of this, and if it be true, as Thackeray
maintains, that Dennis's description of Sir John

Edgar bears a dreadful resemblance to Steele, there
is certainly an equally dreadful truth in Mande-
ville's happy phrase. Steele performed his duties
as Spectator by mingling freely in clubs and coffee-
houses, while Addison, to use Hurd's expression,
remained *suaviter subridens*, maintaining a dignified
aloofness and viewing others with good-humoured
contempt. He had the national dread of giving
a loose rein to emotion, and never indulges his
readers with the naïve self-revelation of Goldsmith
or of Steele. "When phlegm," however, as M. Taine
has said, "is united to gentleness, as in Addison,
it is as agreeable as it is piquant. We are not
repelled by venomous bitterness, as in Swift, or by
continuous buffoonery, as in Voltaire." As compared with Steele, he was a more careful and therefore a better writer. His early practice in verse
composition, and his study of Cowley and Tillotson,
had trained his ear to appreciate the requirements
of prose cadence. His vocabulary was not unusually extensive any more than were his learning
and critical acumen, his moralizings are not in
advance of Pope's, and his style is purposely loose;
but with all this he possessed a quite exceptional
power of graceful and euphonious expression, and
a complete mastery of polite ridicule. The smooth-
ness of his style often entailed a sacrifice of
strength, and the prim propriety of his language
stands out in striking contrast to the nervous, unpolished vigour of Defoe. Addison's true greatness
lies in his use of a pure and tuneful diction, and in
his power of humorous satire. Irony, in his hands,
was like a fine rapier which can wound without at

once being felt, and no English writer has excelled
him in the deft handling of the weapon.

Besides being the standard model for succeeding
essayists, the *Spectator* in its own day won an
astonishing and unprecedented popularity. As
regards the improvement of English prose, Steele
and Addison occupy only a secondary position.
Cowley, Temple, and Dryden among their predecessors, and Swift and Defoe among their contemporaries, left a more veritable mark than they did
on the progress of style. But Steele and Addison
were the first to combine good style with attractive
matter, and thus to convey a prose ideal to a much
wider circle than had any before. And further,
they diffused a taste for knowledge as none previous had done, they fostered an interest in literary
criticism, and exercised generally an incalculable
educative influence. That the "lesser immoralities",
against which they inveighed, were driven out of
fashion is clear from many sources, and there is
important contemporary evidence which has been
attributed to Gay. "It is impossible to conceive the
effect his (Steele's) writings have had on the town;
how many thousand follies they have either quite
banished or given a very great check to; ... how
entirely they have convinced our fops and young
fellows of the value and advantage of learning."
Reformations of manners and customs are not, however, easily effected by strokes of the pen. This
panegyric must be accepted with some qualification,
but that the *Tatler* and *Spectator* did excellent
service in the way indicated is indisputable, though
it need not be believed that the whole of Queen

Anne society was at once reformed by the fiat of two laughing philosophers. And there was still another result which contemporary estimates could not include, although it is the essay's greatest secondary achievement. It led the way to the perfecting of the English novel. More than a century before the *Spectator* the writing of *Characters* was a fashionable kind of composition. In 1608, Bishop Hall wrote a collection of this kind which gained him from Wotton the title of "our English Seneca", and met with high praise from Fuller for "the pureness, plainness, and fullness of his style". This was followed in 1614 by Sir Thomas Overbury's *Witty Descriptions of the Properties of Sundry Persons*, and in 1628 by Earle's *Microcosmography*. All of these were to some extent the forerunners of La Bruyère, they all display a profusion of epigrammatic and sometimes pedantic word-play, but they all painted with too broad a brush, ignoring the individual for the type. Their characters have no basis in reality, and are merely attempts to body forth the universal by combining a number of individual traits. Of idiosyncrasies they take no account, and accordingly fail to create a personality capable of evoking the slightest sympathy or interest. Overbury, the most representative of these character-writers, has been made the subject of an interesting comparison by Professor Raleigh in his *English Novel*. By making a selection of passages from the Coverley papers, he has framed a character of Sir Roger analogous to Overbury's character of a country squire, and the comparison of this selection with the fully elabo-

rated conception in the *Spectator* reveals as nothing
else could do the magnitude of Addison's advance.
"The dreary 'Character' of the seventeenth century", says Professor Raleigh, "which would have
rendered Sir Roger as 'An Old Country Knight',
and Will Honeycomb as 'A Mere Town Gallant',
has received its death-blow in these sketches, drawn
by men who loved the individual better than the type,
and delighted in precisely those touches of character,
eccentricities and surprises, that give life to a literary
portrait." The essayists quickened the seventeenth-
century lay-figure into life by endowing it with
human emotions and passions, and by making it
not merely an isolated object for contemplation but
also a unit on the crowded stage of a larger drama.
The *Spectator* opens with the rather ambitious aim
of bringing philosophy out of closets and libraries
to dwell in clubs and coffee-houses. Steele's more
modest valedictory words in the *Tatler* give a
truer estimate of the essay's work, and are significant as being such as Richardson might have fitly
used. "I must confess it has been a most exquisite
pleasure to me to frame characters of domestic life,
and put those parts of it which are least observed
into an agreeable view ... in a word, to trace human
life through all its mazes and recesses." The claim
to have framed characters of domestic life is just,
and it strikes the key-note of the English novel.
The inauguration of the latter by Richardson does
not differ from that of other literary forms; the
year 1740 marks not so much the birth-year of
a new kind of literature as a critical period in the
history of a development that had long been going

on. Richardson, like others, had his pioneers, some notable, many forgotten. That his work can be so far resolved into its prime factors is no detraction to any literary creator, no reason for any stinting of the praise due to his original contributions. Just as the *Tatler* shows signs of transition, so *Pamela* displays but partial emancipation from the essay form. It resembles the letters of the *Tatler* and *Spectator*, but with the difference that all are made to revolve round a fixed centre. Even in Fielding's fondness for essay interludes there is a trace of the novel's origin, but Fielding stands to Richardson as the *Spectator* to the *Tatler*—the one carries on the other to an inevitable culmination.

None of the other periodicals conducted by Steele and Addison approach the *Spectator* in point of continuity of interest or brilliancy of execution. The *Guardian*, the most notable of them all, contains nothing by Steele that he had not already surpassed, and is interesting mainly for the contributions of Pope and for the celebrated critiques on pastoral poetry—critiques which are valuable, not only as illustrating the crafty intriguing of Pope, but as having furnished the foundation for the revival of Scottish poetry in the successful pastorals of Allan Ramsay. Pope's essays on Epic Poetry and on Dedications both smack most unmistakably of the *Dunciad*, and their author's own practice in the matter both of epic and of dedication hardly justifies the cheap irony and acrimonious wit. His letters, which with their careful workmanship and obvious insincerity present so vivid a contrast to the pathos of the *Journal to Stella* or to the un-

affected candour of Steele's letters, hold an important place in the history of letter-writing; but
his essays are only imitations, and not even strik
ingly brilliant as that. Keenly alive to the foibles
of his time, and with powers of observation carefully
trained by practice, Pope failed as an essayist for
lack of sympathetic humour and of ability to conceal his art. The same reasons partially hold
good for the comparative failure as an essayist of a
greater contemporary. They hold good only partially, for while it is undeniable that Swift's humour
is generally devoid of any touch of sympathy, there
is no author of whom it can be more confidently
said that he never obtrudes his art. What he invited the *Tatler* to become, he was in large measure
himself, " the instrument of introducing into our
style that simplicity which is the best and truest
ornament of most things in life ". He has left the
best definition of style, but the key to his own success, and the key to all good writing, is contained
in his admirable injunction to make use on all
occasions " of such words as naturally occur on the
subject". It is needful to remember that simplicity
like every other quality of style is subordinate to
the greater law of relativity, that simplicity when
affected or overdone defeats its own end, and that
restraint, which is the sign of the true artist, may
easily pass into weakness. Swift was happy in
avoiding these extremes and in realizing his own
ideal. He could easily sustain his style for any
time at the same pitch, he could always closely
accommodate his manner to his matter, and he
could convey his ideas clearly and forcibly without

distracting the reader's attention to the excellence
of their vehicle of expression. Yet, great as were
his powers of shrewd penetration into character,
Swift wanted the lighter graces necessary to the
essayist. He loved to wage war on man rather
than to instruct him, and used wit not to "enliven
morality" but to increase the venom of his sting
The Laputans were attended by flappers who
awaked them from their day-dreams by gently
striking them with a bladder. As contrasted with
Swift's method, the methods of Steele and Addison
are equally gentle, and yet, as an instrument of
social and literary reform the laugh of Steele or the
raillery of Addison was far more potent than the
loaded bludgeon of Swift. Of some of his papers
it is often hard to say whether they are so much
essays as lampoons. The *Vindication of Bickerstaff*
is thus open to question, but there is little need for
justifying the insertion of so thoroughly typical a
specimen of Swift's skill. The grave irony with
which Partridge is furnished with proofs of his own
death, and the drollery with which he is rebuked
for refusing to see that the question of his existence
is only a matter of ordinary speculation, are excelled
by nothing in literature. It is unnecessary to
charge Swift in this case with uncharitableness.
Partridge was a quack, and did not live in vain to
have given occasion to such a brilliant *jeu d'esprit.*

It is almost a commonplace of criticism to remark
on the difficulty of imitating Swift, so free is he
from those mannerisms which are always apt to be
mistaken for originality of style. Indeed the truest
way to imitate him is to aim constantly at a perfect

naturalness of expression. There was one writer of the time who succeeded in this in a wonderful degree. Arbuthnot, who does not rank as an essayist, so faithfully copied the gravity of the irony and the ease of the style that it remains a difficult problem to disentangle his share from their joint productions. Though the most successful, he is not, however, the only understudy to be met with among the early essayists. Of the few who helped Steele and Addison, Budgell and Hughes deserve prominent mention, both for the quantity of their work and for the ability they showed in writing in conformity with the *Spectator's* design. In neither case is the illusion ever quite complete; the copy has certain characteristics of its own, and it has not all those of the original, but in the case of Budgell, at least, the resemblance is so good as to lend plausibility to the assertion made so often on Johnson's authority that the proofs were revised and amended by Addison himself. Little importance attaches to the minor periodicals of Steele and Addison which extend beyond the limits of Queen Anne's reign. Party passion ran so high that even the essayists with one accord rushed into the fray with political diatribes. The one interesting exception is Addison's *Freeholder*, and in it the one interesting character is the Tory Foxhunter, who furnishes an excellent comparison with Sir Roger de Coverley. The political motive here becomes plainly apparent, the same old skill in character delineation is equally marked; but there is no longer any button on the foil, and humorous exaggeration has broadened into caricature.

Ten years had elapsed since the appearance of the *Tatler* when Addison died and Defoe produced his immortal novel. This decade forms the first great period in the history of the essay, the period that comprises both its rise and its culmination. The essay form was now firmly established, thoroughly attuned to the genius of the language; and however great their diversity, all essays henceforth could trace their lineage back to the reign of Queen Anne. Defoe, whose meteoric incursions into the domain of letters during a period of forty years are so bewildering to the lover of an orderly historical outline, not only had helped to lay the foundation of the essay, but took the chief part after the close of this first great epoch in maintaining it during the interval that elapsed between the *Spectator* and the *Rambler*. In one of his last writings he refers ironically to the falling off in periodical essays. "Is there no wit or humour left, because they are gone? Is the spirit of the Spectators all lost, and their mantle fallen upon nobody? Have they said all that can be said? Has the world offered no variety, and presented no new scenes since they retired from us? Or did they leave off, because they were quite exhausted, and had no more to say? We think quite otherwise." Defoe did not allow sufficiently for the damping effect of the *Spectator's* excellence. A crowd of imitations follows in the wake of every striking literary success, but, if that success be a sufficiently prolonged one, imitation will gradually cease, and the literary energies of the time will revive some older form, or will strike out some new line of development, rather than continue in a course in which it seems impossible to excel, impossible to completely avoid the dulness that is inseparable from all mere imitations of a successful model. Defoe's essays have their faults, but they show no lack of originality. That on the Instability of Human Glory is a good example of his serious vein and illustrates some of his merits and shortcomings. It contains a good deal that is natural and eloquent, but as a whole it is formless, and is marred by ludicrous associations out of keeping with the sublimity of the subject. The flavour of journalism permeates all his essays. "In a word, the character of a good writer, wherever he is to be found, is this, viz. that he writes so as to please and serve at the same time." This is how Defoe has stated his literary ideal. It is patently a journalist's one, in which perfection of style holds only a secondary place; but such as it is Defoe realized it, and with all their imperfections his contributions to *Mist's* and *Applebee's* journals are not seriously rivalled by any similar publications in the ten years after Addison's death. The last year of Defoe's life is one of some importance in the history of the periodical essay. It was in 1731 that Edward Cave started the *Gentleman's Magazine*, which, though its immediate effect was small, was destined ultimately to put an end to the separate publication of essays. The plan of the *Spectator*, even when under able management, was fitted to weary readers by its unrelieved monotony, and after one more vigorous attempt to resuscitate the older design, the scheme of Sylvanus Urban was generally adopted, and the essay found its proper place as only one element in a miscellaneous magazine. On Defoe's death, it was left to Henry Fielding to maintain the continuity of the essay until Johnson was ready to accept the trust, and he did so with characteristic ability in the *Champion*, the *Jacobite's Journal*, the *True Patriot*, and the *Covent Garden Journal*, from 1739 to 1752. The last especially contains many excellent essays on literature and morals, characterized by their author's robust common-sense, his vigorous, easy style, and his good-humoured, racy wit. Most of the topics he had already handled in his novels, for while it is inexpedient to dislocate them from their proper setting, the prefatory and incidental discourses in *Tom Jones* are Fielding's best essays. His desultory criticism is as sound as it is original, and whatever differences of opinion there may be as to the value of his fiction, there can be none as to the faithfulness with which he adheres in his novels to the theories which his essays propound.

It was natural, after the *Tatler* and *Spectator* had fallen into oblivion, that some attempt should have been made to start a paper which might do for the Georgian era what they had done for the reign of Queen Anne. That the fame of the *Spectators* was now no longer a serious obstacle to original effort, as Defoe asserted, is tolerably plain from contemporary evidence. In 1750 Richardson candidly states that he "never found time to read them all", and Sylvanus Urban in reply makes the same admission. It was in this same year that the *Rambler* made the first attempt at revival, and began the second epoch of the English essay. Johnson, who

was born in the year of the *Tatler's* appearance,
decided at last, to use Boswell's phrase, "to come
forth in the character for which he was eminently
qualified, a majestic teacher of moral and religious
wisdom". "The *Tatler, Spectator*, and *Guardian*",
continues Boswell, "were the last of the kind published in England, which had stood the test of a
long trial; and such an interval had now elapsed
since their publication, as made him justly think
that to many of his readers this form of instruction
would in some degree have the advantage of
novelty." It is scarcely accurate to say that
Johnson's aim was identical with that of the earlier
essayists. "As it has been my principal design",
he wrote, "to inculcate wisdom or piety, I have
allotted few papers to the idle sports of imagination;
. . . but scarcely any man is so steadily serious as
not to complain that the severity of dictatorial instruction has been too seldom relieved." By the
time that Johnson wrote this, he had found that, in
spite of the encomiums of the best judges, the public
was not prepared to welcome his instruction with
anything like the avidity formerly shown for the
lucubrations of Bickerstaff. Nor is there any cause
for surprise in this. The wonder is that Johnson
should have managed to continue it for two years,
and that with its many obvious defects he should
have been able to win for it at last a very substantial popularity. Too much stress is sometimes laid
on the pomposity of his diction. For serious topics,
which were avowedly his chief aim, his style is well
suited, and his use of a balanced, periodic structure,
if ludicrous when misapplied, is certainly impressive

when it is made the vehicle of his moralizings. In
the *Rambler* and *Adventurer*, the latter of which
shows its editor, Hawkesworth, as faithful an imitator of Johnson as Arbuthnot was of Swift or Hughes
of Addison, his serious papers are undoubtedly the
best. The story is told of him that at one time
he was driven to eke out his income by writing
sermons, and most of his essays certainly resemble
utterances from the pulpit rather than from the
editorial easy-chair.   The essays in the *Rambler*
are not by any means his best, but they are the
most Johnsonian—in the worst sense, in the sense
with which tradition has rather unfairly invested
the term.   An illustration of this is found in the
essay on Literary Courage, which closes with a
passage that a manual of rhetoric might quote as
typical. "By this descent from the pinnacles of
art, no honour will be lost; for the condescensions
of learning are always overpaid by gratitude.   An
elevated genius employed in little things appears,
to use the simile of Longinus, like the sun in his
evening declination: he remits his splendour but
retains his magnitude, and pleases more though he
dazzles less."   Johnson was far from being a
pedant, but he wanted the agility to make a graceful descent from the pinnacles of art, and he had
not the supreme requisite of being able to conceal
the condescensions of learning.   The central idea
in the essay on Living in a Garret is sufficiently
ludicrous, and the humour is able even to break
through the heavy cloud of words that envelops it.
" He that upon level ground stagnates in silence, or
creeps in narrative, might, at the height of half a

mile, ferment into merriment, sparkle with repartee, and froth with declamation." Johnson is seldom so successful as this in his acrobatic feats, and the *Rambler* as a whole, judged by this novel criterion of his own, compels one to think that it had been written for the most part upon the ground floor. An improvement observable in his contributions to the *Adventurer* becomes very apparent in the *Idler* —a collection of papers published weekly for two years in the *Universal Chronicle.* The increased sprightliness of manner and the simpler mode of expression were probably the result only of Johnson's having more accurately gauged the nature of the public demand. Of other causes the most likely is the influence of the *Connoisseur*, which preceded the *Idler* by four years. When Johnson describes Dick Minim he comes very near to the playful irony of Addison, and his two papers on this subject form a good comparison with the *Tatler's* account of Ned Softly. It must always remain a puzzle to account for the two-sidedness of Johnson's literary character. As conversationalist, letter-writer and poet, he wielded a trenchant and incisive style, while in his essays he was seldom able to free himself from the trammels of a cumbrous mannerism. There was sound criticism in Goldsmith's jest that he would make little fishes talk like whales. With this one irreparable deficiency he had every qualification that can be imagined necessary for an essayist. Even more than Steele or Addison he was "a club-able man"; he knew London and loved London as no one else has done; his dictatorship was more powerful and more unquestioned than ever Dryden's

was; and he had besides a passionate love of literature for its own sake, a fund of genuine wit, and a
faculty of acute and eminently sensible criticism.
" No periodical writer", says Addison, "who always
maintains his gravity, and does not sometimes
sacrifice to the Graces, must expect to keep in
vogue for any considerable time." This statement
gives at once the key to the *Spectator's* success and
to the *Rambler's* failure. Johnson's style was frozen
in " the pinnacles of art", while Addison's easy,
flexible English adapted itself to every loose sally
of the mind.

For ten years after the *Rambler*, the essay was
revived with a vigour that almost rivalled that of
the Queen Anne epoch; but, with only one great
exception, all Johnson's contemporaries in essay-
writing were eclipsed by the magnitude of his personality. Yet it might well be argued that no
periodical during this revival resembles the *Tatler*
as closely in many of its outstanding features as
the *Connoisseur* of Colman and Thornton. These
writers, who according to their own statement collaborated in every essay, achieved no brilliant innovation either in form or in matter, but their
magazine is far and away superior to any of Johnson's as a faithful and graphic picture of Georgian
life, and deserves to be remembered for its literary
value as well as for the fact that Cowper was one
of its correspondents. Two other celebrated letter-
writers, Lord Chesterfield and Horace Walpole,
were the most brilliant contributors to the *World*,
but they suffered from the constraint of the essay-
form, and were unable within its scope to display

the graceful negligence and cynical wit that characterize the letters of both. They avoided, however,
what was the besetting sin of the *Rambler's* immediate successors. Johnson's style had a good
effect as a corrective of loose and formless expression, but its influence was baneful upon writers of
less calibre than himself, who neglected the important difference between sound and sense. The
mannerism was so easy to acquire, and it possessed
such sonorous dignity, that many besides Hawkesworth used it successfully to screen their poverty of
matter, and to fob their readers off with platitudes
arrayed in swelling Johnsonese. The one great
writer whom Johnson could not eclipse was Oliver
Goldsmith, who, amidst the general contamination,
stood out as the exponent of a pure and almost
faultless prose style. It is questionable whether
Goldsmith's essays have generally received the attention they merit, for they are easily the best of
their time. Boswell, who highly appreciated Johnson's " labour of language ", and was irritated by the
Idler's comparative simplicity, makes the solemn
assurance that to him "and many others it appeared
that he studiously copied the manner of Johnson,
though indeed upon a smaller scale ". There is
fine, unintentional humour in his honest contempt
for the small scale of Goldsmith's imitation, and in
his manifest anxiety to allow no little fishes to dis-
port themselves quite in the manner of the whale.
And yet, strange as it appears, Boswell could have
produced some evidence in support of his conten-
tion. The first number of the *Bee*, Goldsmith's first
effort at periodical writing, exhibits the ludicrous

spectacle of its author masquerading in Johnsonian
buckram. "In this situation, however, a periodical-
writer often finds himself upon his first attempt to
address the public in form. All his power of pleasing is damped by solicitude, and his cheerfulness
dashed with apprehension. Impressed with the
terrors of the tribunal, his natural terror turns to
pertness, and for real wit he is obliged to substitute
vivacity." A reader coming bolt on such a passage
as this might well rub his eyes, and ask if it could
possibly be the work of that cunning hand which
pictured "the idyllic grace of the Vicar's home".
It was, however, but a momentary yielding to a
prevailing fashion, and very soon Goldsmith's exquisite literary taste provided him with a medium of
expression more pure and limpid than any that had
yet been evolved. His style, which charms by its
inimitable grace and astonishes by its continuous
excellence, was the product of careful workmanship
and of a familiar acquaintance with the best work
of his predecessors. He recognized what was admirable in Dryden, Cowley, and Tillotson; he saw
that vigour was as lacking in Addison as it was
excessive in Johnson; and he acutely observed that
Steele was at his best in the *Tatler*, when he wrote
simply and naturally without making any futile
attempt to imitate Addison's emotional restraint.
His early efforts met with so little encouragement
that his fame "hardly travelled beyond the region
of Bow-bell", but he found "great satisfaction in
considering the delicacy and discernment" of such
readers as he had. This, however, cannot have
continued long, for when he came to collect his

fugitive essays, he found that some of them had been reprinted sixteen times and claimed by different authors as their own. The absence of any national prejudice is a trait of Goldsmith's character in striking contrast to Johnson's insularity of view. His sturdy faith in Fleet Street is inseparable from our conception of Johnson, and no one would have it otherwise; yet it often hurried him into dogmatic assertions out of keeping with his truer judgment. On the other hand, Goldsmith's vagabondage was a notable part of his education; it broadened his sympathies, quickened his sense of humour, and made him, as he loved to think, a citizen of the world. It was under this title that he collected the series of papers by which he had made the fame of the *Public Ledger*, and upon which his reputation as an essayist is most firmly based. The idea of satirizing the failings of one's countrymen in the character of a foreigner was no new one. It began with the *Turkish Spy*, attributed to Marana, and it was put to brilliant use in the *Persian Letters* of Montesquieu, but neither of these was probably the actual source of Goldsmith's inspiration. Mr. Austin Dobson has shown beyond the possibility of doubt that the origin of the Chinese Letters is to be found in a pamphlet by Horace Walpole, consisting of " A Letter from Xo Ho, a Chinese Philosopher in London, to his friend Lien Chi, at Peking ". In the character of the observant and witty oriental, Lien Chi Altangi, Goldsmith came nearer than any other essayist to the plan of the *Spectator*, and he fully equalled his model in the accuracy of his criticism of life and in the gentle humour of his reproof. He possessed in a wonderful degree the art of miniature painting, and the Chinese Letters are full of that same skill in brief but pointed characterization which makes *Retaliation* unique in English poetry. Of the fourth Letter, with its droll exposure of the inconsistency and brusqueness of the national character, Mr. Dobson remarks that " it is Goldsmith, and Goldsmith only, who could have imagined the admirable humour of the dialogue on liberty between a prisoner (through his grating), a porter pausing from his burden to denounce slavery and the French, and a soldier who, with a tremendous oath, advocates, above all, the importance of religion ". In this same essay Goldsmith observed that " the English confer their kindness with an appearance of indifference, and give away benefits with an air as if they despised them ", and it is this characteristic which he proceeded to illustrate more fully in his description of the Man in Black. It is one of the chief charms of Goldsmith's essays that he constantly draws on the fund of his own varied experience, and that in them, just as in the *Deserted Village*, the most amiable traits in his creations are porrowed from his loving recollections of his own Irish home. Writing of the *Vicar of Wakefield*, Mr. Gosse has said " that it is more like an extended episode in the *Spectator* manner than a story, and that Fielding would have discoursed in vain if the British novel, after its superb start, had gracefully trotted back again into its stable in this way ". This is surely an exaggerated expression of a real truth; but for our present purpose it is more per-

tinent to point out that the statement holds good
in the inverse, and that Goldsmith's essay-charac-
ters are like single threads unravelled from the
tangled skein of a complete novel.   The Man in
Black is Goldsmith's first portrait of this kind, and
it is easy to see in it not only a careful delineation
of his father, but also not a few traces of his own
character.   Both as men and as writers there are
many strong points of resemblance between Goldsmith and Steele, and the hundred and eighty-first
Tatler, with its confession that pity was the weakness of its author's heart, affords an interesting
comparison with the twenty-sixth Chinese Letter,
which describes Goldsmith as a "mere machine of
pity".   If not one of his most highly finished
sketches, the Man in Black is thoroughly characteristic of the author, and no better description has
ever been given of one who with his right hand
shakes the fist of righteous indignation at an object
of charity, and furtively bestows alms with the left.
More graphic and much more humorous are the
three papers in which Goldsmith drew the inimitable picture of Beau Tibbs, the prince of all shabby-
genteel gentlemen, who dwelt in what he facetiously
styled the first floor down the chimney.   Like Tony
Lumpkin's pot-house friend, who danced his bear
only to the genteelest of tunes, the beau could not
bear anything *low*; he had a mythical acquaintance
with Lord Mudler and Lady Grogram, and he designed his six-year-old daughter for my Lord
Drumstick's eldest son.   The beau is at his best
when he visits Vauxhall along with his wife, Lien
Chi, the Man in Black, and the pawnbroker's

widow. Lady Teazle riding double, behind the
butler, on a docked coach-horse, is not more ludicrous than the picture of Mr. Tibbs being whirled
to Vauxhall seated on his wife's lap, and the whole
of the little comedy is in keeping with the opening
scene. Equally successful are Goldsmith's attempts
at club portraiture. Not Steele, nor Addison, nor
Johnson, intimately as each knew the humours of
club life, has left anything so vivid as the meeting
of Grub Street hacks, where the poet tables one
and sixpence to be allowed to read his doggerel,
and where another member, evidently a very near
kinsman of Goldsmith, tells how he was duped by
a most splendid message from the Earl of Doomsday into leaving his lodgings, only to alight at a
sponging-house, where a bailiff with a devil's face
came out to meet him. Passages of genuine humour
such as these are scattered broadcast over the
Citizen of the World, but, though predominant,
they do not make up the whole total of its merits.
Goldsmith's sway, as Johnson said, was equally
powerful whether smiles were to be moved or
tears, and the essay, "A City Night Piece", is an
admirable example of his exquisite tenderness.
The simple solemnity of its opening, with its striking anticipation of Macaulay's New Zealander, is
followed up by reflections full of the same delicacy as shines through the humour of Lamb, and
the conclusion is perhaps the most self-revealing
passage in all Goldsmith's works. "Why was this
heart of mine formed with such sensibility? or why
was not my fortune adapted to its impulse?" This
is the key to the greater part of his character; it

accounts for the miseries of his life, for the crowded staircase at Brick Court, and for his unique hold on his readers' affections; and it points also to one of the elements which charm in his style. It was Steele's boast that he aimed at giving his essays the air of common speech by using incorrectness of style, but Goldsmith contrived to sacrifice to the graces without making any such unnecessary surrender. When Swift attempted a homely style he often became coarse, while Addison in the same endeavour frequently succumbed to weakness. Goldsmith easily avoided these pitfalls, and it is not hazardous to say that he is unexcelled by any English prose writer in the purity, simplicity, and melody of his diction. An undoubted archaism lurks in the *Spectator*, but Goldsmith is essentially modern, and when he writes his very best he combines the grace of Addison and the artlessness of Steele.

When Goldsmith died, the reign of Johnson was not yet over, and there was only Burke left to dispute the sovereignty. But Burke was wiser than to descend from the pinnacles of art, and did not attempt any lop-sided union between his fiery rhetoric and the essayist's familiar themes. Indeed, after the *Citizen of the World*, the history of the essay repeats itself, and just as half a century elapsed between the *Tatler* and the *Rambler*, it was not till after a similar period that the nineteenth century effected another brilliant resuscitation of the form. The reasons for this decline are entirely similar to those which previously operated. The essays of Goldsmith and Johnson set up a standard beyond the reach of mediocre craftsmen,

and rendered it inevitable that the centre of literary
interest should be shifted from the essay to other
developments.   The novel had once already, in
the hands of Richardson and Fielding, usurped
the essay's place, and now, after having enjoyed
a second decade of success, the essay gave way
once more to fiction as represented by the *Vicar
of Wakefield, Tristram Shandy*, and the *Castle of
Otranto*, and did not retrieve its position until the
end of the half-century which witnessed the rapid
development of historical and domestic novels.
Selections have been made from the *Gentleman's
Magazine*, and much might be gleaned from other
miscellanies of the time, but it must be an antiquarian rather than a literary interest that prompts
the choice.   Many readers would rejoice like Elia
to find these old magazines in an inn, but when
their contents are read "in a cool hour", most
critics would regard them with the same leniency
and reverence as are paid to the fardingale and
the full-bottomed periwig. Most of these magazine
writers were like Sir Fretful Plagiary "so unlucky
as not to have the skill even to steal with taste",
and, avoiding the graces of Goldsmith, plodded on
industriously in the footsteps of Johnson.   The
futility of their attempt cannot be better expressed
than in the trenchant language of Burke, no matter
though it is an example of Satan reproving sin:—
"No, no, it is not a good imitation of Johnson; it
has all his pomp without his force; it has all the
nodosities of the oak without its strength; it has
all the contortions of the sibyl without the inspiration".   Indeed, only one feeble flicker lights up

the gloom which enveloped the essay during the rest of the century. Long before its appearance, Allan Ramsay had carried pastoral poetry north of the Tweed, but he had shrewdly adapted it to its new environment, substituting Patie and Jenny for Phyllis and Corydon. When Henry Mackenzie attempted a similar feat with the English essay, he made no such requisite changes, and the *Mirror*, the *Lounger*, and the *Observer* are but echoes of the *Tatler*, *Spectator*, and *Connoisseur*. Addison and Sterne are supposed to have been his models, but the contortions of the sibyl are more apparent than the inspiration. The Man of Feeling had nothing of Sterne's subtle humour, which plays round his pathos like a lambent flame; he "resolved", like Steele, "to be sorrowful"; but he nurses his grief so carefully, and toys with it so long, that true pathos is at last insulted by the mummery. *Crambe repetita* is not an appetizing dish, and Simon Softly, and Tom Sanguine, and Mary Muslin, and Mary Plain are names that strike cruelly on the jaded ear. His characters are, indeed, for the most part anachronisms, and are as "cruel dull and dry" as the piping swains in a third-rate pastoral.

By the beginning of this century the face of society had changed, and the essay could no longer afford to confine its scope to "the town". As much as poetry the essay reflects the spirit of the age, and while the former was striking many new notes, the other, leaving aside antiquated scandal and pinchbeck sentimentalism, was being pressed into the service of political and philosophical exposition. When Leigh Hunt commenced to write essays, he was plainly under the spell of a past age, and the *Connoisseur* was admittedly his model. Nor did he ever wholly succeed in throwing off the faded garments of the eighteenth century, and there is always present in his style a touch of archaism which makes one rank him with the earlier essayists rather than with his own vigorous contemporaries. In 1812 he was known only as an unusually capable dramatic critic, and it was not till seven years later that he began in the *Indicator* to revive the essay on the lines of Addison and Goldsmith. He cannot, however, be placed in the first rank of English essayists. In all his work there is a lack of virility, and he had no special endowment of pathos or of humour. When it is said that he could write commonplace gracefully, his merits and defects are summarized. His essays bear nowhere the impress of a strong personality, they contain no fresh creations, and they scarcely ever deviate from one level of unemotional calm. Yet he had indubitable skill in writing on familiar subjects, and he wielded a simple style that on rare occasions became even eloquent. The essays *On Sleep*, and *On the Deaths of Little Children* are his finest pieces of word-painting. The former, if disfigured by some patches of cheap moralizing, concludes with two paragraphs of singular beauty, while the other, though not displaying Steele's pathos, nor Lamb's April blending of tears and smiles, is a masterpiece of tender imagery and artistic restraint. Leigh Hunt was a genuine man of letters, with no very strong feelings and with but little imagination, loving books and flowers, and able to treat any subject in a pleasant and cultured style. The indisputable decline of his reputation is to be accounted for by his want of any striking originality, and by his being overshadowed by his greater contemporaries. Prior to the appearance of the *Indicator*, Hazlitt had done some of his best critical work, while Lamb, having given the results of his loving study of the early dramatists, was on the point of coming forward in the character of Elia. The exclusion of critical papers necessarily gives a totally inadequate representation of Hazlitt, who wrote his best only when art or literature was his theme. In him, much more distinctly than in Hunt or Lamb, a modern spirit is apparent. Save for a certain exuberance of style, there is nothing in his essays to suggest even now the flavour of antiquity; he approached his subjects with perfect originality and freshness ; his style cannot be definitely linked to any prototype; and, as critics of his own day were quick to observe, "his taste was not the creature of schools and canons, it was begotten of Enthusiasm by Thought". It is enthusiasm, indeed, that is the most obvious characteristic of the essays—and they are his best essays— which he contributed between 1820 and 1830 to the *Examiner* and other papers. The traditional limits of the periodical essay, however, were somewhat narrow for the full display of Hazlitt's genius. He craved for "more elbow-room and fewer encumbrances", and, as Professor Saintsbury has said, "what he could do, as hardly any other man has ever done in England, was a *causerie* of about the

same length as Sainte-Beuve's ". None of his
writings display those emotional qualities on which
the reputation of the chief English essayists is
based, and his success must be attributed to the
virile excellence of his style, and to his passionate
and unaffected love of letters. "My sun", he wrote,
" arose with the first dawn of liberty. . . . The
new impulse to ardour given to men's minds imparted a congenial warmth and glow to mine; we
were strong to run a race together." Burke was the
one author whom he never wearied of commending,
and it was at the torch of Burke's eloquence that
the fire of his own style was kindled. Fortunately
for literature, it was to it and not to politics that
Hazlitt directed his enthusiasm, with the result
that, in spite of some prejudices and exaggerations,
his writings are unrivalled as a stimulating introduction to the study of literature. His knowledge
of books was as extensive as his devotion was
profound; they were to him "the first and last,
the most home-felt, the most heart-felt of all our
enjoyments ". Hazlitt's position among the essayists depends on the fact that he devoted himself
less to the delineation of character than to the exposition of literature. If not the first, he was the
most influential of those who bent the essay to this
purely literary purpose, and he may be regarded
as standing midway between the old essayists and
the new. It was a fashion in his own time, and
one that has often since been followed, to insist too
strongly on Hazlitt's limitations as a critic. Yet,
after all has been said, his method was essentially
the same as Sainte-Beuve's, and his essays cannot

even now be safely neglected by students of the
literary developments with which they deal. It is
impossible to read them without catching something
of the ardour of his own enthusiasm, and it says
much for the soundness of his taste and judgment
that the great majority of his criticisms emerged
undistorted from the glowing crucible of his thought.

While there is a strong egotism in his essays,
Hazlitt can scarcely be called a "personal essayist",
for he had no Jonsonian "humour", and he rode no
Shandean hobby-horse. With him, indeed, any
survey of the essay's history might end, for it
would be possible to trace some affinity between
him or some of his predecessors, and any of those
who have subsequently used the essay form. At
least one exception must be made in favour of
Charles Lamb, who occupies in so many ways a
unique place in the development, and who more
closely than any other went back to the practice of
Montaigne in allowing his personality to colour
everything he wrote. The *Essays of Elia* began in
1822, at a time when Sydney Smith had already a
secure reputation as a wit, and Christopher North
was beginning to make the fame of *Blackwood's
Magazine* by his riotous humour. Unlike either of
these, Lamb was an anachronism. Everywhere
around him literature was striking out new channels,
and exaggerated protests were being made against
the alleged artificiality of the previous century.
Except at the demands of private friendship Lamb
took little interest in contemporary writing; he remained constant to his first love for the past, and
drew his inspiration from the pure wells of Eliza-

bethan literature. He had mined deeply in Burton
and in Fuller, in the old dramatists, and in the
writers of artificial comedy; their idioms became
his idioms, and he unconsciously brocaded his
language with their quaint conceits and similitudes.
" He evades the present ", in the words of Hazlitt,
" he mocks the future. . . . He pitches his tent in
the suburbs of existing manners . . . and occupies
that nice point between egotism and disinterested
humanity." In his own phrase, he venerated an
honest obliquity of understanding, and due weight
must always be attached to the influence of his
idiosyncrasies upon his style. As the works of
Goldsmith and Hood derive new meaning when
interpreted in the light of the records of their lives,
so the *Essays of Elia* must be viewed against the
tragic background of their author's life, before due
appreciation can be made of the delicacy of their
humour and of the infinite tenderness of their
unobtrusive pathos. It leads rather to a miscon-
ception of Lamb to associate him only with so
hackneyed an essay as the *Dissertation on Roast
Pig.* Exquisite fooling, no doubt, it is, but it has
not the recondite beauties, the quaint paradoxes,
the felicitous characterization, the intermingling of
humour and pathos, that are everywhere apparent
in his best essays. The descriptions of *Mrs. Battle*
and of the *Convalescent* are masterpieces which more
readily than most of his essays can be directly compared with the work of Addison and Goldsmith;
Dream-Children is typical of Lamb's whimsical
pathos and of the extreme delicacy of his touch;
Thoughts on Books is the most charming confession

extant of a literary creed; while *All Fools' Day* and
the *New Year's Coming of Age* depict him in his
most fantastic mood, toying with his subject, and
wresting from it innumerable pleasantries. Lamb
can scarcely be classed along with any other
essayist; the archness and piquancy of his humour,
if they sometimes remind one of Sterne, had for
the most part an ancestry older than Addison and
Steele, and it is only by going back to the writers
of the seventeenth century that one fully detects
the atavism of his style. "There is an inward
unction, a marrowy vein both in the thought and
feeling, an intuition deep and lively of his subject,
that carries off any quaintness or awkwardness
arising from an antiquated style and dress." In
these happy words Hazlitt has pointed out the
most indefinable feature in Lamb's essays—the
rich marrowiness of their style. With their extraordinary nimbleness of fancy and grace of expression the *Essays of Elia* are indeed "a paradise
of dainty devices", redolent of the sweetness and
old-world air of Cowley. His quaint paradoxes,
too, seem to rise naturally from the subject and do
not grate on the ear with the metallic ring of
modern epigram. The obliquity of Lamb's genius
precluded in his own day, as it still precludes, the
possibility of successful imitation; he created no
new school of essayists, and he left no abiding
mark on the development of English prose; but
he is within certain well-defined limits one of the
most artistic exponents of the essay, and the power
of fully appreciating the delicacy of his work is one
of the surest indications of a literary epicure.

In the case of a continuous development, as that of the essay must necessarily be, it is inevitable that one of the boundaries of the field surveyed should be arbitrarily imposed. The latter half of this century has shown little regard for the older style of essays on abstract subjects; the essay has more and more become associated with literary criticism; and it might almost be said that fiction has again entered into combat with it, and in the form of the short story has ousted it from popular regard. Yet, in spite of powerful rivals, the essay is still a vital literary form. What the sonnet is to the poet, the same and more is the essay to the prose artist, requiring similar compression of thought, and affording similar scope for brilliancy of execution. It would be hazardous to suppose that criticism of the future will regard the present age as marking a revival in the history of the development; but it is tolerably certain that no future collection of the best British essayists will ignore the work of Robert Louis Stevenson. For the purpose, however, of the present volume it is scarcely necessary to extend the survey beyond Leigh Hunt and Lamb. By that time the essay had reached its full maturity, and had furnished examples of all its possible forms. The real history of the essay coincides with the period of a century and a half which elapsed between the appearance of the *Tatler* and the year of Leigh Hunt's death. During that time its progress was more than once arrested, and it is a gain to clearness with small sacrifice of accuracy to regard the three critical periods in the essay's history as being the begin-

ning, the middle, and the end of the eighteenth
century — periods connected with the names of
Steele and Addison, Johnson, and Goldsmith, Hazlitt and Lamb.   If not the greatest, the essay is
certainly the most characteristic literary form of
the eighteenth century.   It owed its origin to the
club-life of Queen Anne society, and true to its
original purpose, it faithfully mirrored the manners
of the day, when fiction presented nothing but
ideals, and artificial comedy only caricature.   It
may be doubted, too, if any other literary development has been so prolific of results.   No doubt the
essay's greatest secondary achievement was the
fillip it gave to the inauguration of the novel, but
it founded, also, a requisite medium for literary
criticism and created the miscellaneous magazine.
Not, however, that the fame of the essay requires
to be propped up by that of its various descendants.
It has been the favourite medium of many of the
greatest masters of English prose, who have lavished
on it the best of their artistic skill and all the re-
sources of their wisdom and humour.   There is no
end to the variety of subjects which the English
essayists have handled; no foible escaped their
laughter, no abuse their scorn; for their motto has
been, as it must continue to be, that which Steele
selected for the first English periodical—

> " Quicquid agunt homines . . . . .
>   .   .   . nostri est farrago libelli "

ENGLISH ESSAYS.

FRANCIS BACON, LORD VERULAM.

(1561-1626.)

I. OF SEEMING WISE.

IT hath been an opinion, that the French are wiser than
they seem, and the Spaniards seem wiser than they
are; but howsoever it be between nations, certainly it is so
between man and man. For, as the Apostle saith of godliness, 'having a show of godliness, but denying the power
thereof', so certainly there are, in points of wisdom and
sufficiency[1], that do nothing or little very solemnly;
Magno conatu nugas.[2] It is a ridiculous thing and fit
for a satire to persons of judgment, to see what shifts
these formalists[3] have, and what prospectives to make
superficies to seem body that hath depth and bulk.
Some are so close and reserved, as they will not show
their wares but by a dark light, and seem always to keep
back somewhat: and when they know within themselves
they speak of that they do not well know, would nevertheless seem to others to know of that which they may
not well speak. Some help themselves with countenance
and gesture, and are wise by signs; as Cicero saith of
Piso, that when he answered him he fetched one of his
brows up to his forehead, and bent the other down to
his chin; *Respondes, altero ad frontem sublato, altero ad
mentum depresso supercilio, crudelitatem tibi non placere.*

---

[1] ability.   [2] Terence, *Heaut.* iv. 1. 8.   [3] *i.e.* the seeming wise.

1

Some think to bear it by speaking a great word, and
being peremptory; and go on, and take by admittance
that which they cannot make good. Some, whatsoever
is beyond their reach, will seem to despise or make
light of it, as impertinent or curious[1], and so would
have their ignorance seem judgment. Some are never
without a difference, and commonly by amusing men
with a subtilty, blanch[2] the matter; of whom A. Gellius
saith; *Hominem delirum, qui verborum minutiis rerum
frangit pondera.*[3] Of which kind also Plato, in his
Protagoras, bringeth in Prodicus in scorn and maketh
him make a speech that consisteth of distinctions from
the beginning to the end. Generally, such men in all
deliberations find ease to be of the negative side, and
affect a credit to object and foretell difficulties: for when
propositions are denied there is an end of them; but if
they be allowed, it requireth a new work: which false
point of wisdom is the bane of business. To conclude,
there is no decaying merchant or inward beggar[4] hath
so many tricks to uphold the credit of their wealth as
these empty persons have to maintain the credit of their
sufficiency. Seeming wise men may make shift to get
opinion: but let no man choose them for employment;
for certainly you were better take for business a man
somewhat absurd[5] than over formal[6].

II. OF STUDIES.

STUDIES serve for delight, for ornament, and for ability.
Their chief use for delight, is in privateness and
retiring; for ornament, is in discourse; and for ability, is in

---

[1] irrelevant or trifling.   [2] evade.
[3] The quotation is not from Gellius, but from Quintilian on Seneca,
iv. 1. (Whately).
[4] one secretly a bankrupt (Whately).   [5] defective in judgment.
[6] too pretentious.

the judgment and disposition of business. For expert men can execute, and perhaps judge of particulars, one by one; but the general counsels, and the plots and marshalling of affairs, come best from those that are learned. To spend too much time in studies, is sloth; to use them too much for ornament, is affectation; to make judgment wholly by their rules is the humour of a scholar. They perfect nature and are perfected by experience: for natural abilities are like natural plants, that need pruning by study: and studies themselves do give forth directions too much at large, except they be bounded in by experience. Crafty men contemn studies; simple men admire them; and wise men use them: for they teach not their own use; but that is a wisdom without them, and above them, won by observation. Read not to contradict and confute, nor to believe and take for granted, nor to find talk and discourse, but to weigh and consider. Some books are to be tasted, others to be swallowed, and some few to be chewed and digested: that is some books are to be read only in parts; others to be read, but not curiously[1]; and some few to be read wholly, and with diligence and attention. Some books also may be read by deputy, and extracts made of them by others: but that would be only in the less important arguments, and the meaner sort of books: else distilled books are, like common distilled waters, flashy[2] things. Reading maketh a full man, conference a ready man, and writing an exact man. And therefore, if a man write little, he had need have a great memory; if he confer little, he had need have a present wit; and if he read little, he had need have much cunning, to seem to know that he doth

---

[1] attentively.

[2] Bacon uses the word in the sense of 'tasteless'. In his *Nat. Hist.* he remarks that the most offensive tastes are "bitter, sour, harsh, waterish, or flashy".

not. Histories make men wise; poets witty; the mathematics subtle; natural philosophy deep; moral, grave;
logic and rhetoric able to contend: *Abeunt studia in
mores.* Nay, there is no stond[1] or impediment in the
wit, but may be wrought out by fit studies: like as
diseases of the body may have appropriate exercises.
Bowling is good for the stone and reins; shooting for
the lungs and breast; a gentle walking for the stomach;
riding for the head; and the like. So, if a man's wits be
wandering, let him study the mathematics; for in demon-
strations, if his wit be called away never so little, he must
begin again: if his wit be not apt to distinguish or find
differences, let him study the school-men; for they are
Cymini sectores[2]. If he be not apt to beat over matters,
and to call up one thing to prove and illustrate another,
let him study the lawyer's cases: so every defect of the
mind may have a special receipt.

ABRAHAM COWLEY.

(1618–1667.)

III. OF MYSELF.

IT is a hard and nice subject for a man to write of
himself;[3] it grates his own heart to say anything of
disparagement and the reader's ears to hear anything of
praise from him. There is no danger from me of offend-
ing him in this kind; neither my mind, nor my body, nor
my fortune allow me any materials for that vanity. It is

---

[1] obstacle.

[2] hair-splitters: lit. "dividers of cummin seed, which is one of the
least seeds " (Bacon).

[3] Cf. *Spectator*, No. 562, where Addison discourses on Egotism, and
misquotes this sentence from Cowley.

sufficient for my own contentment that they have preserved me from being scandalous, or remarkable on the
defective side. But besides that, I shall here speak of
myself only in relation to the subject of these precedent
discourses,[1] and shall be likelier thereby to fall into the
contempt than rise up to the estimation of most people.
As far as my memory can return back into my past life,
before I knew or was capable of guessing what the world,
or glories, or business of it were, the natural affections of
my soul gave me a secret bent of aversion from them, as
some plants are said to turn away from others, by an
antipathy imperceptible to themselves and inscrutable to
man's understanding. Even when I was a very young
boy at school,[2] instead of running about on holidays and
playing with my fellows, I was wont to steal from them
and walk into the fields, either alone with a book, or with
some one companion, if I could find any of the same
temper. I was then, too, so much an enemy to all constraint, that my masters could never prevail on me, by
any persuasions or encouragements, to learn without
book the common rules of grammar, in which they dispensed with me alone, because they found I made a
shift to do the usual exercise out of my own reading and
observation. That I was then of the same mind as I am
now (which I confess I wonder at myself) may appear by
the latter end of an ode[3] which I made when I was but
thirteen years old, and which was then printed with many
other verses. The beginning of it is boyish, but of this
part which I here set down, if a very little were corrected,
I should hardly now be much ashamed.

---

[1] "Of Myself" is the last of eleven essays comprised under the title,
"Several Discourses by way of Essays in Prose and Verse".

[2] Cowley entered Westminster School when about ten years old. In
1636 he became a scholar of Trinity College, Cambridge.

[3] The stanzas quoted form the conclusion of a poem entitled "A
Vote", which appeared in *Sylva* of 1636.

IX.

This only grant me, that my means may lie
Too low for envy, for contempt too high.
　　Some honour I would have,
Not from great deeds, but good alone.
The unknown are better than ill known.
　　Rumour can ope the grave;
Acquaintance I would have, but when 't depends
Not on the number, but the choice of friends.

X.

Books should, not business, entertain the light,
And sleep, as undisturbed as death, the night.
　　My house a cottage, more
Than palace, and should fitting be
For all my use, no luxury.
　　My garden painted o'er
With Nature's hand, not Art's; and pleasures yield,
Horace might envy in his Sabine field.

XI.

Thus would I double my life's fading space,
For he that runs it well, twice runs his race.
　　And in this true delight,
These unbought sports, this happy state,
I would not fear, nor wish my fate,
　　But boldly say each night,
To-morrow let my sun his beams display,
Or in clouds hide them—I have lived to-day.

You may see by it I was even then acquainted with
the poets (for the conclusion is taken out of Horace[1]),
and perhaps it was the immature and immoderate love
of them which stamped first, or rather engraved, these
characters in me. They were like letters cut into the
bark of a young tree, which with the tree still grow pro-
portionably. But how this love came to be produced in
me so early is a hard question. I believe I can tell the
particular little chance that filled my head first with such

---

[1] *Odes*, III. xxix. 41.

chimes of verse as have never since left ringing there.
For I remember when I began to read, and to take some
pleasure in it, there was wont to lie in my mother's parlour (I know not by what accident, for she herself never
in her life read any book but of devotion), but there was
wont to lie Spenser's works; this I happened to fall upon,
and was infinitely delighted with the stories of the knights,
and giants, and monsters, and brave houses, which I
found everywhere there (though my understanding had
little to do with all this); and by degrees with the tinkling
of the rhyme and dance of the numbers, so that I think
I had read him all over before I was twelve years old,
and was thus made a poet as irremediably as a child is
made an eunuch. With these affections of mind, and my
heart wholly set upon letters, I went to the university,
but was soon torn from thence by that violent public
storm [1] which would suffer nothing to stand where it did,
but rooted up every plant, even from the princely cedars
to me, the hyssop. Yet I had as good fortune as could
have befallen me in such a tempest; for I was cast by it
into the family of one of the best persons, and into the
court of one of the best princesses of the world. Now
though I was here engaged in ways most contrary to the
original design of my life, that is, into much company,
and no small business, and into a daily sight of greatness,
both militant and triumphant, for that was the state then
of the English and French courts; yet all this was so far
from altering my opinion, that it only added the confirmation of reason to that which was before but natural
inclination. I saw plainly all the paint of that kind of
life, the nearer I came to it; and that beauty which I did
not fall in love with when, for aught I knew, it was real,

---

[1] In 1643 Cowley, as a Loyalist, had to leave Cambridge. A year
after, he went to Paris as secretary to Lord Jermyn, the adviser of
Queen Henrietta Maria.

was not like to bewitch or entice me when I saw that it was adulterate. I met with several great persons, whom I liked very well, but could not perceive that any part of their greatness was to be liked or desired, no more than I would be glad or content to be in a storm, though I saw many ships which rid safely and bravely in it. A storm would not agree with my stomach, if it did with my courage. Though I was in a crowd of as good company as could be found anywhere, though I was in business of great and honourable trust, though I ate at the best table, and enjoyed the best conveniences for present subsistence that ought to be desired by a man of my condition in banishment and public distresses, yet I could not abstain from renewing my old schoolboy's wish in a copy of verses to the same effect.

> Well then; I now do plainly see,
> This busy woild and I shall ne'er agree, &c.[1]

And I never then proposed to myself any other advantage from His Majesty's happy restoration, but the getting into some moderately convenient retreat in the country, which I thought in that case I might easily have compassed, as well as some others, with no greater probabilities or pretences, have arrived to extraordinary fortunes. But I had before written a shrewd prophecy against myself, and I think Apollo inspired me in the truth, though not in the elegance of it.

> Thou, neither great at court nor in the war,
> Nor at th' exchange shalt be, nor at the wrangling bar;
> Content thyself with the small barren praise,
> Which neglected verse does raise, &c.[2]

However, by the failing of the forces which I had

---

[1] The opening lines of "The Wish", one of the poems published in 1647 under the collective name of *The Mistress*.

[2] From "Destiny", the seventh of Cowley's fifteen *Pindarique Odes* published in 1656.

expected, I did not quit the design which I had resolved on; I cast myself into it *A corps perdu*, without making capitulations or taking counsel of fortune. But God laughs at a man who says to his soul, "Take thy ease": I met presently not only with many little encumbrances and impediments, but with so much sickness (a new misfortune to me) as would have spoiled the happiness of an emperor as well as mine. Yet I do neither repent nor alter my course. *Non ego perfidum dixi sacramentum.* Nothing shall separate me from a mistress which I have loved so long, and have now at last married, though she neither has brought me a rich portion, nor lived yet so quietly with me as I hoped from her.

> ————*Nec vos, dulcissima mundi*
> *Nomina, vos Musæ, libertas, otia, libri,*
> *Hortique sylvæque anima remanente relinquam.*

> Nor by me e'er shall you,
> You of all names the sweetest, and the best,
> You Muses, books, and liberty, and rest;
> You gardens, fields, and woods forsaken be,
> As long as life itself forsakes not me.

But this is a very petty ejaculation. Because I have concluded all the other chapters with a copy of verses, I will maintain the humour to the last.

MARTIAL, LIB. 10, EP. 47.

Vitam quæ faciunt beatiorem, etc.

SINCE, dearest friend, 't is your desire to see
A true receipt of happiness from me;
These are the chief ingredients, if not all:
Take an estate neither too great nor small,
Which *quantum sufficit* the doctors call;
Let this estate from parents' care descend:
The getting it too much of life does spend.
Take such a ground, whose gratitude may be
A fair encouragement for industry.

Let constant fires the winter's fury tame,
And let thy kitchens be a vestal flame.
Thee to the town let never suit at law,
And rarely, very rarely, business draw.
Thy active mind in equal temper keep,
In undisturbèd peace, yet not in sleep.
Let exercise a vigorous health maintain,
Without which all the composition's vain.
In the same weight prudence and innocence take,
Ana[1] of each does the just mixture make.
But a few friendships wear, and let them be
By Nature and by Fortune fit for thee.
Instead of art and luxury in food,
Let mirth and freedom make thy table good.
If any cares into thy daytime creep,
At night, without wine's opium, let them sleep.
Let rest, which Nature does to darkness wed,
And not lust, recommend to thee thy bed.
Be satisfied, and pleased with what thou art;
Act cheerfully and well the allotted part.
Enjoy the present hour, be thankful for the past,
And neither fear, nor wish the approaches of the last.

MARTIAL, LIB. 10, EP. 96.

ME, who have lived so long among the great,
You wonder to hear talk of a retreat:
And a retreat so distant, as may show
No thoughts of a return when once I go.
Give me a country, how remote so e'er,
Where happiness a moderate rate does bear,
Where poverty itself in plenty flows
And all the solid use of riches knows.
The ground about the house maintains it there,
The house maintains the ground about it here.
Here even hunger's dear, and a full board
Devours the vital substance of the lord.
The land itself does there the feast bestow,
The land itself must here to market go.
Three or four suits one winter here does waste,
One suit does there three or four winters last.

[1] an equal quantity.

Here every frugal man must oft be cold,
And little lukewarm fires are to you sold.
There fire's an element as cheap and free
Almost as any of the other three.
Stay you then here, and live among the great,
Attend their sports, and at their tables eat.
When all the bounties here of men you score:
The Place's bounty there, shall give me more.

DANIEL DEFOE.

(1661-1731.)

IV. THE INSTABILITY OF HUMAN GLORY.[1]

SIR, I have employed myself of late pretty much in the
study of history, and have been reading the stories
of the great men of past ages, Alexander the Great, Julius
Cæsar, the great Augustus, and many more down, down,
down, to the still greater Louis XIV., and even to the
still greatest John, Duke of Marlborough[2].   In my way
I met with Tamerlane[3], the Scythian, Tomornbejus[4], the
Egyptian, Solyman[5], the Magnificent, and others of the
Mahometan or Ottoman race; and after all the great

[1] This essay appeared on July 21, 1722, in *The Original Weekly
Journal and Saturday's Post*, started by Applebee on 2nd Oct. 1714.
From 1720 to 1726 Defoe contributed weekly articles in the form of
'letters introductory". These letters—admittedly the prototypes of
'leading articles"—were first introduced by Defoe in the sixty-eighth
number of *Mist's Journal*, 1718.

[2] The Duke died five weeks before the date of Defoe's essay.

[3] Timour (1336-1405) made war on the whole world in support of
what he regarded as the true Mahometan faith. He defeated the Ottoman Sultan, and died when preparing to invade China.

[4] Tumanbeg or Tumanbai, the last Mameluke Sultan, was defeated
and put to death by Selim in 1517.

[5] Suleiman, the Magnificent, the Lawgiver (1490-1566), was the greatest constructor of the Ottoman power. The capture of Rhodes, the
invasion of Hungary, and the siege of Vienna were his most famous
exploits.

things they have done I find it said of them all, one after
another, AND THEN HE DIED, all dead, dead, dead!
hic jacet is the finishing part of their history.   Some lie
in the bed of honour, and some in honour's truckle bed;
some were bravely slain in battle on the field of honour,
some in the storm of a counterscarp and died in the ditch
of honour; some here, some there;—the bones of the bold
and the brave, the cowardly and the base, the hero and
the scoundrel, are heaped up together;—there they lie in
oblivion, and under the ruins of the earth, undistinguished
from one another, nay, even from the common earth.

> " Huddled in dirt the blust'ring engine lies,
>   That was so great, and thought himself so wise."

How many hundreds of thousands of the bravest fellows
then in the world lie on heaps in the ground, whose bones
are to this day ploughed up by the rustics, or dug up by
the labourer, and the earth their more noble vital parts are
converted to has been perhaps applied to the meanest uses!

How have we screened the ashes of heroes to make
our mortar, and mingled the remains of a Roman general
to make a hog sty!   Where are the ashes of a Cæsar, and
the remains of a Pompey, a Scipio, or a Hannibal?   All
are vanished, they and their very monuments are mouldered
into earth, their dust is lost, and their place knows them
no more.   They live only in the immortal writings of
their historians and poets, the renowned flatterers of the
age they lived in, and who have made us think of the
persons, not as they really were, but as they were pleased
to represent them.

As the greatest men, so even the longest lived.   The
Methusalems of the antediluvian world—the accounts of
them all end with the same.   Methusalem lived nine
hundred sixty and nine years and begat sons and daughters
—and what then?   AND THEN HE DIED.

> " Death like an overflowing stream
> Sweeps us away; our life's a dream."

We are now solemnizing the obsequies of the great Marlborough; all his victories, all his glories, his great projected schemes of war, his uninterrupted series of conquests, which are called his, as if he alone had fought and conquered by his arm, what so many men obtained for him with their blood—all is ended, where other men, and, indeed, where all men ended: HE IS DEAD.

Not all his immense wealth, the spoils and trophies of his enemies, the bounty of his grateful Mistress, and the treasure amassed in war and peace, not all that mighty bulk of gold—which some suggest is such, and so great, as I care not to mention—could either give him life, or continue it one moment, but he is dead; and some say the great treasure he was possessed of here had one strange particular quality attending it, which might have been very dissatisfying to him if he had considered much on it, namely, that he could not carry much of it with him.

We have now nothing left us of this great man that we can converse with but his monument and his history. He is now numbered among things passed. The funeral as well as the battles of the Duke of Marlborough are like to adorn our houses in sculpture as things equally gay and to be looked on with pleasure. Such is the end of human glory, and so little is the world able to do for the greatest men that come into it, and for the greatest merit those men can arrive to.

What then is the work of life? What the business of great men, that pass the stage of the world in seeming triumph as these men, we call heroes, have done? Is it to grow great in the mouth of fame and take up many pages in history? Alas! that is no more than making a tale for the reading of posterity till it turns into fable and romance. Is it to furnish subject to the poets, and live in their immortal rhymes, as they call them? That is, in short, no more than to be hereafter turned into ballad and song and be sung by old women to quiet children, or at the corner of a street to gather crowds in aid of the pickpocket and the poor. Or is their business rather to add virtue and piety to their glory, which alone will pass them into eternity and make them truly immortal? What is glory without virtue? A great man without religion is no more than a great beast without a soul. What is honour without merit? And what can be called true merit but that which makes a person be a good man as well as a great man?

If we believe in a future state of life, a place for the rewards of good men and for the punishment of the haters of virtue, how few of heroes and famous men crowd in among the last! How few crowned heads wear the crowns of immortal felicity!

Let no man envy the great and glorious men, as we call them! Could we see them now, how many of them would move our pity rather than call for our congratulations! These few thoughts, Sir, I send to prepare your readers' minds when they go to see the magnificent funeral of the late Duke of Marlborough.

v. DESCRIPTION OF A QUACK DOCTOR.[1]

M. MIST, Passing occasionally the other day through a little village, at some distance from town, I was entertained with the view of a very handsome equipage moving towards me. The gravity of the gentleman who sat in it, and the eagerness wherewith the coachman drove

[1] This essay appeared on Dec. 5, 1719, in Nathaniel Mist's *Weekly Journal or Saturday's Post*, started on 15th Dec. 1716. On March 29, 1718, Defoe contributed the first leading article. The paper ran until 1728, when it passed into the hands of Fog. Mist was a Jacobite, and a "vender of Scandal and Sedition", and in January, 1728, "took the opportunity of slinking away in a mist".

along, engaged my whole attention; and I immediately
concluded that it could be nothing less than some minister
of state, who was posting this way upon some very important affair. They were now got about the middle of the
place, when making a full stand, the footman, deserting his
station behind and making up abreast of his master, gave
us a very fine blast with a trumpet. I was surprised to
see a skip[1] transformed so speedily into a trumpeter, and
began to wonder what should be the meaning of such an
unusual phenomenon; when the coachman, jumping from
his box, laying by his whip, and slipping off his great
coat, in an instant rose up a complete merry-andrew.
My surprise was now heightened, and though honest
pickle[2] with a world of grimace and gesticulation endeavoured to move my gaiety, I began to be very fearful
where the metamorphosis might end. I looked very
earnestly first at the horse and then at the wheels, and
expected every minute to have seen them take their turn
in the farce, and laying aside their present appearances
assume other shapes. By this time the gentleman, who
had hitherto appeared wonderfully sedate and composed,
began to throw off his disguise; and having pocketed all
his former modesty and demureness, and flushed his
forehead with all the impudence of a thorough-paced
quack, I immediately discovered him to be a very
eminent and learned mountebank.

   This discovery raised my curiosity as much as it abated
my surprise, so that being very desirous to hear what new
proposal the doctor had to make, or what new *arcanum*
in physic he had found out, I quitted my former station
and joined myself to the crowd that encompassed him.
After a short preamble, he began to open the design of

---

[1] lackey.
[2] A harlequin in O. G. comedy. The fuller form of the word is pickle-
herring.

his embassy, setting forth at large the great affection which
he bore in particular to the people of that place; ampli-
fying on his own merits and qualifications, specifying
great numbers of cures which he had wrought on incurable
distempers, expatiating on the extreme danger of being
without his physic, and offering health and immortality
to sale for the price of a tester.

You'd have burst your sides, Mr. Mist, had you but
heard the foolish allusions, quaint expressions, and in-
consistent metaphors, which fell from the mouth of this
eloquent declaimer. For my part I should have wondered
where he could have raked up nonsense enough to
furnish out such a wordy harangue, but that I am told he
has studied the *Flying Post*[1] with a great deal of application, and that most of the silly things in his speech are
borrowed from that excellent author. Sometimes he'd
creep in the most vulgar phrases imaginable, by and by
he'd soar out of sight and traverse the spacious realms
of fustian and bombast. He was, indeed, very sparing
of his Latin and Greek, as (God knows) having a very
slender stock of those commodities; but then, for hard
words and terms, which neither he, nor you, nor I, nor
anybody else understand, he poured them out in such
abundance that you'd have sworn he had been rehearsing
some of the occult philosophy of Agrippa[2] or Rosicrusius,
or reading a lecture out of Cabala.

After the doctor had given such ample indications of
the greatest humanity, skill, and erudition, who d'ye think
would be so incredulous as not to believe him, or so

---

[1] This is obviously a thrust at Defoe's enemy, George Ridpath, the
writer of the *Flying Post*. Defoe contributed to another paper of the
same name, hence Ridpath's scornful allusion to a "Sham Flying Post".
" To dulness Ridpath is as dear as Mist ".

(*Dunciad*, I. 208.)

[2] Henry Cornelius Agrippa (1486, Cologne) was a famous alchemist,
author of *De Occulta Philosophia*, &c.

uncourteous as to refuse to purchase one of his packets?
Lest any of us, however, should be too tenacious of our
money to part with it on these considerations, he had
one other motive which did not fail to do the business;
this was by persuading us that there were the seeds of
some malignant distemper lurking in every one of our
bodies, and that there was nothing in nature could save
us but some one or other of his medicines. He threatened
us with death in case of refusal, and assured us with a
prophetic air that without his physic every mother's son
of us would be in our graves by that day twelve-month.
The poor people were infinitely terrified with the imminent
danger they found themselves under, but were as much
pleased to find how easy it was to be evaded; so that,
without more ado, every man bought his packet, and
turned the doctor adrift to pursue further adventures.

The scene being now removed, I was at leisure to
reflect on what had passed, and could really have either
cry'd or laugh'd very heartily at what I had seen. The
arrogance of the doctor and the silliness of his patients
were each of them ridiculous enough to have set a person
of more gravity than myself a-laughing; but then to
consider the tragical issue to which these things tended,
and the fatal effect so many murthering medicines might
have on several of his majesty's good subjects, would have
made the merriest buffoon alive serious. I have not often
observed a more hale, robust crowd of people than that
which encircled this doughty doctor, methinks one might
have read health in their very faces, and there was not a
countenance among them which did not give the lie to
the doctor's suggestions. Could but one see a little into
futurity, and observe the condition they will be in a few
months hence, what an alteration would one find! How
many of those brawny youths are already puking in
chimney corners? And how many rosy complexioned

girls are by this time reduced to the paleness of a cockney?

I propose in a little time to make a second journey to this place in order to see how the doctor's physic has operated. By searching the parish register and comparing the number of funerals made weekly before the doctor's visit with those which have followed, it will be easy to form an estimate of the havoc which this itinerant man-slayer made in the space of two hours. I shall then proceed to compute the number of quacks[1] in the three kingdoms, from which it will be no hard matter to determine the number of people carried off *per annum* by the whole fraternity. Lastly, I shall calculate the loss which the government sustains by the death of every subject; from all of which the immense damages accruing to his majesty will evidently appear, and the public will be fully convinced of the truth of what I have heretofore asserted, viz. that the quacks contribute more towards keeping us poor than all our national debts, and that to suppress the former would be an infallible means of redeeming the latter. The whole scheme shall be drawn up in due form and presented to the parliament in the ensuing session, and that august assembly, I don't doubt, will pay all regard thereto, which the importance of the subject and the weight of my argument shall require.

Methinks the course of justice, which has hitherto obtained among us, is chargeable with great absurdities. Petty villains are hanged or transported, while great ones are suffered to pass *impune*. A man cannot take a purse upon the highway, or cut a single throat, but he must presently be called to answer for it at the Old Bailey, and perhaps to suffer for it at Tyburn; and yet, here are

---

[1] Cf. *Tatler*, 240, and *Spectator*, 572. The latter by Zachary Pearce is largely similar to Defoe's essay. Defoe had reason to know about the subject, as his Review was filled with quack advertisements.

wretches suffered to commit murthers by wholesale, and
to plunder, not only private persons and pockets, but
even the king and the Exchequer, without having any
questions asked! Pray, Mr. Mist, what were gibbets,
gallows, and whipping posts made for?

But to return to Doctor Thornhill. I have had the
curiosity to examine several of his medicines in a re-
verberatory, reducing compounds into their simples by a
chemical analysis, and have constantly found a considerable proportion of some poisonous plant or mineral in
every one of them. Arsenic, wolf's-bane, mercury, and
hemlock are *sine quibus non*, and he could no more make
up a medicament without some of these than remove a
mountain. Accordingly as they are variously mixed and
disposed among other drugs, he gives them various names,
calling them pills, boluses, electuaries, etc. His pills I
would prescribe as a *succedaneum* to a halter, so that such
persons as are weary of this troublesome world and would
willingly quit it for a better, but are too squeamish to take
up with that queer old-fashioned recipe called hanging,
may have their business done as securely and more
decently by some of these excellent pills. His bolus, too,
is very good in its kind; I have made experiments with
it on several animals, and find that it poisons to a miracle.
A moderate dose of it has perfectly silenced a bawling
dog that used to disturb my morning slumbers, and a like
quantity of it has quieted several other snarling curs in
my neighbourhood. And then, if you be troubled with
rats, Mr. Mist, there's the doctor's electuary is an infallible
remedy, as I myself have experienced. I have effectually
cleared my house of those troublesome animals by disposing little packets of it in the places they frequent, and
do recommend it to you and your readers as the most
powerful ratsbane in the world. It would be needless to
enumerate all the virtues of the doctor's several medicines,

but I dare affirm that what the ancients fabulously reported of Pandora's box is strictly true of the doctor's packet, and that it contains in it the seeds and principles of all diseases.

I must ask your pardon, Mr. Mist, for being so grave on so ludicrous a subject and spending so many words on an empty quack.   Mr. Mist, Your humble servant, Philygeia.

SIR RICHARD STEELE.

(1671-1729.)

VI. A SCENE OF DOMESTIC FELICITY.

Interea dulces pendent circum oscula nati,
Casta pudicitiam servat domus.
—Virg. Georg. ii. 523.

His cares are eas'd with intervals of bliss;
His little children, climbing for a kiss,
Welcome their father's late return at night,
His faithful bed is crown'd with chaste delight.
—Dryden.

THERE are several persons who have many pleasures and entertainments in their possession, which they do not enjoy. It is, therefore, a kind and good office to acquaint them with their own happiness, and turn their attention to such instances of their good fortune as they are apt to overlook.   Persons in the married state often want such a monitor; and pine away their days, by looking upon the same condition in anguish and murmur, which carries with it in the opinion of others a complication of all the pleasures of life, and a retreat from its inquietudes.

I am led into this thought by a visit I made an old friend, who was formerly my school-fellow.   He came to town last week with his family for the winter, and yesterday morning sent me word his wife expected me to dinner

I am, as it were, at home at that house, and every member
of it knows me for their well-wisher. I cannot, indeed,
express the pleasure it is, to be met by the children with
so much joy as I am when I go thither. The boys and
girls strive who shall come first, when they think it is I
that am knocking at the door; and that child which loses
the race to me runs back again to tell the father it is Mr.
Bickerstaff[1]. This day I was led in by a pretty girl, that
we all thought must have forgot me, for the family has
been out of town these two years. Her knowing me
again was a mighty subject with us, and took up our
discourse at the first entrance. After which, they began
to rally me upon a thousand little stories they heard in
the country, about my marriage to one of my neighbour's
daughters. Upon which the gentleman, my friend, said,
"Nay, if Mr. Bickerstaff marries a child of any of his old
companions, I hope mine shall have the preference; there
is Mrs. Mary is *now sixteen*, and would make him as fine
a widow as the best of them. But I know him too well:
he is so enamoured with the very memory of those who
flourished in our youth, that he will not so much as look
upon the modern beauties. I remember, old gentleman, how often you went home in a day to refresh your
countenance and dress when Teraminta reigned in your
heart. As we came up in the coach, I repeated to my wife
some of your verses on her." With such reflections on
little passages which happened long ago, we passed our
time, during a cheerful and elegant meal. After dinner,
his lady left the room, as did also the children. As soon
as we were alone, he took me by the hand; "Well, my
good friend," says he, "I am heartily glad to see thee; I
was afraid you would never have seen all the company

---

[1] Swift borrowed the name from a locksmith's sign, and Steele adopted
it because, from Swift's use of it, it was sure to gain " an audience of all
who had any taste of wit ".

that dined with you to-day again. Do not you think the
good woman of the house a little altered, since you
followed her from the playhouse, to find out who she was,
for me?" I perceived a tear fall down his cheek as he
spoke, which moved me not a little. But, to turn the
discourse, I said, "She is not indeed quite that creature
she was, when she returned me the letter I carried from
you; and told me, 'she hoped, as I was a gentleman, I
would be employed no more to trouble her, who had
never offended me; but would be so much the gentleman's friend, as to dissuade him from a pursuit, which he
could never succeed in'. You may remember, I thought
her in earnest; and you were forced to employ your cousin
Will, who made his sister get acquainted with her, for
you. You cannot expect her to be for ever fifteen."
"Fifteen!" replied my good friend: "Ah! you little understand, you that have a lived a bachelor, how great, how
exquisite a pleasure there is, in being really beloved! It
is impossible, that the most beauteous face in nature
should raise in me such pleasing ideas, as when I look
upon that excellent woman. That fading in her countenance is chiefly caused by her watching with me in my
fever. This was followed by a fit of sickness, which had
like to have carried her off last winter. I tell you sin-
cerely, I have so many obligations to her, that I cannot,
with any sort of moderation, think of her present state of
health. But as to what you say of fifteen, she gives me
every day pleasures beyond what I ever knew in the
possession of her beauty, when I was in the vigour of
youth. Every moment of her life brings me fresh instances of her complacency to my inclinations, and her
prudence in regard to my fortune. Her face is to me
much more beautiful than when I first saw it; there is no
decay in any feature, which I cannot trace, from the very
instant it was occasioned by some anxious concern for

my welfare and interests. Thus, at the same time, me-thinks, the love I conceived towards her for what she was, is heightened by my gratitude for what she is. The love of a wife is as much above the idle passion commonly called by that name, as the loud laughter of buffoons is inferior to the elegant mirth of gentlemen. Oh, she is an inestimable jewel! In her examination of her household affairs, she shows a certain fearfulness to find a fault, which makes her servants obey her like children; and the meanest we have has an ingenuous shame for an offence, not always to be seen in children in other families. I speak freely to you, my old friend; ever since her sick-ness, things that gave me the quickest joy before, turn now to a certain anxiety. As the children play in the next room, I know the poor things by their steps, and am considering what they must do, should they lose their mother in their tender years. The pleasure I used to take in telling my boy stories of battles, and asking my girl questions about the disposal of her baby, and the gossiping of it, is turned into inward reflection and melancholy."

He would have gone on in this tender way, when the good lady entered, and with an inexpressible sweetness in her countenance told us, "she had been searching her closet for something very good, to treat such an old friend as I was" Her husband's eye sparkled with pleasure at the cheerfulness of her countenance; and I saw all his fears vanish in an instant. The lady observing some-thing in our looks which showed we had been more serious than ordinary, and seeing her husband receive her with great concern under a forced cheerfulness, im-mediately guessed at what we had been talking of; and applying herself to me, said, with a smile, "Mr. Bickerstaff, do not believe a word of what he tells you; I shall still live to have you for my second, as I have often promised you, unless he takes more care of himself than he has done since his coming to town. You must know, he tells me he finds London is a much more healthy place than the country; for he sees several of his old acquaintances and schoolfellows are here young fellows with fair full-bottomed periwigs[1]. I could scarce keep him this morning from going out open-breasted[1]". My friend, who is always extremely delighted with her agreeable humour, made her sit down with us. She did it with that easiness which is peculiar to women of sense; and to keep up the good humour she had brought in with her, turned her raillery upon me. "Mr. Bickerstaff, you remember you followed me one night from the play-house: suppose you should carry me thither to-morrow night, and lead me into the front box." This put us into a long field of discourse about the beauties, who were mothers to the present, and shined in the boxes twenty years ago. I told her, "I was glad she had transferred so many of her charms, and I did not question but her eldest daughter was within half a year of being a toast[2]."

We were pleasing ourselves with this fantastical preferment of the young lady, when on a sudden we were alarmed with the noise of a drum, and immediately entered my little godson to give me a point of war. His mother, between laughing and chiding, would have put him out of the room; but I would not part with him so. I found, upon conversation with him, though he was a little noisy in his mirth, that the child had excellent parts, and was a great master of all the learning on the

---

[1] A privilege allowed only to young beaux. In *Tatler*, No. 246, Steele reproves "a fat fellow for wearing his breast open in the midst of winter out of an affectation of youth".

[2] An institution that first came into vogue in Anne's reign. At the age of seventeen every young lady of quality expected to become a toast at some club, more especially at the Kit-Cat. The *locus classicus* on the subject is in the 24th *Tatler*.

other side eight years old. I perceived him a very great
historian in Æsop's Fables: but he frankly declared to
me his mind, "that he did not delight in that learning,
because he did not believe they were true;" for which
reason I found he had very much turned his studies, for
about a twelvemonth past, into the lives and adventures
of Don Bellianis of Greece, Guy of Warwick, the Seven
Champions, and other historians of that age. I could not
but observe the satisfaction the father took in the for-
wardness of his son; and that these diversions might
turn to some profit, I found the boy had made remarks
which might be of service to him during the course of
his whole life. He would tell you the mismanagements
of John Hickathrift, find fault with the passionate temper
in Bevis of Southampton, and loved Saint George for
being the champion of England; and by this means had
his thoughts insensibly moulded into the notions of discretion, virtue, and honour. I was extolling his accomplishments, when his mother told me that the little girl
who led me in this morning was in her way a better scholar
than he. "Betty", said she, "deals chiefly in fairies and
sprites, and sometimes in a winter night will terrify the
maids with her accounts, until they are afraid to go up to
bed."

I sat with them until it was very late, sometimes in
merry, sometimes in serious discourse, with this particular
pleasure, which gives the only true relish to all conversation, a sense that every one of us liked each other. I
went home considering the different conditions of a
married life and that of a bachelor; and I must confess
it struck me with a secret concern, to reflect, that whenever
I go off I shall leave no traces behind me. In this
pensive mood I return to my family: that is to say, to
my maid, my dog, and my cat, who only can be the
better or worse for what happens to me.

VII.—A DEATH-BED SCENE.

Ut in vita, sic in studiis, pulcherrimum et humanissimum existime
severitatem comitatemque miscere, ne illa in tristitiam, haec in petulan-
*tiam procedat.—*Pliny.

As in a man's life, so in his studies, I think it the most beautiful and
humane thing in the world, so to mingle gravity with pleasantry, that
the one may not sink into melancholy, nor the other rise up into
wantonness.

I WAS walking about my chamber this morning in a
very gay humour, when I saw a coach stop at my door,
and a youth about fifteen alighting out of it, whom I perceived to be the eldest son of my bosom friend that I
gave some account of in my paper of the seventeenth
of the last month. I felt a sensible pleasure rising in me
at the sight of him, my acquaintance having begun with
his father when he was just such a stripling, and about
that very age. When he came up to me he took me by
the hand, and burst out in tears. I was extremely moved,
and immediately said, " Child, how does your father do?"
He began to reply, "My mother—" but could not go on
for weeping. I went down with him into the coach, and
gathered out of him, "that his mother was then dying;
and that, while the holy man was doing the last offices to
her, he had taken that time to come and call me to his
father, who, he said, would certainly break his heart, if I
did not go and comfort him ". The child's discretion in
coming to me of his own head, and the tenderness he
showed for his parents, would have quite overpowered
me, had I not resolved to fortify myself for the seasonable
performances of those duties which I owed to my friend.
As we were going, I could not but reflect upon the
character of that excellent woman, and the greatness of
his grief for the loss of one who has ever been the support
to him under all other afflictions. How, thought I, will
he be able to bear the hour of her death, that could not,

when I was lately with him, speak of a sickness, which was then past, without sorrow? We were now got pretty far into Westminster, and arrived at my friend's house. At the door of it I met Favonius, not without a secret satisfaction to find he had been there. I had formerly conversed with him at this house; and as he abounds with that sort of virtue and knowledge which makes religion beautiful, and never leads the conversation into the violence and rage of party-disputes, I listened to him with great pleasure. Our discourse chanced to be upon the subject of death, which he treated with such a strength of reason, and greatness of soul, that, instead of being terrible, it appeared to a mind rightly cultivated, altogether to be contemned, or rather to be desired. As I met him at the door, I saw in his face a certain glowing of grief and humanity, heightened with an air of fortitude and resolution, which, as I afterwards found, had such an irresistible force, as to suspend the pains of the dying, and the lamentation of the nearest friends who attended her. I went up directly to the room where she lay, and was met at the entrance by my friend, who, notwithstanding his thoughts had been composed a little before, at the sight of me turned away his face and wept. The little family of children renewed the expressions of their sorrow according to their several ages and degrees of under-standing. The eldest daughter was in tears, busied in attendance upon her mother; others were kneeling about the bedside; and what troubled me most, was, to see a little boy, who was too young to know the reason, weeping only because his sisters did. The only one in the room who seemed resigned and comforted was the dying person. At my approach to the bed side she told me, with a low broken voice, "This is kindly done—take care of your friend—do not go from him". She had before taken leave of her husband and children, in a manner proper

for so solemn a parting, and with a gracefulness peculiar
to a woman of her character. My heart was torn in
pieces, to see the husband on one side suppressing and
keeping down the swellings of his grief, for fear of dis-
turbing her in her last moments; and the wife, even at
that time, concealing the pains she endured, for fear of
increasing his affliction. She kept her eyes upon him
for some moments after she grew speechless, and soon
after closed them for ever. In the moment of her
departure, my friend, who had thus far commanded
himself, gave a deep groan, and fell into a swoon by her
bed side.[1] The distraction of the children, who thought
they saw both their parents expiring together, and now
lying dead before them, would have melted the hardest
heart; but they soon perceived their father recover, whom
I helped to remove into another room, with a resolution
to accompany him until the first pangs of his affliction
were abated. I knew consolation would now be impertinent, and therefore contented myself to sit by him, and
condole with him in silence. For I shall here use the
method of an ancient author[2], who, in one of his epistles,
relating the virtues and death of Macrinus's wife, expresses
himself thus: "I shall suspend my advice to this best of
friends until he is made capable of receiving it by those
three great remedies, the necessity of submission, length
of time, and satiety of grief".

In the mean time, I cannot but consider, with much
commiseration, the melancholy state of one who has had

---

[1] With this sentence Steele's share in the paper stops. The rest has
always been assigned to Addison, and it is instructive to compare his
conclusion with Steele's in *Tatler*, 281. Steele's emotion kept pace with
his imagination, while Addison constantly checked his from an over-
regard for "elegant" expression. Thus, while Addison ends this essay
incongruously with a fragment of criticism, Steele is quite overcome,
and "commended the hamper of wine until two of the clock this
morning".

[2] Seneca.

such a part of himself torn from him, and which he misses in every circumstance of life. His condition is like that of one who has lately lost his right arm, and is every moment offering to help himself with it. He does not appear to himself the same person in his house, at his table, in company, or in retirement; and loses the relish of all the pleasures and diversions that were before entertaining to him by her participation of them. The most agreeable objects recall the sorrow for her with whom he used to enjoy them. This additional satisfaction, from the taste of pleasures in the society of one we love, is admirably described by Milton, who represents Eve, though in Paradise itself, no further pleased with the beautiful objects around her, than as she sees them in company with Adam, in that passage so inexpressibly charming:

> "With thee conversing, I forget all time;
> All seasons, and their change; all please alike.
> Sweet is the breath of morn, her rising sweet
> With charm of earliest birds; pleasant the sun,
> When first on this delightful land he spreads
> His orient beams, on herb, tree, fruit, and flower,
> Glistering with dew; fragrant the fertile earth
> After soft showers; and sweet the coming on
> Of grateful evening mild; the silent night,
> With this her solemn bird, and this fair moon,
> And these the gems of heaven, her starry train.
> But neither breath of morn when she ascends
> With charm of earliest birds; nor rising sun
> On this delightful land; nor herb, fruit, flower,
> Glistering with dew; nor fragrance after showers;
> Nor grateful evening mild; nor silent night,
> With this her solemn bird, nor walk by moon,
> Or glittering star-light, without thee is sweet."

The variety of images in this passage is infinitely pleasing, and the recapitulation of each particular image, with a little varying of the expression, makes one of the finest turns of words that I have ever seen; which I rather

mention because Mr. Dryden[1] has said, in his preface to
Juvenal, that he could meet with no turn of words in
Milton.

It may be further observed, that though the sweetness
of these verses has something in it of a pastoral, yet it
excels the ordinary kind, as much as the scene of it is
above an ordinary field or meadow.   I might here, since
I am accidentally led into this subject, show several
passages in Milton that have as excellent turns of this
nature as any of our English poets whatsoever; but shall
only mention that which follows, in which he describes
the fallen angels engaged in the intricate disputes of pre-
destination, free-will, and fore-knowledge; and, to humour
the perplexity, makes a kind of labyrinth in the very
words that describe it.

> "Others apart sat on a hill retir'd,
>   In thoughts more elevate, and reason'd high
>   Of providence, fore-knowledge, will, and fate,
>   Fix'd fate, free-will, fore-knowledge absolute,
>   And found no end, in wandering mazes lost."

VIII. THE TRUMPET CLUB.[2]

*Habeo senectuti magnam gratiam, quae mihi sermonis aviditatem
auxit, potionis et cibi sustulit.*—Cicero, de Sen.
I am much beholden to old age, which has increased my eagerness
for conversation, in proportion as it has lessened my appetites of hunger
and thirst.

AFTER having applied my mind with more than ordinary attention to my studies, it is my usual custom
to relax and unbend it in the conversation of such as are

---

[1] Near the end of his Discourse on Satire, Dryden says that he
searched the older poets in quest of "beautiful turns of thoughts and
words", but that he found none in Cowley or in Milton.

[2] As clubs are of some interest to students of the English Essay,
reference may be made to Timbs' *History of Clubs and Club Life*, and to
Ashton's *Social Life in the Reign of Queen Anne*. To the latter excellent
book the present writer has to express special obligations.

rather easy than shining companions. This I find particularly necessary for me before I retire to rest, in order
to draw my slumbers upon me by degrees, and fall asleep
insensibly. This is the particular use I make of a set of
heavy honest men, with whom I have passed many hours
with much indolence, though not with great pleasure.
Their conversation is a kind of preparative for sleep; it
takes the mind down from its abstractions, leads it into
the familiar traces of thought, and lulls it into that state
of tranquillity, which is the condition of a thinking man,
when he is but half awake. After this, my reader will
not be surprised to hear the account which I am about to
give of a club of my own contemporaries, among whom I
pass two or three hours every evening. This I look upon
as taking my first nap before I go to bed. The truth of
it is, I should think myself unjust to posterity, as well as
to the society at the *Trumpet*[1], of which I am a member, did not I in some part of my writings give an account
of the persons among whom I have passed almost a sixth
part of my time for these last forty years. Our club consisted originally of fifteen; but, partly by the severity of
the law in arbitrary times, and partly by the natural effects
of old age, we are at present reduced to a third part of
that number; in which, however, we have this consolation,
that the best company is said to consist of five persons.
I must confess, besides the aforementioned benefit which
I meet with in the conversation of this select society, I
am not the less pleased with the company, in that I find
myself the greatest wit among them, and am heard as
their oracle in all points of learning and difficulty.

Sir Jeoffery Notch, who is the oldest of the club, has
been in possession of the right-hand chair time out of
mind, and is the only man among us that has the liberty

---

[1] A tavern in Shire Lane, near the new Courts of Justice. The Kit
Cat Club also originated here about 1700.

of stirring the fire. This our foreman is a gentleman of an ancient family, that came to a great estate some years before he had discretion, and run it out in hounds, horses, and cock-fighting; for which reason he looks upon himself as an honest, worthy gentleman, who has had misfortunes in the world, and calls every thriving man a pitiful upstart.

Major Matchlock is the next senior, who served in the last civil wars, and has all the battles by heart. He does not think any action in Europe worth talking of since the fight of Marston Moor; and every night tells us of having been knocked off his horse at the rising[1] of the London apprentices; for which he is in great esteem among us.

Honest old Dick Reptile is the third of our society. He is a good-natured indolent man, who speaks little himself, but laughs at our jokes; and brings his young nephew along with him, a youth of eighteen years old, to show him good company, and give him a taste of the world. This young fellow sits generally silent; but whenever he opens his mouth, or laughs at anything that passes, he is constantly told by his uncle, after a jocular manner, "Ay, ay, Jack, you young men think us fools; but we old men know you are".

The greatest wit of our company, next to myself, is a bencher of the neighbouring inn, who in his youth frequented the ordinaries[2] about Charing-cross, and pretends to have been intimate with Jack Ogle. He has about ten distichs of Hudibras without book, and never leaves the club until he has applied them all. If any modern wit be mentioned, or any town-frolic spoken of, he shakes his head at the dulness of the present age, and tells us a story of Jack Ogle.

---

[1] July 14, 1647.
[2] Locket's Ordinary at Charing Cross was one of the fashionable restaurants of the time. Cf. *Tale of a Tub*, Sec. 2.

For my own part, I am esteemed among them, because they see I am something respected by others; though at the same time I understand by their behaviour, that I am considered by them as a man of a great deal of learning, but no knowledge of the world; insomuch, that the major sometimes, in the height of his military pride, calls me the Philosopher: and Sir Jeoffery, no longer ago than last night, upon a dispute what day of the month it was then in Holland, pulled his pipe out of his mouth, and cried, "What does the scholar say to it?"

Our club meets precisely at *six o'clock in the evening*; but I did not come last night until half an hour after seven, by which means I escaped the battle of Naseby, which the major usually begins at about three quarters after six: I found also, that my good friend the bencher had already spent three of his distichs; and only waited an opportunity to hear a sermon spoken of, that he might introduce the couplet where "a stick" rhymes to "ecclesiastic". At my entrance into the room, they were naming a red petticoat and a cloak, by which I found that the bencher had been diverting them with a story of Jack Ogle.

I had no sooner taken my seat, but Sir Jeoffery, to show his goodwill towards me, gave me a pipe of his own tobacco, and stirred up the fire. I look upon it as a point of morality, to be obliged by those who endeavour to oblige me; and therefore, in requital for his kindness, and to set the conversation a-going, I took the best occasion I could to put him upon telling us the story of old Gantlett[1], which he always does with very particular concern. He traced up his descent on both sides for several generations, describing his diet and manner of life, with his several battles, and particularly that in which

---

[1] Cock-fighting was then a favourite pastime. As much as 500 guineas was staked on an inter-county match.

he fell. This Gantlett was a game cock, upon whose
head the knight, in his youth, had won five hundred
pounds, and lost two thousand. This naturally set the
major upon the account of Edge-hill fight, and ended in
a duel of Jack Ogle's.

Old Reptile was extremely attentive to all that was
said, though it was the same he had heard every night
for these twenty years, and, upon all occasions, winked
upon his nephew to mind what passed.

This may suffice to give the world a taste of our innocent conversation, which we spun out until about ten of
the clock, when my maid came with a lantern to light me
home.   I could not but reflect with myself, as I was
going out, upon the talkative humour of old men, and
the little figure which that part of life makes in one who
cannot employ his natural propensity in discourses which
would make him venerable.   I must own, it makes me
very melancholy in company, when I hear a young man
begin a story; and have often observed, that one of a
quarter of an hour long in a man of five-and-twenty,
gathers circumstances every time he tells it, until it
grows into a long Canterbury tale of two hours by that
time he is threescore.

The only way of avoiding such a trifling and frivolous
old age, is to lay up in our way to it such stores of
knowledge and observation, as may make us useful and
agreeable in our declining years.   The mind of man in a
long life will become a magazine of wisdom or folly,
and will consequently discharge itself in something
impertinent or improving.   For which reason, as there
is nothing more ridiculous than an old trifling story-teller,
so there is nothing more venerable than one who has
turned his experience to the entertainment and advantage
of mankind.

In short, we, who are in the last stage of life, and are

apt to indulge ourselves in talk, ought to consider if what we speak be worth being heard, and endeavour to make our discourse like that of Nestor, which Homer compares to the flowing of honey for its sweetness.

I am afraid I shall be thought guilty of this excess I am speaking of, when I cannot conclude without observing that Milton certainly thought of this passage in Homer, when, in his description of an eloquent spirit, he says:—

> " His tongue dropped manna ".

IX. ON THE DEATH OF FRIENDS.

Dies, ni fallor, adest, quem semper acerbum,
Semper honoratum, sic dii voluistis, habebo.
—Virg. *Aen.* v. 49.

And now the rising day renews the year,
A day for ever sad, for ever dear.—*Dryden.*

THERE are those among mankind, who can enjoy no relish of their being, except the world is made acquainted with all that relates to them, and think everything lost that passes unobserved; but others find a solid delight in stealing by the crowd, and modelling their life after such a manner as is as much above the approbation as the practice of the vulgar. Life being too short to give instances great enough of true friendship or goodwill, some sages have thought it pious to preserve a certain reverence for the Manes of their deceased friends; and have withdrawn themselves from the rest of the world at certain seasons, to commemorate in their own thoughts such of their acquaintance who have gone before them out of this life. And indeed, when we are advanced in years, there is not a more pleasing entertainment, than to recollect in a gloomy moment the many we have parted with that have been dear and agreeable to us, and to cast a melancholy thought or two after those with whom, perhaps, we have indulged ourselves in whole nights of mirth and jollity. With such inclinations in my heart I went to my closet yesterday in the evening, and resolved to be sorrowful; upon which occasion I could not but look with disdain upon myself, that though all the reasons which I had to lament the loss of many of my friends are now as forcible as at the moment of their departure, yet did not my heart swell with the same sorrow which I felt at that time; but I could, without tears, reflect upon many pleasing adventures I have had with some, who have long been blended with common earth. Though it is by the benefit of nature that length of time thus blots out the violence of afflictions; yet, with tempers too much given to pleasure, it is almost necessary to revive the old places of grief in our memory; and ponder step by step on past life, to lead the mind into that sobriety of thought which poises the heart, and makes it beat with due time, without being quickened by desire, or retarded with despair, from its proper and equal motion. When we wind up a clock that is out of order, to make it go well for the future, we do not immediately set the hand to the present instant, but we make it strike the round of all its hours, before it can recover the regularity of its time. Such, thought I, shall be my method this evening; and since it is that day of the year which I dedicate to the memory of such in another life as I much delighted in when living, an hour or two shall be sacred to sorrow and their memory, while I run over all the melancholy circumstances of this kind which have occurred to me in my whole life.

The first sense of sorrow I ever knew was upon the death of my father[1], at which time I was not quite five years of age; but was rather amazed at what all the house

---

[1] Steele's father was a lawyer, and was once secretary to the Duke of Ormond, who procured the essayist a foundation at the Charterhouse, where his friendship with Addison began.

meant than possessed with a real understanding why nobody was willing to play with me. I remember I went into the room where his body lay, and my mother sat weeping alone by it. I had my battledore in my hand, and fell a-beating the coffin, and calling papa; for, I know not how, I had some slight idea that he was locked up there. My mother catched me in her arms, and, transported beyond all patience of the silent grief she was before in, she almost smothered me in her embraces; and told me in a flood of tears, "Papa could not hear me, and would play with me no more, for they were going to put him under ground, whence he could never come to us again". She was a very beautiful woman, of a noble spirit, and there was a dignity in her grief amidst all the wildness of her transport which, methought, struck me with an instinct of sorrow, that, before I was sensible of what it was to grieve, seized my very soul, and has made pity the weakness of my heart ever since. The mind in infancy is, methinks, like the body in embryo; and receives impressions so forcible, that they are as hard to be removed by reason as any mark with which a child is born is to be taken away by any future application. Hence it is that good-nature in me is no merit; but having been so frequently overwhelmed with her tears before I knew the cause of any affliction, or could draw defences from my own judgment, I imbibed commiseration, remorse, and an unmanly gentleness of mind, which has since insnared me into ten thousand calamities; from whence I can reap no advantage, except it be that, in such a humour as I am now in, I can the better indulge myself in the softness of humanity, and enjoy that sweet anxiety which arises from the memory of past afflictions.

We, that are very old, are better able to remember things which befell us in our distant youth than the passages of later days. For this reason it is that the

companions of my strong and vigorous years present
themselves more immediately to me in this office of sorrow.
Untimely and unhappy deaths are what we are most apt
to lament; so little are we able to make it indifferent
when a thing happens, though we know it must happen.
Thus we groan under life, and bewail those who are
relieved from it. Every object that returns to our imagination raises different passions, according to the
circumstance of their departure. Who can have lived
in an army, and in a serious hour reflect upon the many
gay and agreeable men that might long have flourished
in the arts of peace, and not join with the imprecations
of the fatherless and widow on the tyrant to whose ambition they fell sacrifices? But gallant men, who are cut
off by the sword, move rather our veneration than our
pity; and we gather relief enough from their own contempt
of death, to make that no evil, which was approached with
so much cheerfulness, and attended with so much honour.
But when we turn our thoughts from the great parts of
life on such occasions, and instead of lamenting those
who stood ready to give death to those from whom they
had the fortune to receive it; I say, when we let our
thoughts wander from such noble objects, and consider
the havoc which is made among the tender and the
innocent, pity enters with an unmixed softness, and
possesses all our souls at once.

Here (were there words to express such sentiments with
proper tenderness) I should record the beauty, innocence,
and untimely death of the first object my eyes ever beheld
with love. The beauteous virgin! how ignorantly did she
charm, how carelessly excel! Oh Death! thou hast right
to the bold, to the ambitious, to the high, and to the
haughty; but why this cruelty to the humble, to the meek,
to the undiscerning, to the thoughtless? Nor age, nor
business, nor distress can erase the dear image from my

imagination. In the same week, I saw her dressed for a ball, and in a shroud. How ill did the habit of death become the pretty trifler! I still behold the smiling earth——A large train of disasters were coming on to my memory, when my servant knocked at my closet-door, and interrupted me with a letter, attended with a hamper of wine, of the same sort with that which is to be put to sale on Thursday next at Garraway's coffee-house [1]. Upon the receipt of it I sent for three of my friends. We are so intimate that we can be company in whatever state of mind we meet, and can entertain each other without expecting always to rejoice. The wine we found to be generous and warming, but with such a heat as moved us rather to be cheerful than frolicsome. It revived the spirits, without firing the blood. We commended it until two of the clock this morning; and having to-day met a little before dinner, we found that, though we drank two bottles a man, we had much more reason to recollect than forget what had passed the night before.

x. THE SPECTATOR CLUB.

Ast alii sex
Et plures uno conclamant ore.—Juv. Sat. vii. 166.

Six more at least join their consenting voice.

THE first of our society is a gentleman of Worcester-shire, of an ancient descent, a baronet, his name Sir Roger de Coverley [2]. His great-grandfather was in-ventor of that famous country-dance which is called after him. All who know that shire are very well acquainted with the parts and merits of Sir Roger. He is a gentleman

---

[1] A noted coffee-house in Change Alley, Cornhill. It was opened about 1660 by Thomas Garway, who was the first to sell tea.

[2] The tune and dance are said to have been named after a Yorkshire knight, Roger Calverley, who lived in the reign of Richard I. (Chappell's *Music of the Olden Time*).

that is very singular in his behaviour, but his singularities
proceed from his good sense, and are contradictions to
the manners of the world, only as he thinks the world is
in the wrong. However, this humour creates him no
enemies, for he does nothing with sourness or obstinacy;
and his being unconfined to modes and forms makes him
but the readier and more capable to please and oblige all
who know him. When he is in town he lives in Soho
Square. It is said he keeps himself a bachelor by reason
he was crossed in love by a perverse beautiful widow of
the next county to him. Before this disappointment, Sir
Roger was what you call a fine gentleman[1], had often
supped with my Lord Rochester[2] and Sir George
Etherege[3], fought a duel upon his first coming to town,
and kicked bully Dawson[4] in a public coffee-house for
calling him youngster. But being ill-used by the above-
mentioned widow, he was very serious for a year and a
half; and though, his temper being naturally jovial, he at
last got over it, he grew careless of himself and never
dressed afterwards. He continues to wear a coat and
doublet of the same cut that were in fashion at the time

[1] This describes those whom Steele calls "ambitious young men, every
night employed in roasting Porters, smoking Coblers, knocking down
Watchmen, overturning Constables, etc." (*Tatler*, 77).

[2] John Wilmot, Earl of Rochester (1647-1680), a poet of some ability.
Rochester and Sedley anticipated the Mohocks of Queen Anne's reign,
and were notorious even in the Restoration age.

[3] This dramatist (1634-1694) closely resembled the two writers men-
tioned above. His plays are of little value, but one of them, *The
Comical Revenge* (1664), has the distinction of having founded the
English Comedy of Manners.

[4] A tavern swashbuckler, who is represented in Brown's *Letters from
the Living to the Dead* as thus challenging a rival bully:—"If ever you
intend to be my Rival in Glory, you must fight a Bailiff once a Day,
Stand Kick and Cuff once a Week, Challenge some Coward or Other
once a Month, Bilk your Lodgings once a Quarter, and Cheat a Taylor
once a Year. Never till then will the fame of W-n (Wharton?) ring
like Dawson's in every coffee-house, and be the merry subject of every
Tavern Tittle Tattle."

of his repulse, which, in his merry humours, he tells us,
has been in and out twelve times since he first wore it.
It is said Sir Roger grew humble in his desires after he
had forgot his cruel beauty, in so much that it is reported
he has frequently offended with beggars and gypsies; but
this is looked upon, by his friends, rather as matter of
raillery than truth. He is now in his fifty-sixth year,
cheerful, gay, and hearty; keeps a good house both in
town and country; a great lover of mankind; but there
is such a mirthful cast in his behaviour, that he is
rather beloved than esteemed[1]. His tenants grow rich,
his servants look satisfied, all the young women profess
love to him, and the young men are glad of his company.
When he comes into a house, he calls the servants by
their names, and talks all the way upstairs to a visit. I
must not omit that Sir Roger is a justice of the quorum;
that he fills the chair at a quarter-session with great
abilities, and three months ago gained universal applause,
by explaining a passage in the Game Act.

The gentleman next in esteem and authority among us

---

[1] The Coverley papers properly amount to thirty-one in number, of
which Addison wrote sixteen, Steele seven, Budgell three, and Tickell
one. (No. 410, signed T, has been ascribed to Steele, but internal
evidence favours its assignment to Tickell.) The natural outcome of
this joint-authorship is the presence of some incongruities in the sketch.
To mention but one example, the simple knight who makes guileless
comments on the Tombs (Add. *Spect.* 329) could never have been such
a beau in his youth as to have supped with Etherege and Rochester
(Steele, *Spect.* 2). It can hardly be doubted that Addison indulged in
some irony at the knight's expense, thereby aiming a left-handed blow
at Tory squiredom. It is only hero-worship that could make a critic see
in Addison's picture nothing but "a sweet image of simplicity and good-
ness" (Arnold's *Spectator.*) Nor is it quite just to say, as Mr. Gosse
does, that Sir Roger is "the peculiar property of Addison". This is
merely to re-echo what Mr. Forster truly called "the braying of Hurd".
Some of the finest touches in the picture are entirely due to Steele, and
a very competent critic, after a subtle analysis of the character, arrived
at the conclusion that "all that is amiable in the conception belongs to
Steele" (Minto's *Manual of Eng. Prose Lit.*, p. 457.)

is another bachelor, who is a member of the Inner Temple,
a man of great probity, wit, and understanding; but he
has chosen his place of residence rather to obey the direction of an old humorsome father than in pursuit of his
own inclinations.   He was placed there to study the laws
of the land, and is the most learned of any of the house
in those of the stage.   Aristotle and Longinus are much
better understood by him than Littleton or Coke.   The
father sends up every post questions relating to marriage-
articles, leases, and tenures, in the neighbourhood; all
which questions he agrees with an attorney to answer and
take care of in the lump.   He is studying the passions
themselves, when he should be enquiring into the debates
among men which arise from them.   He knows the
argument of each of the orations of Demosthenes and
Tully, but not one case in the reports of our own courts.
No one ever took him for a fool; but none, except his
intimate friends, know he has a great deal of wit.   This
turn makes him at once both disinterested and agreeable.
As few of his thoughts are drawn from business, they are
most of them fit for conversation.   His taste for books
is a little too just for the age he lives in; he has read all
but approves of very few.   His familiarity with the customs,
manners, actions, and writings of the ancients, makes him
a very delicate observer of what occurs to him in the
present world.   He is an excellent critic, and the time
of the play is his hour of business; exactly at five he
passes through New-Inn, crosses through Russell-court,
and takes a turn at Will's till the play begins; he has his
shoes rubbed and his periwig powdered at the barber's
as you go into the Rose.   It is for the good of the audience when he is at the play, for the actors have an ambition to please him.

The person of next consideration is Sir Andrew Freeport, a merchant of great eminence in the city of London;

a person of indefatigable industry, strong reason, and great experience. His notions of trade are noble and generous, and (as every rich man has usually some sly way of jesting, which would make no great figure were he not a rich man) he calls the sea the British Common. He is acquainted with commerce in all its parts, and will tell you that it is a stupid and barbarous way to extend dominion by arms; for true power is to be got by arts and industry. He will often argue that, if this part of our trade were well cultivated, we should gain from one nation; and if another, from another. I have heard him prove that diligence makes more lasting acquisitions than valour, and that sloth has ruined more nations than the sword. He abounds in several frugal maxims, amongst which the greatest favourite is, "A penny saved is a penny got". A general trader of good sense is pleasanter company than a general scholar; and Sir Andrew having a natural unaffected eloquence, the perspicuity of his discourse gives the same pleasure that wit would in another man. He has made his fortune himself; and says that England may be richer than other kingdoms by as plain methods as he himself is richer than other men; though at the same time I can say this of him, that there is not a point in the compass but blows home a ship in which he is an owner.

Next to Sir Andrew in the club-room sits Captain Sentry, a gentleman of great courage, good understanding, but invincible modesty. He is one of those that deserve very well, but are very awkward at putting their talents within the observation of such as should take notice of them. He was some years a captain, and behaved himself with great gallantry in several engagements and at several sieges; but having a small estate of his own, and being next heir to Sir Roger, he has quitted a way of life in which no man can rise suitably to his merit, who is

not something of a courtier as well as a soldier. I have
heard him often lament that, in a profession where merit
is placed in so conspicuous a view, impudence should
get the better of modesty. When he has talked to this
purpose, I never heard him make a sour expression, but
frankly confess that he left the world, because he was not
fit for it. A strict honesty and an even regular behaviour
are in themselves obstacles to him that must press through
crowds, who endeavour at the same end with himself,
the favour of a commander. He will, however, in his
way of talk excuse generals for not disposing according
to men's desert, or enquiring into it; for, says he, that
great man who has a mind to help me has as many to
break through to come to me as I have to come at him:
therefore he will conclude that the man who would make
a figure, especially in a military way, must get over all
false modesty, and assist his patron against the impor-
tunity of other pretenders, by a proper assurance in his
own vindication. He says it is a civil cowardice to be
backward in asserting what you ought to expect, as it is
a military fear to be slow in attacking when it is your
duty. With this candour does the gentleman speak of
himself and others. The same frankness runs through
all his conversation. The military part of his life has
furnished him with many adventures, in the relation of
which he is very agreeable to the company; for he is
never overbearing, though accustomed to command men
in the utmost degree below him; nor ever too obsequious,
from an habit of obeying men highly above him.

But that our society may not appear a set of humourists,
unacquainted with the gallantries and pleasures of the
age, we have amongst us the gallant Will Honeycomb,
a gentleman who, according to his years, should be in the
decline of his life; but having ever been very careful of
his person, and always had a very easy fortune, time has

made but a very little impression, either by wrinkles on his forehead, or traces on his brain. His person is well turned, and of a good height. He is very ready at that sort of discourse with which men usually entertain women. He has all his life dressed very well, and remembers habits as others do men. He can smile when one speaks to him, and laughs easily. He knows the history of every mode, and can inform you from which of the French king's wenches our wives and daughters had this manner of curling their hair, that way of placing their hoods; whose frailty was covered by such a sort of petticoat, and whose vanity to show her foot made that part of the dress so short in such a year. In a word, all his conversation and knowledge have been in the female world. As other men of his age will take notice to you what such a minister said upon such and such an occasion, he will tell you when the Duke of Monmouth danced at court, such a woman was then smitten, another was taken with him at the head of his troop in the park. In all these important relations, he has ever about the same time received a kind glance, or a blow of a fan from some celebrated beauty, mother of the present Lord Such-a-one. If you speak of a young commoner that said a lively thing in the House, he starts up, " He has good blood in his veins; Tom Mirable begot him; the rogue cheated me in that affair; that young fellow's mother used me more like a dog than any woman I ever made advances to". This way of talking of his very much enlivens the conversation among us of a more sedate turn, and I find there is not one of the company, but myself, who rarely speak at all, but speaks of him as of that sort of man who is usually called a well-bred fine gentleman. To conclude his character, where women are not concerned, he is an honest worthy man.

I cannot tell whether I am to account him, whom I am

next to speak of, as one of our company; for he visits us but seldom, but when he does, it adds to every man else a new enjoyment of himself. He is a clergyman, a very philosophic man, of general learning, great sanctity of life, and the most exact good breeding. He has the misfortune to be of a very weak constitution, and consequently cannot accept of such cares and business as preferments in his function would oblige him to; he is therefore among divines what a chamber - counsellor is among lawyers. The probity of his mind, and the integrity of his life, create him followers, as being eloquent or loud advances others. He seldom introduces the subject he speaks upon; but we are so far gone in years that he observes, when he is among us, an earnestness to have him fall on some divine topic, which he always treats with much authority, as one who has no interest in this world, as one who is hastening to the object of all his wishes, and conceives hope from his decays and infirmities. These are my ordinary companions..

XI. THE UGLY CLUB.

Tetrum ante omnia vultum.—Juv., *Sat.* x. 191.

A visage rough,
Deform'd, unfeatur'd.—*Dryden.*

SINCE our persons are not of our own making, when they are such as appear defective or uncomely, it is, methinks, an honest and laudable fortitude to dare to be ugly; at least to keep ourselves from being abashed with a consciousness of imperfections which we cannot help, and in which there is no guilt. I would not defend a haggard beau for passing away much time at a glass, and giving softness and languishing graces to deformity: all I intend is, that we ought to be contented with our countenance and shape, so far as never to give ourselves an uneasy reflection on that subject. It is to the ordinary people, who are not accustomed to make very proper remarks on any occasion, matter of great jest if a man enters with a prominent pair of shoulders into an assembly, or is distinguished by an expansion of mouth, or obliquity of aspect. It is happy for a man that has any of these oddnesses about him, if he can be as merry upon himself as others are apt to be upon that occasion. When he can possess himself with such a cheerfulness, women and children, who are at first frightened at him, will afterwards be as much pleased with him. As it is barbarous in others to rally him for natural defects, it is extremely agreeable when he can jest upon himself for them.

Madame Maintenon's first husband[1] was an hero in this kind, and has drawn many pleasantries from the irregularity of his shape, which he describes as very much resembling the letter Z. He diverts himself likewise by representing to his reader the make of an engine and pulley, with which he used to take off his hat. When there happens to be anything ridiculous in a visage, and the owner of it thinks it an aspect of dignity, he must be of very great quality to be exempt from raillery. The best expedient, therefore, is to be pleasant upon himself. Prince Harry and Falstaff, in Shakespeare, have carried the ridicule upon fat and lean as far as it will go. Falstaff is humorously called woolsack, bedpresser, and hill of flesh; Harry, a starveling, an elfskin, a sheath, a bowcase, and a tuck. There is, in several incidents of the conversation between them, the jest still kept up upon the person. Great tenderness and sensibility in this point is one of the greatest weaknesses of self-love. For my own part, I am a little unhappy in the mould of my face, which is not quite so long as it is broad. Whether this might not partly arise from my opening my mouth much

[1] Scarron.

seldomer than other people, and by consequence not so much lengthening the fibres of my visage, I am not at leisure to determine. However it be, I have been often put out of countenance by the shortness of my face,[1] and was formerly at great pains in concealing it by wearing a periwig with a high fore-top, and letting my beard grow. But now I have thoroughly got over this delicacy, and could be contented with a much shorter, provided it might qualify me for a member of the merry club, which the following letter gives me an account of. I have received it from Oxford, and as it abounds with the spirit of mirth and good humour, which is natural to that place, I shall set it down word for word as it came to me.

"Most Profound Sir,

"Having been very well entertained, in the last of your speculations that I have yet seen, by your specimen upon clubs, which I therefore hope you will continue, I shall take the liberty to furnish you with a brief account of such a one as, perhaps, you have not seen in all your travels, unless it was your fortune to touch upon some of the woody parts of the African continent, in your voyage to or from Grand Cairo. There have arose in this university (long since you left us without saying anything) several of these inferior hebdomadal societies, as the Punning Club, the Witty Club, and, amongst the rest, the Handsome Club; as a burlesque upon which, a certain merry species that seem to have come into the world in masquerade, for some years last past have associated themselves together, and assumed the name of the Ugly Club. This ill-favoured fraternity consists of a president and twelve fellows; the choice of which is not confined by

---

[1] This was made use of by the savage John Dennis in his attack on Steele, who had, he said, "a shape like the picture of somebody over a farmer's chimney". Steele vanquished his surly critic with the suavest good humour.

patent to any particular foundation (as St. John's men would have the world believe, and have therefore erected a separate society within themselves), but liberty is left to elect from any school in Great Britain, provided the candidates be within the rules of the club, as set forth in a table entitled, 'The Act of Deformity', a clause or two of which I shall transmit to you.

" 'I. That no person whatsoever shall be admitted without a visible queerity in his aspect, or peculiar cast of countenance; of which the president and officers for the time being are to determine, and the president to have the casting voice.

" 'II. That a singular regard be had upon examination to the gibbosity of the gentlemen that offer themselves as founder's kinsmen; or to the obliquity of their figure, in what sort soever.

" 'III. That if the quantity of any man's nose be eminently miscalculated, whether as to length or breadth, he shall have a just pretence to be elected.

" 'Lastly, That if there shall be two or more competitors for the same vacancy, *cæteris paribus*, he that has the thickest skin to have the preference.'

" Every fresh member, upon his first night, is to entertain the company with a dish of cod-fish, and a speech in praise of Æsop, whose portraiture they have in full proportion, or rather disproportion, over the chimney; and their design is, as soon as their funds are sufficient, to purchase the heads of Thersites, Duns Scotus[1], Scarron, Hudibras[2], and the old gentleman in Oldham,[3] with all

---

[1] The disciples of Aquinas maligned the personal appearance as well as the doctrines of Duns Scotus.

[2] Admitted to the club for the sake of his beard, which was a mixture of whey, orange, and grey.

[3] Ignatius Loyola as described in the third of the *Satires upon the Jesuits* by John Oldham, 1679.

the celebrated ill faces of antiquity, as furniture for the club-room.

"As they have always been professed admirers of the other sex, so they unanimously declare that they will give all possible encouragement to such as will take the benefit of the statute, though none yet have appeared to do it.

"The worthy president, who is their most devoted champion, has lately shown me two copies of verses, composed by a gentleman of his society; the first, a congratulatory ode, inscribed to Mrs. Touchwood, upon the loss of her two fore-teeth; the other, a panegyric upon Mrs. Andiron's left shoulder. Mrs. Vizard, he says, since the small-pox, has grown tolerably ugly, and a top toast in the club; but I never heard him so lavish of his fine things as upon old Nell Trot, who constantly officiates at their table; her he even adores and extols as the very counterpart of Mother Shipton; in short, Nell, says he, is one of the extraordinary works of nature; but as for complexion, shape, and features, so valued by others, they are all mere outside and sym-metry, which is his aversion. Give me leave to add that the president is a facetious, pleasant gentleman, and never more so than when he has got (as he calls them) his dear mummers about him; and he often protests it does him good to meet a fellow with a right genuine grimace in his air (which is so agreeable in the generality of the French nation); and, as an instance of his sincerity in this particular, he gave me a sight of a list in his pocket-book of all this class, who for these five years have fallen under his observation, with himself at the head of them, and in the rear (as one of a promising and improving aspect), Sir,

"Your obliged and humble servant,
         "ALEXANDER CARBUNCLE.

"OXFORD, *March* 12, 1710."

XII. SIR ROGER AND THE WIDOW.

Hærent infixi pectore vultus.—Virg. *Æn.* iv. 4.

Her looks were deep imprinted in his heart.

IN my first description of the company in which I pass
most of my time, it may be remembered that I mentioned a great affliction which my friend Sir Roger had
met with in his youth, which was no less than a disappointment in love. It happened this evening that we
fell into a very pleasing walk at a distance from his house.
As soon as we came into it, "It is," quoth the good old
man, looking round him with a smile, "very hard that
any part of my land should be settled upon one who has
used me so ill as the perverse widow[1] did; and yet I am
sure I could not see a sprig of any bough of this whole
walk of trees, but I should reflect upon her and her
severity. She has certainly the finest hand of any woman
in the world. You are to know this was the place
wherein I used to muse upon her; and by that custom
I can never come into it, but the same tender sentiments
revive in my mind as if I had actually walked with that
beautiful creature under these shades. I have been fool
enough to carve her name on the bark of several of these
trees; so unhappy is the condition of men in love to
attempt the removing of their passion by the methods
which serve only to imprint it deeper. She has certainly
the finest hand of any woman in the world."

Here followed a profound silence; and I was not dis-
pleased to observe my friend falling so naturally into a
discourse, which I had ever before taken notice he industriously avoided. After a very long pause, he entered

---

[1] It has been conjectured that the widow—and also, with less proba-
bility, the sweetheart alluded to in *Tatler* 181—was Mrs. Catherine
Bovey, to whom Steele dedicated the second volume of his *Lady's
Library.*

upon an account of this great circumstance in his life,
with an air which I thought raised my idea of him above
what I had ever had before; and gave me the picture of
that cheerful mind of his before it received that stroke
which has ever since affected his words and actions. But
he went on as follows:

"I came to my estate in my twenty-second year, and
resolved to follow the steps of the most worthy of my
ancestors who have inhabited this spot of earth before
me, in all the methods of hospitality and good neighbourhood, for the sake of my fame; and in country
sports and recreations, for the sake of my health. In
my twenty-third year, I was obliged to serve as Sheriff
of my county; and in my servants, officers, and whole
equipage, indulged the pleasure of a young man (who
did not think ill of his own person) in taking that
public occasion of showing my figure and behaviour to
advantage. You may easily imagine to yourself what
appearance I made, who am pretty tall, rode well, and was
very well dressed, at the head of a whole county, with
music before me, a feather in my hat, and my horse well
bitted. I can assure you I was not a little pleased with
the kind looks and glances I had from all the balconies
and windows as I rode to the hall where the assizes were
held. But when I came there, a beautiful creature, in a
widow's habit, sat in court to hear the event of a cause
concerning her dower. This commanding creature (who
was born for the destruction of all who beheld her) put
on such a resignation in her countenance, and bore the
whispers of all around the court with such a pretty uneasiness, I warrant you, and then recovered herself from
one eye to another, until she was perfectly confused by
meeting something so wistful in all she encountered, that
at last, with a murrain to her, she cast her bewitching
eye upon me. I no sooner met it but I bowed, like a

great surprised booby; and knowing her cause to be
the first which came on, I cried, like a captivated calf
as I was, 'Make way for the defendant's witnesses'.
This sudden partiality made all the county see the sheriff
also was become a slave to the fine widow. During the
time her cause was upon trial, she behaved herself, I
warrant you, with such a deep attention to her business,
took opportunities to have little billets handed to her counsel, then would be in such a pretty confusion, occasioned,
you must know, by acting before so much company,
that not only I, but the whole court, was prejudiced in her
favour; and all that the next heir to her husband had to
urge was thought so groundless and frivolous that when
it came to her counsel to reply, there was not half so
much said as every one besides in the court thought he
could have urged to her advantage. You must understand, sir, this perverse woman is one of those unaccountable creatures that secretly rejoice in the admiration of
men, but indulge themselves in no further consequences.
Hence it is that she has ever had a train of admirers,
and she removes from her slaves in town to those in the
country according to the seasons of the year. She is a
reading lady, and far gone in the pleasures of friendship.
She is always accompanied by a confidant who is witness
to her daily protestations against our sex, and consequently a bar to her first steps towards love, upon the
strength of her own maxims and declarations.

"However, I must needs say, this accomplished mistress
of mine has distinguished me above the rest, and has
been known to declare Sir Roger de Coverley was the
tamest and most humane of all the brutes in the country.
I was told she said so by one who thought he rallied me;
but upon the strength of this slender encouragement of
being thought least detestable, I made new liveries, new-
paired my coach-horses, sent them all to town to be

bitted, and taught to throw their legs well, and move all together, before I pretended to cross the country and wait upon her. As soon as I thought my retinue suitable to the character of my fortune and youth, I set out from hence to make my addresses. The particular skill of this lady has ever been to inflame your wishes, and yet command respect. To make her mistress of this art, she has a greater share of knowledge, wit, and good sense than is usual even among men of merit. Then she is beautiful beyond the race of women. If you will not let her go on with a certain artifice with her eyes, and the skill of beauty, she will arm herself with her real charms, and strike you with admiration instead of desire. It is certain that if you were to behold the whole woman, there is that dignity in her aspect, that composure in her motion, that complacency in her manner, that if her form makes you hope, her merit makes you fear. But then again she is such a desperate scholar that no country gentleman can approach her without being a jest. As I was going to tell you, when I came to her house, I was admitted to her presence with great civility; at the same time she placed herself to be first seen by me in such an attitude as I think you call the posture of a picture, that she discovered new charms, and I at last came towards her with such an awe as made me speechless. This she no sooner observed but she made her advantage of it, and began a discourse to me concerning love and honour, as they both are followed by pretenders, and the real votaries to them. When she discussed these points in a discourse, which I verily believe was as learned as the best philosopher in Europe could possibly make, she asked me whether she was so happy as to fall in with my sentiments on these important particulars. Her confidant sat by her, and upon my being in the last confusion and silence, this malicious aid of hers, turning to her, says, ‘ I am very glad to observe Sir Roger pauses upon this subject, and seems resolved to deliver all his sentiments upon the matter when he pleases to speak'. They both kept their countenances, and after I had sat half an hour meditating how to behave before such profound casuists, I rose up and took my leave. Chance has since that time thrown me very often in her way, and she as often has directed a discourse to me which I do not understand. This barbarity has kept me ever at a distance from the most beautiful object my eyes ever beheld. It is thus also she deals with all mankind, and you must make love to her, as you would conquer the sphinx, by posing her. But were she like other women, and that there were any talking to her, how constant must the pleasure of that man be who would converse with a creature—But, after all, you may be sure her heart is fixed on some one or other; and yet I have been credibly informed—but who can believe half that is said?—after she had done speaking to me she put her hand to her bosom and adjusted her tucker. Then she cast her eyes a little down upon my beholding her too earnestly. They say she sings excellently: her voice in her ordinary speech has something in it inexpressibly sweet. You must know I dined with her at a public table the day after I first saw her, and she helped me to some tansy in the eye of all the gentlemen in the country. She has certainly the finest hand of any woman in the world. I can assure you, sir, were you to behold her you would be in the same condition; for as her speech is music, her form is angelic. But I find I grow irregular while I am talking of her; but indeed it would be stupidity to be unconcerned at such perfection. Oh, the excellent creature! she is as inimitable to all women as she is inaccessible to all men—"

I found my friend begin to rave, and insensibly led him towards the house that we might be joined by some other company; and am convinced that the widow is the secret cause of all that inconsistency which appears in some parts of my friend's discourse; though he has so much command of himself as not directly to mention her, yet, according to that of Martial, which one knows not how to render into English, *Dum tacet, hanc loquitur;* I shall end this paper with that whole epigram, which represents with much humour my honest friend's condition:—

> *Quicquid agit Rufus, nihil est nisi Nævia Rufo,*
> *Si gauaet, si flet, si tacet, hanc loquitur:*
> *Cœnat, propinat, poscit, negat, innuit, una est*
> *Nævia: si non sit Nævia, mutus erit.*
> *Scriberet hesternâ patri cum luce salutem,*
> *Nævia lux, inquit, Nævia! lumen, ave.*—Epig. i. 69.

> "Let Rufus weep, rejoice, stand, sit, or walk,
> Still he can nothing but of Nævia talk;
> Let him eat, drink, ask questions or dispute,
> Still he must speak of Nævia, or be mute.
> He writ to his father, ending with this line,
> I am, my lovely Nævia, ever thine."

JOSEPH ADDISON.
(1672-1719.)

XIII. THE CHARACTER OF NED SOFTLY.

> *Idem inficeto est inficetior rure,*
> *Simul poemata attigit; neque idem unquam*
> *Aeque est beatus, ac poema cum scribit:*
> *Tam gaudet in se, tamque se ipse miratur.*
> *Nimirum idem omnes fallimur; neque est quisquam*
> *Quem non in aliqua re videre Suffenum*
> *Possis.* —Catul. *de Suffeno,* xx. 14.

Suffenus has no more wit than a mere clown when he attempts to write verses; and yet he is never happier than when he is scribbling: so much does he admire himself and his compositions. And, indeed, this is the foible of every one of us; for there is no man living who is not a Suffenus in one thing or other.

I YESTERDAY came hither about two hours before the company generally make their appearance, with a design to read over all the newspapers; but, upon my sitting down, I was accosted by Ned Softly, who saw me from a corner in the other end of the room, where I found he had been writing something. " Mr. Bickerstaff," says he, " I observe by a late paper of yours, that you and I are just of a humour; for you must know, of all impertinences, there is nothing which I so much hate as news. I never read a gazette in my life; and never trouble my head about our armies, whether they win or lose, or in what part of the world they lie encamped." Without giving me time to reply, he drew a paper of verses out of his pocket, telling me, " that he had something which would entertain me more agreeably; and that he would desire my judgment upon every line, for that we had time enough before us until the company came in."

Ned Softly is a very pretty poet, and a great admirer of easy lines. Waller is his favourite: and as that admirable writer has the best and worst verses of any among our great English poets, Ned Softly has got all the bad ones without book: which he repeats upon occasion, to show his reading, and garnish his conversation. Ned is indeed a true English reader, incapable of relishing the great and masterly strokes of this art; but wonderfully pleased with the little Gothic ornaments of epigrammatical conceits, turns, points, and quibbles, which are so frequent in the most admired of our English poets, and practised by those who want genius and strength to represent, after the manner of the ancients, simplicity in its natural beauty and perfection.

Finding myself unavoidably engaged in such a conversation, I was resolved to turn my pain into a pleasure, and to divert myself as well as I could with so very odd a fellow. " You must understand," says Ned, " that the sonnet I am going to read to you was written upon a lady, who showed me some verses of her own making, and is, perhaps, the best poet of our age. But you shall hear it."

Upon which he began to read as follows:

TO MIRA, ON HER INCOMPARABLE POEMS.

I.

When dress'd in laurel wreaths you shine,
  And tune your soft melodious notes,
You seem a sister of the Nine,
  Or Phœbus' self in petticoats.

II.

I fancy, when your song you sing,
  (Your song you sing with so much art)
Your pen was pluck'd from Cupid's wing;
  For, ah! it wounds me like his dart.

"Why," says I, "this is a little nosegay of conceits, a very lump of salt: every verse has something in it that piques; and then the *dart* in the last line is certainly as pretty a sting in the tail of an epigram, for so I think you critics call it, as ever entered into the thought of a poet." "Dear Mr. Bickerstaff," says he, shaking me by the hand, "everybody knows you to be a judge of these things; and to tell you truly, I read over Roscommon's translation of Horace's *Art of Poetry* three several times before I sat down to write the sonnet which I have shown you. But you shall hear it again, and pray observe every line of it; for not one of them shall pass without your approbation.

When dress'd in laurel wreaths you shine,

"That is," says he, "when you have your garland on; when you are writing verses." To which I replied, "I know your meaning; a metaphor!" "The same," said he, and went on.

And tune your soft melodious notes,

"Pray observe the gliding of that verse; there is scarce a consonant in it; I took care to make it run upon liquids. Give me your opinion of it." "Truly," said I,

" I think it as good as the former."   " I am very glad to hear you say so," says he, " but mind the next."

> You seem a sister of the Nine,

" That is," says he, " you seem a sister of the Muses; for, if you look into ancient authors, you will find it was their opinion that there were nine of them."   " I remember it very well," said I; " but pray proceed."

> Or Phœbus' self in petticoats.

" Phœbus ", says he, " was the god of poetry.   These little instances, Mr. Bickerstaff, show a gentleman's reading.   Then, to take off from the air of learning, which Phœbus and the Muses had given to this first stanza, you may observe, how it falls all of a sudden into the familiar, ' in petticoats!'

" Let us now," says I, " enter upon the second stanza; I find the first line is still a continuation of the metaphor."

> I fancy, when your song you sing,

" It is very right," says he; " but pray observe the turn of words in those two lines.   I was a whole hour in adjusting of them, and have still a doubt upon me whether in the second line it should be, ' Your song you sing;' or, 'You sing your song.'   You shall hear them both"·

> I fancy, when your song you sing
> (Your song you sing with so much art);

or,

> I fancy, when your song you sing,
> (You sing your song with so much art).

" Truly," said I, " the turn is so natural either way, that you have made me almost giddy with it."   " Dear sir," said he, grasping me by the hand, " you have a great deal of patience; but pray what do you think of the next verse?"

> Your pen was pluck'd from Cupid's wing:

"Think!" says I, "I think you have made Cupid look like a little goose." "That was my meaning," says he, "I think the ridicule is well enough hit off. But we come now to the last, which sums up the whole matter."

For, ah ! it wounds me like his dart.

" Pray how do you like that *Ah !* doth it not make a pretty figure in that place ? *Ah !*—it looks as if I felt the dart, and cried out as being pricked with it.

For, ah ! it wounds me like his dart.

"My friend, Dick Easy," continued he, "assured me he would rather have written that *Ah !* than to have been the author of the *Æneid*. He indeed objected, that I made Mira's pen like a quill in one of the lines, and like a dart in the other. But as to that—" "Oh ! as to that," says I, "it is but supposing Cupid to be like a porcupine, and his quills and darts will be the same thing." He was going to embrace me for the hint; but half a dozen critics coming into the room, whose faces he did not like, he conveyed the sonnet into his pocket, and whispered me in the ear, "he would show it me again as soon as his man had written it over fair".

xiv. NICOLINI AND THE LIONS.

Dic mihi, si fueris tu leo, qualis eris?—Mart.
Were you a lion, how would you behave?

THERE is nothing that of late years has afforded matter of greater amusement to the town than Signor Nicolini's [1] combat with a lion in the Haymarket,

---

[1] The Cavaliere Nicolino Grimaldi, a Neapolitan, came to London in 1708. He performed first in *Pyrrhus and Demetrius* in 1710, the last of the mongrel Anglo-Italian operas. In 1712 he left England, after gaining the name of being "the greatest performer in dramatick music that is now living, or that perhaps ever appeared on a stage" (*Spect.* 405). He is alluded to by Addison in *Spect.* 5, as acting in the opera *Rinaldo* by 'Mynheer Handel'.

which has been very often exhibited to the general satisfaction of most of the nobility and gentry in the kingdom of Great Britain. Upon the first rumour of his intended combat, it was confidently affirmed, and is still believed, by many in both galleries, that there would be a tame lion sent from the Tower every opera night in order to be killed by Hydaspes.[1] This report, though altogether groundless, so universally prevailed in the upper regions of the playhouse that some of the most refined politicians in those parts of the audience gave it out in whisper that the lion was a cousin-german of the tiger who made his appearance in King William's days, and that the stage would be supplied with lions at the public expense during the whole session. Many likewise were the conjectures of the treatment which this lion was to meet with from the hands of Signor Nicolini; some supposed that he was to subdue him in recitativo, as Orpheus used to serve the wild beasts in his time, and afterwards to knock him on the head; some fancied that the lion would not pretend to lay his paws upon the hero, by reason of the received opinion, that a lion will not hurt a virgin. Several, who pretended to have seen the opera in Italy, had informed their friends that the lion was to act a part in high Dutch, and roar twice or thrice to a thorough bass before he fell at the feet of Hydaspes. To clear up a matter that was so variously reported, I have made it my business to examine whether this pretended lion is really the savage he appears to be, or only a counterfeit.

But before I communicate my discoveries, I must acquaint the reader, that upon my walking behind the scenes last winter, as I was thinking on something else, I accidentally jostled against a monstrous animal that extremely startled me, and, upon my nearer survey of it, appeared to be a lion rampant. The lion seeing me very

---

[1] An opera by Francesco Mancini, produced at the Haymarket, 1710.

much surprised told me, in a gentle voice, that I might
come by him if I pleased; "For", says he, "I do not intend
to hurt anybody". I thanked him very kindly, and passed
by him: and in a little time after saw him leap upon the
stage, and act his part with very great applause. It has
been observed by several that the lion has changed his
manner of acting twice or thrice since his first appearance; which will not seem strange when I acquaint my
reader that the lion has been changed upon the audience
three several times. The first lion was a candle-snuffer,
who, being a fellow of a testy choleric temper, overdid
his part, and would not suffer himself to be killed as
easily as he ought to have done; besides, it was observed
of him, that he grew more surly every time that he came
out of the lion; and having dropt some words in ordinary
conversation, as if he had not fought his best, and that
he suffered himself to be thrown upon his back in the
scuffle, and that he would wrestle with Mr. Nicolini for
what he pleased, out of his lion's skin, it was thought
proper to discard him: and it is verily believed to this
day, that had he been brought upon the stage another
time, he would certainly have done mischief. Besides,
it was objected against the first lion, that he reared himself so high upon his hinder paws, and walked in so erect
a posture, that he looked more like an old man than a
lion.

The second lion was a tailor by trade, who belonged
to the playhouse, and had the character of a mild and
peaceable man in his profession. If the former was too
furious, this was too sheepish for his part; insomuch,
that after a short modest walk upon the stage, he would
fall at the first touch of Hydaspes, without grappling
with him, and giving him an opportunity of showing
his variety of Italian trips. It is said, indeed, that he
once gave him a rip in his flesh-coloured doublet: but

this was only to make work for himself, in his private character of a tailor. I must not omit that it was this second lion who treated me with so much humanity behind the scenes.

The acting lion at present is, as I am informed, a country gentleman, who does it for his diversion, but desires his name may be concealed. He says very handsomely in his own excuse, that he does not act for gain, that he indulges an innocent pleasure in it; and that it is better to pass away an evening in this manner than in gaming and drinking: but at the same time says, with a very agreeable raillery upon himself, that if his name should be known, the ill-natured world might call him, "The ass in the lion's skin". This gentleman's temper is made out of such a happy mixture of the mild and the choleric that he outdoes both his predecessors, and has drawn together greater audiences than have been known in the memory of man.

I must not conclude my narrative without first taking notice of a groundless report that has been raised to a gentleman's disadvantage of whom I must declare myself an admirer; namely, that Signor Nicolini and the lion have been seen sitting peaceably by one another, and smoking a pipe together behind the scenes; by which their common enemies would insinuate that it is but a sham combat which they represent upon the stage: but upon inquiry I find, that if any such correspondence has passed between them, it was not till the combat was over, when the lion was to be looked upon as dead, according to the received rules of the drama. Besides, this is what is practised every day in Westminster Hall, where nothing is more usual than to see a couple of lawyers, who have been tearing each other to pieces in the court, embracing one another as soon as they are out of it.

I would not be thought in any part of this relation to reflect upon Signor Nicolini, who in acting this part only complies with the wretched taste of his audience; he knows very well that the lion has many more admirers than himself; as they say of the famous equestrian statue on the Pont-Neuf at Paris, that more people go to see the horse than the king who sits upon it. On the contrary, it gives me a just indignation to see a person whose action gives new majesty to kings, resolution to heroes, and softness to lovers, thus sinking from the greatness of his behaviour, and degraded into the character of the London 'prentice. I have often wished that our tragedians would copy after this great master of action. Could they make the same use of their arms and legs, and inform their faces with as significant looks and passions, how glorious would an English tragedy appear with that action, which is capable of giving dignity to the forced thoughts, cold conceits, and unnatural expressions of an Italian opera! In the meantime, I have related this combat of the lion, to show what are at present the reigning entertainments of the politer part of Great Britain.

Audiences have often been reproached by writers for the coarseness of their tastes, but our present grievance does not seem to be the want of a good taste, but of common sense.

xv. FANS.

Lusus animo debent aliquando dari,
Ad cogitandum melior ut redeat sibi.
—Phaedr. *Fab.* xiv. 5.

The mind ought sometimes to be diverted, that it may return the better to thinking.

I DO not know whether to call the following letter a satire upon coquettes, or a representation of their several fantastical accomplishments, or what other title to give it; but, as it is, I shall communicate it to the public. It will sufficiently explain its own intentions, so that I shall give it my reader at length, without either preface or postscript.

"Mr. Spectator,

"Women are armed with fans as men with swords, and sometimes do more execution with them. To the end therefore that ladies may be entire mistresses of the weapons which they bear, I have erected an academy for the training up of young women in the exercise of the fan, according to the most fashionable airs and motions that are now practised at court. The ladies who carry fans under me are drawn up twice a day in my great hall, where they are instructed in the use of their arms, and exercised by the following words of command:—Handle your fans, Unfurl your fans, Discharge your fans, Ground your fans, Recover your fans, Flutter your fans. By the right observation of these few plain words of command, a woman of a tolerable genius, who will apply herself diligently to her exercise for the space of but one half-year, shall be able to give her fan all the graces that can possibly enter into that little modish machine.

"But to the end that my readers may form to themselves a right notion of this exercise, I beg leave to explain it to them in all its parts. When my female regiment is drawn up in array, with every one her weapon in her hand, upon my giving the word to Handle their fans, each of them shakes her fan at me with a smile, then gives her right-hand woman a tap upon the shoulder, then presses her lips with the extremity of her fan, then lets her arms fall in an easy motion, and stands in readiness to receive the next word of command. All this is done with a close fan, and is generally learned in the first week.

"The next motion is that of unfurling the fan, in which

are comprehended several little flirts and vibrations, as
also gradual and deliberate openings, with many voluntary
fallings asunder in the fan itself, that are seldom learned
under a month's practice.   This part of the exercise
pleases the spectators more than any other, as it discovers
on a sudden an infinite number of cupids, garlands,
altars, birds, beasts, rainbows, and the like agreeable
figures, that display themselves to view, whilst every one
in the regiment holds a picture in her hand.

" Upon my giving the word to Discharge their fans,
they give one general crack that may be heard at a
considerable distance when the wind sits fair.   This is
one of the most difficult parts of the exercise, but I have
several ladies with me, who at their first entrance could
not give a pop loud enough to be heard at the farther
end of a room, who can now discharge a fan in such a
manner, that it shall make a report like a pocket-pistol.
I have likewise taken care (in order to hinder young
women from letting off their fans in wrong places or on
unsuitable occasions) to show upon what subject the crack
of a fan may come in properly: I have likewise invented
a fan, with which a girl of sixteen, by the help of a little
wind which is inclosed about one of the largest sticks,
can make as loud a crack as a woman of fifty with an
ordinary fan.

" When the fans are thus discharged, the word of
command in course is to Ground their fans.   This teaches
a lady to quit her fan gracefully when she throws it aside
in order to take up a pack of cards, adjust a curl of hair,
replace a falling pin, or apply herself to any other matter
of importance.   This part of the exercise, as it only
consists in tossing a fan with an air upon a long table
(which stands by for that purpose), may be learned in
two days' time as well as in a twelvemonth.

" When my female regiment is thus disarmed, I gene-

rally let them walk about the room for some time; when
on a sudden (like ladies that look upon their watches
after a long visit) they all of them hasten to their arms,
catch them up in a hurry, and place themselves in their
proper stations upon my calling out, Recover your fans.
This part of the exercise is not difficult, provided a woman
applies her thoughts to it.

"The fluttering of the fan is the last, and indeed the
masterpiece of the whole exercise; but if a lady does not
misspend her time, she may make herself mistress of it in
three months. I generally lay aside the dog-days and the
hot time of the summer for the teaching of this part of the
exercise; for as soon as ever I pronounce Flutter your
fans, the place is filled with so many zephyrs and gentle
breezes as are very refreshing in that season of the year,
though they might be dangerous to ladies of a tender
constitution in any other.

"There is an infinite variety of motions to be made
use of in the flutter of a fan. There is the angry flutter,
the modest flutter, the timorous flutter, the confused
flutter, the merry flutter, and the amorous flutter. Not
to be tedious, there is scarce any emotion in the mind
which does not produce a suitable agitation in the fan;
insomuch, that if I only see the fan of a disciplined lady,
I know very well whether she laughs, frowns, or blushes.
I have seen a fan so very angry, that it would have been
dangerous for the absent lover who provoked it to have
come within the wind of it; and at other times so very
languishing, that I have been glad for the lady's sake
the lover was at sufficient distance from it. I need not
add, that a fan is either a prude or coquette, according
to the nature of the person who bears it. To conclude
my letter, I must acquaint you that I have from my own
observations compiled a little treatise for the use of my
scholars, entitled, The Passions of the Fan; which I will

communicate to you, if you think it may be of use to the public. I shall have a general review on Thursday next; to which you shall be very welcome if you will honour it with your presence.

"I am, &c.

"P.S. I teach young gentlemen the whole art of gallanting a fan.

N.B. I have several little plain fans made for this use, to avoid expense."

xvi. SIR ROGER AT THE ASSIZES.

Comes jucundus in via pro vehiculo est.—Publ. Syr. *Frag.*

An agreeable companion upon the road is as good as a coach.

A MAN'S first care should be to avoid the reproaches of his own heart; his next, to escape the censures of the world. If the last interferes with the former, it ought to be entirely neglected; but otherwise there cannot be a greater satisfaction to an honest mind than to see those approbations which it gives itself seconded by the applauses of the public. A man is more sure of his conduct when the verdict which he passes upon his own behaviour is thus warranted and confirmed by the opinion of all that know him.

My worthy friend Sir Roger is one of those who is not only at peace within himself, but beloved and esteemed by all about him. He receives a suitable tribute for his universal benevolence to mankind in the returns of affection and good-will which are paid him by everyone that lives within his neighbourhood. I lately met with two or three odd instances of that general respect which is shown to the good old knight. He would needs carry Will Wimble and myself with him to the country assizes. As we were upon the road, Will Wimble joined a couple of plain men who rid before us, and conversed with them for some time, during which my friend Sir Roger acquainted me with their characters.

" The first of them," says he, " that has a spaniel by his side, is a yeoman of about a hundred pounds a year, an honest man. He is just within the Game Act, and qualified to kill a hare or a pheasant. He knocks down his dinner with his gun twice or thrice a week; and by that means lives much cheaper than those who have not so good an estate as himself. He would be a good neighbour if he did not destroy so many partridges. In short, he is a very sensible man, shoots flying, and has been several times foreman of the petty jury.

" The other that rides along with him is Tom Touchy, a fellow famous for ' taking the law' of everybody. There is not one in the town where he lives that he has not sued at a quarter sessions. The rogue had once the impudence to go to law with the widow. His head is full of costs, damages, and ejectments. He plagued a couple of honest gentlemen so long for a trespass in breaking one of his hedges, till he was forced to sell the ground it enclosed to defray the charges of the prosecution. His father left him fourscore pounds a year; but he has cast and been cast so often that he is not now worth thirty. I suppose he is going upon the old business of the willow-tree."

As Sir Roger was giving me this account of Tom Touchy, Will Wimble and his two companions stopped short till we came up to them. After having paid their respects to Sir Roger, Will told him that Mr. Touchy and he must appeal to him upon a dispute that arose between them. Will, it seems, had been giving his fellow-traveller an account of his angling one day in such a hole, when Tom Touchy, instead of hearing out his story, told him that Mr. Such-a-one, if he pleased, might " take the law of

him" for fishing in that part of the river. My friend Sir
Roger heard them both upon a round trot; and after
having paused some time, told them, with the air of a man
who would not give his judgment rashly, that "much might
be said on both sides". They were neither of them dis-
satisfied with the knight's determination, because neither
of them found himself in the wrong by it. Upon which
we made the best of our way to the assizes.

The court was sat before Sir Roger came; but notwith-
standing all the justices had taken their places upon the
bench, they made room for the old knight at the head of
them; who, for his reputation in the country, took occasion
to whisper in the judge's ear, "that he was glad his lordship had met with so much good weather in his circuit".
I was listening to the proceeding of the court with much
attention, and infinitely pleased with that great appearance of solemnity which so properly accompanies such a
public administration of our laws; when, after about an
hour's sitting, I observed, to my great surprise, in the
midst of a trial, that my friend Sir Roger was getting up
to speak. I was in some pain for him, until I found he
had acquitted himself of two or three sentences, with a
look of much business and great intrepidity.

Upon his first rising the court was hushed, and a
general whisper ran among the country people that Sir
Roger "was up". The speech he made was so little to
the purpose that I shall not trouble my readers with an
account of it; and I believe was not so much designed
by the knight himself to inform the court, as to give
him a figure in my eye, and keep up his credit in the
country.

I was highly delighted, when the court rose, to see the
gentlemen of the country gathering about my old friend,
and striving who should compliment him most; at the
same time that the ordinary people gazed upon him at a

distance, not a little admiring his courage that was not afraid to speak to the judge.

In our return home we met with a very odd accident, which I cannot forbear relating, because it shows how desirous all who know Sir Roger are of giving him marks of their esteem. When we were arrived upon the verge of his estate, we stopped at a little inn to rest ourselves and our horses. The man of the house had, it seems, been formerly a servant in the knight's family; and to do honour to his old master, had some time since, unknown to Sir Roger, put him up in a sign-post before the door; so that the knight's head had hung out upon the road about a week before he himself knew anything of the matter. As soon as Sir Roger was acquainted with it, finding that his servant's indiscretion proceeded wholly from affection and goodwill, he only told him that he had made him too high a compliment; and when the fellow seemed to think that could hardly be, added with a more decisive look, that it was too great an honour for any man under a duke; but told him at the same time that it might be altered with a very few touches, and that he himself would be at the charge of it. Accordingly they got a painter by the knight's directions to add a pair of whiskers to the face, and by a little aggravation of the features to change it into the Saracen's Head. I should not have known this story had not the innkeeper, upon Sir Roger's alighting, told him in my hearing that his honour's head was brought back last night with the alterations that he had ordered to be made in it. Upon this, my friend, with his usual cheerfulness, related the particulars above-mentioned, and ordered the head to be brought into the room. I could not forbear discovering greater expressions of mirth than ordinary upon the appearance of this monstrous face, under which, notwith-standing it was made to frown and stare in a most extra-

ordinary manner, I could still discover a distant resem
blance to my old friend.   Sir Roger, upon seeing me
laugh, desired me to tell him truly if I thought it possible
for people to know him in that disguise.   I at first kept
my usual silence; but upon the knight's conjuring me to
tell him whether it was not still more like himself than a
Saracen, I composed my countenance in the best manner
I could, and replied that "much might be said on both
sides".

These several adventures, with the knight's behaviour
in them, gave me as pleasant a day as ever I met with in
any of my travels.

XVII. THE VISION OF MIRZA.

Omnem, quae nunc obducta tuenti
Mortales hebetat visus tibi, et humida circum
Caligat, nubem eripiam.   —Virg. *Æn.* ii. 604.

The cloud, which, intercepting the clear light,
Hangs o'er thy eyes, and blunts thy mortal sight,
I will remove.

WHEN I was at Grand Cairo, I picked up several
oriental manuscripts, which I have still by me.
Among others I met with one entitled, *The Visions of
Mirza,* which I have read over with great pleasure.   I
intend to give it to the public when I have no other
entertainment for them, and shall begin with the first
vision, which I have translated word for word as follows:—

"On the fifth day of the moon, which according to
the custom of my forefathers I always keep holy, after
having washed myself and offered up my morning devotions, I ascended the high hills of Bagdad, in order to
pass the rest of the day in meditation and prayer.   As I
was here airing myself on the tops of the mountains, I fell
into a profound contemplation on the vanity of human
life, and passing from one thought to another, 'Surely,'

said I, 'man is but a shadow, and life a dream'. Whilst
I was thus musing, I cast my eyes towards the summit of
a rock that was not far from me, where I discovered one
in the habit of a shepherd, with a little musical instrument in his hand. As I looked upon him he applied it
to his lips, and began to play upon it. The sound of
it was exceeding sweet, and wrought into a variety of
tunes that were inexpressibly melodious and altogether
different from anything I had ever heard. They put me
in mind of those heavenly airs that are played to the
departed souls of good men upon their first arrival in
Paradise, to wear out the impressions of the last agonies,
and qualify them for the pleasures of that happy place.
My heart melted away in secret raptures.

"I had been often told that the rock before me was the
haunt of a genius; and that several had been entertained
with music who had passed by it, but never heard that
the musician had before made himself visible. When he
had raised my thoughts by those transporting airs which
he played, to taste the pleasures of his conversation, as I
looked upon him like one astonished, he beckoned to
me, and by the waving of his hand directed me to
approach the place where he sat. I drew near with that
reverence which is due to a superior nature; and as my
heart was entirely subdued by the captivating strains I
had heard, I fell down at his feet and wept. The genius
smiled upon me with a look of compassion and affability
that familiarized him to my imagination, and at once
dispelled all the fears and apprehensions with which I
approached him. He lifted me from the ground, and
taking me by the hand, 'Mirza,' said he, 'I have heard
thee in thy soliloquies; follow me'.

" He then led me to the highest pinnacle of the rock,
and placing me on the top of it, 'Cast thy eyes east-
ward,' said he, 'and tell me what thou seest'. 'I see,'

said I, 'a huge valley and a prodigious tide of water rolling through it.' 'The valley that thou seest,' said he, 'is the Vale of Misery, and the tide of water that thou seest is part of the great tide of eternity.' 'What is the reason,' said I, 'that the tide I see rises out of a thick mist at one end, and again loses itself in a thick mist at the other?' 'What thou seest,' said he, 'is that portion of eternity which is called time, measured out by the sun, and reaching from the beginning of the world to its consummation. Examine now,' said he, 'this sea that is thus bounded with darkness at both ends, and tell me what thou discoverest in it.' 'I see a bridge,' said I, 'standing in the midst of the tide.' 'The bridge thou seest,' said he, 'is human life; consider it attentively.' Upon a more leisurely survey of it I found that it consisted of more than three-score and ten entire arches, with several broken arches which, added to those that were entire, made up the number to about a hundred. As I was counting the arches, the genius told me that this bridge consisted at first of a thousand arches; but that a great flood swept away the rest, and left the bridge in the ruinous condition I now beheld it. 'But tell me further,' said he, 'what thou discoverest on it.' 'I see multitudes of people passing over it,' said I, 'and a black cloud hanging on each end of it.' As I looked more attentively, I saw several of the passengers dropping through the bridge into the great tide that flowed underneath it; and upon further examination, perceived there were innumerable trap-doors that lay concealed in the bridge, which the passengers no sooner trod upon, but they fell through them into the tide and immediately disappeared. These hidden pit-falls were set very thick at the entrance of the bridge, so that throngs of people no sooner broke through the cloud, but many of them fell into them. They grew thinner towards the middle, but

multiplied and lay closer together towards the end of
the arches that were entire.

"There were indeed some persons, but their number
was very small, that continued a kind of hobbling march
on the broken arches, but fell through one after another,
being quite tired and spent with so long a walk.

"I passed some time in the contemplation of this
wonderful structure, and the great variety of objects which
it presented. My heart was filled with a deep melancholy
to see several dropping unexpectedly in the midst of
mirth and jollity, and catching at everything that stood
by them to save themselves. Some were looking up
towards the heavens in a thoughtful posture, and in the
midst of a speculation stumbled and fell out of sight.
Multitudes were very busy in the pursuit of bubbles that
glittered in their eyes and danced before them, but often
when they thought themselves within the reach of them
their footing failed and down they sunk. In this confusion of objects, I observed some with scimitars in their
hands, and others with urinals, who ran to and fro upon
the bridge, thrusting several persons on trap-doors which
did not seem to lie in their way, and which they might
have escaped had they not been thus forced upon them.

"The genius, seeing me indulge myself on this melancholy prospect, told me I had dwelt long enough upon
it. 'Take thine eyes off the bridge,' said he, 'and tell
me if thou yet seest anything thou dost not comprehend.'
Upon looking up, 'What mean,' said I, 'those great
flights of birds that are perpetually hovering about the
bridge, and settling upon it from time to time? I see
vultures, harpies, ravens, cormorants, and among many
other feathered creatures several little winged boys that
perch in great numbers upon the middle arches.' 'These,'
said the genius, 'are Envy, Avarice, Superstition, Despair,
Love, with the like cares and passions that infest human life.'

"I here fetched a deep sigh. 'Alas,' said I, 'man was made in vain: how is he given away to misery and mortality, tortured in life, and swallowed up in death!' The genius being moved with compassion towards me, bid me quit so uncomfortable a prospect. 'Look no more,' said he, 'on man in the first stage of his existence, in his setting out for eternity; but cast thine eye on that thick mist into which the tide bears the several generations of mortals that fall into it. I directed my sight as I was ordered, and (whether or no the good genius strengthened it with any supernatural force, or dissipated part of the mist that was before too thick for eye to penetrate) I saw the valley opening at the farther end, and spreading forth into an immense ocean that had a huge rock of adamant running through the midst of it, and dividing it into two equal parts. The clouds still rested on one half of it, insomuch that I could discover nothing in it; but the other appeared to me a vast ocean planted with innumerable islands, that were covered with fruits and flowers, and interwoven with a thousand little shining seas that ran among them. I could see persons dressed in glorious habits with garlands upon their heads, passing among the trees, lying down by the sides of fountains, or resting on beds of flowers; and could hear a confused harmony of singing birds, falling waters, human voices, and musical instruments. Gladness grew in me upon the discovery of so delightful a scene. I wished for the wings of an eagle that I might fly away to those happy seats; but the genius told me there was no passage to them except through the gates of death that I saw opening every moment upon the bridge. 'The islands,' said he, 'that lie so fresh and green before thee, and with which the whole face of the ocean appears spotted as far as thou canst see, are more in number than the sands on the sea-shore; there are myriads of islands behind those which thou here discoverest, reaching farther than thine eye, or even thine imagination can extend itself. These are the mansions of good men after death, who, according to the degree and kinds of virtue in which they excelled, are distributed among these several islands, which abound with pleasures of different kinds and degrees suitable to the relishes and perfections of those who are settled in them; every island is a paradise accommodated to its respective inhabitants. Are not these, O Mirza, habitations worth contending for? Does life appear miserable that gives thee opportunities of earning such a reward? Is death to be feared that will convey thee to so happy an existence? Think not man was made in vain who has such an eternity reserved for him.' I gazed with inexpressible pleasure on these happy islands. At length, said I, 'Show me now, I beseech thee, the secrets that lie hid under those dark clouds which cover the ocean on the other side of the rock of adamant'. The genius making me no answer, I turned me about to address myself to him a second time, but I found that he had left me; I then turned again to the vision which I had been so long contemplating; but, instead of the rolling tide, the arched bridge, and the happy islands, I saw nothing but the long valley of Bagdad, with oxen, sheep, and camels grazing upon the sides of it."

The end of the first Vision of Mirza.

XVIII. THE ART OF GRINNING.

Remove fera monstra, tuaeque
Saxificos vultus, quaecunque ea, tolle Medusae.—Ovid, *Met.* v. 216.

Hence with those monstrous features, and, O! spare
That Gorgon's look, and petrifying stare.—P.

IN a late paper I mentioned the project of an ingenious author for the erecting of several handicraft prizes to be contended for by our British artisans, and the influence they might have towards the improvement of our several manufactures. I have since that been very much surprised by the following advertisement, which I find in the *Post-Boy* [1] of the 11th instant, and again repeated in the *Post-Boy* of the 15th:—

"On the 9th of October next will be run for upon Coleshill-heath in Warwickshire, a plate of six guineas value, three heats, by any horse, mare, or gelding, that hath not won above the value of 5*l.*, the winning horse to be sold for 10*l.* To carry 10 stone weight, if 14 hands high; if above or under to carry or be allowed weight for inches, and to be entered Friday the 15th at the Swan in Coleshill, before six in the evening. Also a plate of less value to be run for by asses. The same day a gold ring to be grinned for by men."

The first of these diversions that is to be exhibited by the 10*l.* race-horses, may probably have its use; but the two last, in which the asses and men are concerned, seem to me altogether extraordinary and unaccountable. Why they should keep running asses at Coleshill, or how making mouths turns to account in Warwickshire, more than in any other parts of England, I cannot comprehend. I have looked over all the Olympic games, and do not find anything in them like an ass-race, or a match at grinning. However it be, I am informed that several asses are now kept in body-clothes, and sweated every morning upon the heath; and that all the country-fellows within ten miles of the Swan grin an hour or two in their glasses every morning, in order to qualify themselves for the 9th of October. The prize which is proposed to be grinned for has raised such an ambition among the common people of out-grinning one another, that many very discerning persons are afraid it should spoil most of the faces in the county; and that a Warwickshire man will

[1] A tri-weekly which began in May, 1695.

be known by his grin, as Roman Catholics imagine a Kentish man is by his tail. The gold ring, which is made the prize of deformity, is just the reverse of the golden apple that was formerly made the prize of beauty, and should carry for its poesy the old motto inverted:

'Detur tetriori'.

Or, to accommodate it to the capacity of the combatants,

The frightfull'st grinner
Be the winner.

In the meanwhile I would advise a Dutch painter to be present at this great controversy of faces, in order to make a collection of the most remarkable grins that shall be there exhibited.

I must not here omit an account which I lately received of one of these grinning-matches from a gentleman, who, upon reading the above-mentioned advertisement, entertained a coffee-house with the following narrative:—Upon the taking of Namur[1], amidst other public rejoicings made on that occasion, there was a gold ring given by a whig justice of peace to be grinned for. The first competitor that entered the lists was a black swarthy Frenchman, who accidentally passed that way, and being a man naturally of a withered look, and hard features, promised himself good success. He was placed upon a table in the great point of view, and looking upon the company like Milton's death,

'Grinn'd horribly a ghastly smile'.

His muscles were so drawn together on each side of his face, that he showed twenty teeth at a grin, and put the country in some pain, lest a foreigner should carry away the honour of the day; but upon a farther trial they found he was master only of the merry grin.

[1] Captured by William in 1695.

The next that mounted the table was a malcontent in those days, and a great master in the whole art of grinning, but particularly excelled in the angry grin. He did his part so well that he is said to have made half a dozen women miscarry; but the justice being apprised by one who stood near him that the fellow who grinned in his face was a Jacobite, and being unwilling that a disaffected person should win the gold ring, and be looked upon as the best grinner in the country, he ordered the oaths to be tendered unto him upon his quitting the table, which the grinner refusing, he was set aside as an unqualified person. There were several other grotesque figures that presented themselves, which it would be too tedious to describe. I must not however omit a ploughman, who lived in the farther part of the country, and being very lucky in a pair of long lantern-jaws[1], wrung his face into such a hideous grimace, that every feature of it appeared under a different distortion. The whole company stood astonished at such a complicated grin, and were ready to assign the prize to him, had it not been proved by one of his antagonists that he had practised with verjuice for some days before, and had a crab found upon him at the very time of grinning; upon which the best judges of grinning declared it as their opinion that he was not to be looked upon as a fair grinner, and therefore ordered him to be set aside as a cheat.

The prize it seems at length fell upon a cobbler, Giles Gorgon by name, who produced several new grins of his own invention, having been used to cut faces for many years together over his last. At the very first grin he cast every human feature out of his countenance, at the second he became the face of a spout, at the third a baboon, at the fourth a head of a bass-viol, and at the

---

[1] "A term used of a thin visage, such as if a candle were burning in the mouth might transmit the light" (Johnson).

fifth a pair of nut-crackers. The whole assembly wondered at his accomplishments, and bestowed the ring
upon him unanimously; but, what he esteemed more
than all the rest, a country wench, whom he had wooed
in vain for above five years before, was so charmed with
his grins, and the applauses which he received on all
sides, that she married him the week following, and to
this day wears the prize upon her finger, the cobbler
having made use of it as his wedding-ring.

This paper might perhaps seem very impertinent, if it
grew serious in the conclusion. I would nevertheless
leave to the consideration of those who are the patrons
of this monstrous trial of skill, whether or no they are not
guilty, in some measure, of an affront to their species, in
treating after this manner the "human face divine", and
turning that part of us, which has so great an image impressed upon it, into the image of a monkey; whether
the raising such silly competitions among the ignorant,
proposing prizes for such useless accomplishments, filling
the common people's heads with such senseless ambitions,
and inspiring them with such absurd ideas of superiority
and pre-eminence, has not in it something immoral as
well as ridiculous.

XIX. SIR ROGER AT THE ABBEY.

Ire tamen restat Numa quò devenit et Ancus.—Hor. *Ep.* i. 6, 27.

> With Ancus, and with Numa, kings of Rome,
> We must descend into the silent tomb.

My friend Sir Roger de Coverley told me t' other
night, that he had been reading my paper[1] upon Westminster Abbey, in which, says he, there are a great many
ingenious fancies. He told me at the same time that he
observed I had promised another paper upon the tombs,

[1] *Spectator*, 26.

and that he should be glad to go and see them with me, not having visited them since he had read history. I could not imagine how this came into the knight's head, till I recollected that he had been very busy all last summer upon *Baker's Chronicle*, which he has quoted several times in his disputes with Sir Andrew Freeport since his last coming to town. Accordingly, I promised to call upon him the next morning, that we might go together to the abbey.

I found the knight under his butler's hands, who always shaves him. He was no sooner dressed than he called for a glass of the Widow Trueby's water, which he told me he always drank before he went abroad. He recommended to me a dram of it at the same time, with so much heartiness, that I could not forbear drinking it. As soon as I had got it down, I found it very unpalatable; upon which the knight, observing that I had made several wry faces, told me that he knew I should not like it at first, but that it was the best thing in the world against the stone or gravel.

I could have wished indeed that he had acquainted me with the virtues of it sooner; but it was too late to complain, and I knew what he had done was out of good will. Sir Roger told me further, that he looked upon it to be very good for a man whilst he staid in town, to keep off infection, and that he got together a quantity of it upon the first news of the sickness being at Dantzic; when, of a sudden, turning short to one of his servants, who stood behind him, he bid him call a hackney-coach and take care it was an elderly man that drove it.

He then resumed his discourse upon Mrs. Trueby's water, telling me that the Widow Trueby was one who did more good than all the doctors and apothecaries in the county; that she distilled every poppy that grew within five miles of her; that she distributed her water gratis among all sorts of people: to which the knight added that she had a very great jointure, and that the whole country would fain have it a match between him and her: "and truly," says Sir Roger, "if I had not been engaged, perhaps I could not have done better".

His discourse was broken off by his man's telling him he had called a coach. Upon our going to it, after having cast his eye upon the wheels, he asked the coachman if his axle-tree was good: upon the fellow's telling him he would warrant it, the knight turned to me, told me he looked like an honest man, and went in without further ceremony.

We had not gone far, when Sir Roger, popping out his head, called the coachman down from his box, and upon presenting himself at the window, asked him if he smoked. As I was considering what this would end in, he bid him stop by the way at any good tobacconist's, and take in a roll of their best Virginia. Nothing material happened in the remaining part of our journey, till we were set down at the west end of the abbey.

As we went up the body of the church, the knight pointed at the trophies upon one of the new monuments, and cried out, "A brave man, I warrant him!" Passing afterwards by Sir Cloudsley Shovel,[1] he flung his hand that way, and cried "Sir Cloudsley Shovel! a very gallant man". As we stood before Busby's[2] tomb, the knight uttered himself again after the same manner: "Dr. Busby! a great man: he whipped my grandfather; a very great man! I should have gone to him myself, if I had not been a blockhead—a very great man!"

We were immediately conducted into the little chapel on the right hand. Sir Roger, planting himself at our historian's elbow, was very attentive to everything he

[1] Drowned off the Scilly Isles, Oct. 22, 1707.
[2] Headmaster of Westminster (b. 1606, d. 1695).

said, particularly to the account he gave us of the lord who had cut off the king of Morocco's head. Among several other figures, he was very well pleased to see the statesman Cecil upon his knees; and concluding them all to be great men, was conducted to the figure which represents that martyr to good housewifery[1] who died by the prick of a needle. Upon our interpreter's telling us that she was a maid of honour to Queen Elizabeth, the knight was very inquisitive into her name and family; and, after having regarded her finger for some time, "I wonder," says he, "that Sir Richard Baker has said nothing of her in his Chronicle".

We were then conveyed to the two coronation chairs[2], where my old friend, after having heard that the stone underneath the most ancient of them, which was brought from Scotland, was called Jacob's pillow, sat himself down in the chair, and, looking like the figure of an old Gothic king, asked our interpreter, what authority they had to say that Jacob had ever been in Scotland? The fellow, instead of returning him an answer, told him, that he hoped his honour would pay his forfeit. I could observe Sir Roger a little ruffled upon being thus trepanned, but our guide not insisting upon his demand, the knight soon recovered his good humour, and whispered in my ear, that if Will Wimble were with us, and saw those two chairs, it would go hard but he would get a tobacco stopper out of one or t' other of them.

Sir Roger, in the next place, laid his hand upon Edward the Third's sword, and, leaning upon the pommel

---

[1] Lady Eliz. Russel, one of whose sisters married Lord Burleigh, and another was the mother of Francis Bacon. The story here alluded to is an absurd legend.

[2] In the chapel of Edward the Confessor. One of the chairs was made for the coronation of Queen Mary. The other is Edward's chair, the seat of which was carried off from Scone in 1296, and was said by tradition to have been Jacob's pillow.

of it, gave us the whole history of the Black Prince; concluding, that, in Sir Richard Baker's opinion, Edward the
Third was one of the greatest princes that ever sat upon
the English throne.

We were then shown Edward the Confessor's tomb;
upon which Sir Roger acquainted us, that he was the
first who touched for the evil: and afterwards Henry the
Fourth's; upon which he shook his head, and told us
there was fine reading in the casualties of that reign.

Our conductor then pointed to that monument where
there is the figure of one of our English kings without a
head;[1] and upon giving us to know that the head, which
was of beaten silver, had been stolen away several years
since, "Some Whig, I'll warrant you," says Sir Roger;
"you ought to lock up your kings better; they will carry
off the body too, if you don't take care".

The glorious names of Henry the Fifth and Queen
Elizabeth gave the knight great opportunities of shining,
and of doing justice to Sir Richard Baker, who, as our
knight observed with some surprise, had a great many kings
in him, whose monuments he had not seen in the abbey.

For my own part, I could not but be pleased to see
the knight show such an honest passion for the glory of
his country, and such a respectful gratitude to the memory
of its princes.

I must not omit that the benevolence of my good old
friend, which flows out towards every one he converses
with, made him very kind to our interpreter, whom he
looked upon as an extraordinary man: for which reason
he shook him by the hand at parting, telling him that he
should be very glad to see him at his lodgings in Norfolk
Buildings, and talk over these matters with him more at
leisure.

---

[1] The head of Henry V., cast in silver, was stolen at the time of the
Reformation.

xx. SIR ROGER AT THE PLAY.

Respicere exemplar vitae morumque jubebo
Doctum imitatorem, et veras hinc ducere voces.
                                    —Hor. *Ars Poet.*, 317.

Keep Nature's great original in view,
And thence the living images pursue.—*Francis.*

MY friend Sir Roger de Coverley, when we last met together at the club, told me that he had a great mind to see the new tragedy [1] with me, assuring me at the same time that he had not been at a play these twenty years. "The last I saw," said Sir Roger, "was The Committee [2], which I should not have gone to neither, had not I been told beforehand that it was a good Church of England comedy." He then proceeded to inquire of me who this distrest mother was; and upon hearing that she was Hector's widow, he told me that her husband was a brave man, and that when he was a schoolboy he had read his life at the end of the dictionary. My friend asked me, in the next place, if there would not be some danger in coming home late, in case the Mohocks [3] should be abroad. "I assure you," says he, "I thought I had fallen into their hands last night; for I observed two or

---

[1] *The Distrest Mother*, by Ambrose Philips, 1712, founded on Racine's *Andromaque.*

[2] A play (1665) by Sir Robert Howard, who collaborated with Dryden in *The Indian Queen.*

[3] " Who has not trembled at the Mohock's name?
    Was there a watchman took his hourly rounds,
    Safe from their blows or new invented wounds?"
                            (Gay's *Trivia*, Bk. III.)

The Mohocks corresponded to the Restoration Scowrers. See note on Essay x. There was a special scare at the time of this Essay. On March 9, 1712, Swift wrote to Stella that "it is not safe being in the streets at night for them". So great was the alarm that on March 17 a royal proclamation offered £100 reward for their detection.

three lusty black men that followed me half way up Fleet Street, and mended their pace behind me in proportion as I put on to get away from them. You must know," continued the knight with a smile, " I fancied they had a mind to hunt me; for I remember an honest gentleman in my neighbourhood, who was served such a trick in King Charles the Second's time, for which reason he has not ventured himself in town ever since. I might have shown them very good sport, had this been their design; for, as I am an old fox-hunter, I should have turned and dodged and have played them a thousand tricks they had never seen in their lives before." Sir Roger added, that "if these gentlemen had any such intention, they did not succeed very well in it; for I threw them out", says he, "at the end of Norfolk Street, where I doubled the corner, and got shelter in my lodgings before they could imagine what was become of me. However," says the knight, " if Captain Sentry will make one with us to-morrow night, and you will both of you call upon me about four o'clock, that we may be at the house before it is full, I will have my own coach in readiness to attend you, for John tells me he has got the fore-wheels mended."

The captain, who did not fail to meet me there at the appointed hour, bid Sir Roger fear nothing, for that he had put on the same sword which he made use of at the battle of Steenkirk[1]. Sir Roger's servants, and among the rest my old friend the butler, had, I found, provided themselves with good oaken plants, to attend their master upon this occasion. When we had placed him in his coach, with myself at his left hand, the captain before

---

[1] King William was forced to retreat at Steenkirk on July 24, 1692, before the Duke of Luxemburg. The French generals, it is said, were so eager for the fray that they did not take time to adjust their neck-cloths. Hence the fashion in Queen Anne's reign of wearing a scarf with studied negligence.

him, and his butler at the head of his footmen in the
rear, we convoyed him in safety to the playhouse, where,
after having marched up the entry in good order, the
captain and I went in with him, and seated him betwixt
us in the pit. As soon as the house was full, and the
candles lighted, my old friend stood up, and looked about
him with that pleasure which a mind seasoned with
humanity naturally feels in itself, at the sight of a multitude of people who seem pleased with one another, and
partake of the same common entertainment. I could not
but fancy to myself, as the old man stood up in the
middle of the pit, that he made a very proper centre to a
tragic audience. Upon the entering of Pyrrhus, the
knight told me that he did not believe the king of France
himself had a better strut. I was indeed very attentive
to my old friend's remarks, because I looked upon them
as a piece of natural criticism, and was well pleased to
hear him, at the conclusion of almost every scene, telling
me that he could not imagine how the play would end.
One while he appeared much concerned for Andromache;
and a little while after as much for Hermione; and was
extremely puzzled to think what would become of Pyrrhus.

When Sir Roger saw Andromache's obstinate refusal
to her lover's importunities, he whispered me in the ear,
that he was sure she would never have him; to which he
added, with a more than ordinary vehemence, "You
can't imagine, sir, what it is to have to do with a widow".
Upon Pyrrhus's threatening afterwards to leave her, the
knight shook his head, and muttered to himself, "Ay, do
if you can". This part dwelt so much upon my friend's
imagination, that at the close of the third act, as I was
thinking of something else, he whispered me in my ear,
"These widows, sir, are the most perverse creatures in the
world. But pray," says he, " you that are a critic, is the
play according to your dramatic rules, as you call them?

Should your people in tragedy always talk to be understood? Why, there is not a single sentence in this play that I do not know the meaning of."

The fourth act very luckily began before I had time to give the old gentleman an answer. "Well," says the knight, sitting down with great satisfaction, "I suppose we are now to see Hector's ghost." He then renewed his attention, and, from time to time, fell a-praising the widow. He made, indeed, a little mistake as to one of her pages, whom at his first entering he took for Astyanax; but quickly set himself right in that particular, though, at the same time, he owned he should have been very glad to have seen the little boy, who, says he, must needs be a very fine child by the account that is given of him. Upon Hermione's going off with a menace to Pyrrhus, the audience gave a loud clap, to which Sir Roger added, "On my word, a notable young baggage!"

As there was a very remarkable silence and stillness in the audience during the whole action, it was natural for them to take the opportunity of these intervals between the acts to express their opinion of the players and of their respective parts. Sir Roger, hearing a cluster of them praise Orestes, struck in with them, and told them that he thought his friend Pylades was a very sensible man. As they were afterwards applauding Pyrrhus, Sir Roger put in a second time, "And let me tell you," says he, "though he speaks but little, I like the old fellow in whiskers as well as any of them". Captain Sentry, seeing two or three wags who sat near us lean with an attentive ear towards Sir Roger, and fearing lest they should smoke the knight, plucked him by the elbow, and whispered something in his ear, that lasted till the opening of the fifth act. The knight was wonderfully attentive to the account which Orestes gives of Pyrrhus's death. and at the conclusion of it, told me it was such a bloody piece of work that he was glad it was not done upon the stage. Seeing afterwards Orestes in his raving fit, he grew more than ordinarily serious, and took occasion to moralize (in his way) upon an evil conscience, adding, that Orestes, in his madness, looked as if he saw something.

As we were the first that came into the house, so we were the last that went out of it; being resolved to have a clear passage for our old friend, whom we did not care to venture among the jostling of the crowd. Sir Roger went out fully satisfied with his entertainment, and we guarded him to his lodging in the same manner that we brought him to the playhouse; being highly pleased for my own part, not only with the performance of the excellent piece which had been presented, but with the satisfaction which it had given to the good old man.

XXI. THE TORY FOX-HUNTER.[1]

Studiis rudis, sermone barbarus, impetu strenuus, manu promptus,
cogitatione celer.—Vell. Paterc.

FOR the honour of his Majesty, and the safety of his government, we cannot but observe that those who have appeared the greatest enemies to both are of that rank of men who are commonly distinguished by the title of Fox-hunters. As several of these have had no part of their education in cities, camps, or courts, it is doubtful whether they are of greater ornament or use to the nation in which they live. It would be an everlasting reproach to politics should such men be able to overturn an establishment which has been formed by the wisest laws,

---

[1] From *The Freeholder*. This paper was written entirely by Addison, and consisted of fifty-five numbers, from 23rd Dec. 1715, to 29th June, 1716. Its object was purely political, and its main topics were "the enormity of rebellion and the prejudices of ignorance and faction". The Tory Fox-hunter is painted manifestly by a Whig brush.

and is supported by the ablest heads. The wrong notions and prejudices which cleave to many of these country gentlemen, who have always lived out of the way of being better informed, are not easy to be conceived by a person who has never conversed with them.

That I may give my readers an image of these rural statesmen, I shall, without farther preface, set down an account of a discourse I chanced to have with one of them some time ago. I was travelling towards one of the remote parts of England, when about three o'clock in the afternoon, seeing a country gentleman trotting before me with a spaniel by his horse's side, I made up to him. Our conversation opened, as usual, upon the weather, in which we were very unanimous, having both agreed that it was too dry for the season of the year. My fellow-traveller, upon this, observed to me that there had been no good weather since the Revolution. I was a little startled at so extraordinary a remark, but would not interrupt him till he proceeded to tell me of the fine weather they used to have in King Charles the Second's reign. I only answered that I did not see how the badness of the weather could be the king's fault; and, without waiting for his reply, asked him whose house it was we saw upon a rising ground at a little distance from us. He told me it belonged to an old fanatical cur, Mr. Such-a-one. "You must have heard of him," says he, "he's one of the Rump." I knew the gentleman's character upon hearing his name, but assured him that to my knowledge he was a good churchman. "Ay," says he, with a kind of surprise, "we were told in the country that he spoke twice, in the Queen's time, against taking off the duties upon French claret." This naturally led us in the proceedings of late parliaments, upon which occasion he affirmed roundly that there had not been one good law passed since King William's accession to

the throne, except the act for preserving the game.   I had
a mind to see him out, and therefore did not care for
contradicting him.   "Is it not hard," says he, "that
honest gentlemen should be taken into custody of
messengers to prevent them from acting according to
their consciences?   But," says he, "what can we expect
when a parcel of factious sons of —" He was going
on in great passion, but chanced to miss his dog, who
was amusing himself about a bush that grew at some
distance behind us.   We stood still till he had whistled
him up, when he fell into a long panegyric upon his
spaniel, who seemed, indeed, excellent in his kind; but
I found the most remarkable adventure of his life was
that he had once like to have worried a dissenting
teacher[1].   The master could hardly sit on his horse for
laughing all the while he was giving me the particulars of
this story, which I found had mightily endeared his dog
to him, and as he himself told me, had made him a great
favourite among all the honest gentlemen of the country.
We were at length diverted from this piece of mirth by a
post-boy, who winding his horn at us, my companion
gave him two or three curses, and left the way clear for
him.   "I fancy," said I, "that post brings news from
Scotland.   I shall long to see the next Gazette."   "Sir,"
says he, "I make it a rule never to believe any of your
printed news.   We never see, sir, how things go, except
now and then in Dyer's Letter[2], and I read that more for
the style than the news.   The man has a clever pen, it must
be owned.   But is it not strange that we should be

---

[1] Fielding probably profited by Addison's sketch, when twenty-six
years later he described in *Joseph Andrews* the squire who set his dogs
on Parson Adams.

[2] *Dyer's News Letter* began about 1690.   Steele in *Tatler* 18 states that
it was specially esteemed by fox-hunters for the marvels in which it dealt.
Cf. Addison's *Drummer*, act ii. sc. 1. " I believe he is still living, because the news of his death was first published in Dyer's Letter ".

making war upon Church of England men, with Dutch and Swiss soldiers, men of antimonarchical principles? These foreigners will never be loved in England, sir; they have not that wit and good-breeding that we have." I must confess I did not expect to hear my new acquaintance value himself upon these qualifications, but finding him such a critic upon foreigners, I asked him if he had ever travelled. He told me he did not know what travelling was good for, but to teach a man to ride the great horse, to jabber French, and to talk against passive obedience; to which he added that he scarce ever knew a traveller in his life who had not forsook his principles and lost his hunting-seat. "For my part," says he, "I and my father before me have always been for passive obedience, and shall be always for opposing a prince who makes use of ministers that are of another opinion. But where do you intend to inn to-night? (for we were now come in sight of the next town). I can help you to a very good landlord if you will go along with me. He is a lusty jolly fellow, that lives well, at least three yards in the girt, and the best Church of England man upon the road." I had a curiosity to see this High-church inn-keeper, as well as to enjoy more of the conversation of my fellow-traveller, and therefore readily consented to set our horses together for that night. As we rode side by side through the town, I was let into the characters of all the principal inhabitants whom we met in our way. One was a dog, another a whelp, another a cur, and another the son of a bitch, under which several denominations were compre-hended all that voted on the Whig side in the last elec-tion of burgesses. As for those of his own party, he distinguished them by a nod of his head, and asking them how they did by their Christian names. Upon our arrival at the inn my companion fetched out the jolly landlord, who knew him by his whistle. Many endearments and

private whispers passed between them, though it was easy
to see, by the landlord's scratching his head, that things
did not go to their wishes. The landlord had swelled
his body to a prodigious size, and worked up his complexion to a standing crimson by his zeal for the prosperity
of the Church, which he expressed every hour of the day,
as his customers dropt in, by repeated bumpers. He had
not time to go to church himself, but, as my friend told
me in my ear, had headed a mob at the pulling down of
two or three meeting-houses. While supper was preparing, he enlarged upon the happiness of the neighbouring
shire; "For," says he, "there is scarce a Presbyterian in
the whole county, except the bishop". In short, I found
by his discourse that he had learned a great deal of politics,
but not one word of religion, from the parson of his
parish; and, indeed, that he had scarce any other notion
of religion but that it consisted in hating Presbyterians.
I had a remarkable instance of his notions in this particular. Upon seeing a poor decrepit old woman pass
under the window where we sat, he desired me to take
notice of her; and afterwards informed me that she was
generally reputed a witch by the country people, but that,
for his part, he was apt to believe she was a Presbyterian.

Supper was no sooner served in than he took occasion,
from a shoulder of mutton that lay before us, to cry up
the plenty of England, which would be the happiest
country in the world, provided we would live within ourselves. Upon which he expatiated on the inconveniences
of trade, that carried from us the commodities of our
country, and made a parcel of upstarts as rich as men of
the most ancient families of England. He then declared
frankly that he had always been against all treaties and
alliances with foreigners. "Our wooden walls," says he,
"are our security, and we may bid defiance to the whole

world, especially if they should attack us when the militia
is out." I ventured to reply that I had as great an opinion
of the English fleet as he had; but I could not see how
they could be paid, and manned, and fitted out, unless
we encouraged trade and navigation. He replied, with
some vehemence, that he would undertake to prove trade
would be the ruin of the English nation. I would fain
have put him upon it; but he contented himself with
affirming it more eagerly, to which he added two or three
curses upon the London merchants, not forgetting the
directors of the bank. After supper he asked me if I was
an admirer of punch, and immediately called for a sneaker.
I took this occasion to insinuate the advantages of trade
by observing to him that water was the only native of
England that could be made use of on this occasion, but
that the lemons, the brandy, the sugar, and the nutmeg
were all foreigners. This put him into confusion; but
the landlord, who overheard me, brought him off, by
affirming, that for constant use, there was no liquor like
a cup of English water, provided it had malt enough in it.
My squire laughed heartily at the conceit, and made the
landlord sit down with us. We sat pretty late over our
punch; and, amidst a great deal of improving discourse,
drank the healths of several persons in the country, whom
I had never heard of, that, they both assured me, were the
ablest statesmen in the nation: and of some Londoners,
whom they extolled to the skies for their wit, and who,
I knew, passed in town for silly fellows. It being now
midnight, and my friend perceiving by his almanac that
the moon was up, he called for his horses, and took a
sudden resolution to go to his house, which was at three
miles distance from the town, after having bethought himself that he never slept well out of his own bed. He
shook me very heartily by the hand at parting, and discovered a great air of satisfaction in his looks, that he had

met with an opportunity of showing his parts, and left me
a much wiser man than he found me.

JONATHAN SWIFT.
(1667-1745).

XXII. ON STYLE.

THE following letter has laid before me many great
and manifest evils in the world of letters, which
I had overlooked; but they open to me a very busy
scene, and it will require no small care and application
to amend errors which are become so universal. The
affection of politeness is exposed in this epistle with
a great deal of wit and discernment; so that whatever
discourses I may fall into hereafter upon the subjects the
writer treats of, I shall at present lay the matter before
the world, without the least alteration from the words of
my correspondent.

" *To Isaac Bickerstaff, Esquire.*

" Sir,

" There are some abuses among us of great consequence, the reformation of which is properly your
province; though, as far as I have been conversant in
your papers, you have not yet considered them. These
are the deplorable ignorance that for some years hath
reigned among our English writers, the great depravity
of our taste, and the continual corruption of our style.
I say nothing here of those who handle particular sciences,
divinity, law, physic, and the like; I mean the traders in
history, politics, and the *belles lettres*, together with those
by whom books are not translated, but, as the common
expressions are, *done* out of French, Latin, or other
language, and made English. I cannot but observe to

you that until of late years a Grub-street book was always bound in sheep-skin, with suitable print and paper, the price never above a shilling, and taken off wholly by common tradesmen or country pedlars; but now they appear in all sizes and shapes, and in all places. They are handed about from lapfuls in every coffee-house to persons of quality; are shown in Westminster-hall and the Court of Requests. You may see them gilt, and in royal paper of five or six hundred pages, and rated accordingly. I would engage to furnish you with a catalogue of English books, published within the compass of seven years past, which at the first hand would cost you a hundred pounds, wherein you shall not be able to find ten lines together of common grammar or common sense.

"These two evils, ignorance and want of taste, have produced a third; I mean the continual corruption of our English tongue, which, without some timely remedy, will suffer more by the false refinements of twenty years past than it hath been improved in the foregoing hundred. And this is what I design chiefly to enlarge upon, leaving the former evils to your animadversion.

"But instead of giving you a list of the late refinements crept into our language, I here send you the copy of a letter I received, some time ago, from a most accomplished person in this way of writing; upon which I shall make some remarks. It is in these terms:

"'Sir,

"'I *cou'd n't* get the things you sent for all *about town*— I *thot* to *ha* come down myself, and then *I'd h' brot 'um*; but I *ha'nt don 't*, and I believe I *can't do 't*, that's *pozz*— Tom begins to *gi 'mself* airs, because *he's* going with the *plenipo's*—'T is said the *French* king will *bamboozl us agen*, which causes many speculations. The *Jacks* and others of that *kidney* are very *uppish* and *alert upon 't*, as you may

see by their *phizz's*—Will Hazard has got the *hipps*,
having lost *to the tune of* five *hundr'd* pound, *tho'* he
understands play very well, *no body better*.   He has
promis't me upon *rep*, to leave off play; but you know 't is
a weakness *he's* too apt to *give in to, tho'* he has as much
wit as any man, *no body more*.   He has lain *incog* ever
since—The *mob 's* very quiet with us now—I believe you
thot I banter'd you in my last, like a *country put*—I *shan't*
leave town this month, &c.'

"This letter is in every point an admirable pattern of
the present polite way of writing; nor is it of less authority
for being an epistle.   You may gather every flower in it,
with a thousand more of equal sweetness, from the books,
pamphlets, and single papers offered us every day in the
coffee-houses: and these are the beauties introduced to
supply the want of wit, sense, humour, and learning,
which formerly were looked upon as qualifications for a
writer.   If a man of wit, who died forty years ago, were
to rise from the grave on purpose, how would he be able
to read this letter? and after he had got through that
difficulty, how would he be able to understand it?   The
first thing that strikes your eye, is the breaks at the end
of almost every sentence; of which I know not the use,
only that it is a refinement, and very frequently practised.
Then you will observe the abbreviations and elisions, by
which consonants of most obdurate sound are joined
together, without one softening vowel to intervene; and
all this only to make one syllable of two, directly contrary to the example of the Greek and Romans, altogether
of the Gothic strain, and a natural tendency towards
relapsing into barbarity, which delights in monosyllables
and uniting of mute consonants, as it is observable in all
the northern languages.   And this is still more visible in
the next refinement, which consists in pronouncing the
first syllable in a word that has many, and dismissing the

rest, such as *phizz*, *hipps*, *mob*, *pozz*, *rep*, and many more, when we are already overloaded with monosyllables, which are the disgrace of our language. Thus we cram one syllable, and cut off the rest, as the owl fattened her mice after she had bit off their legs to prevent them from running away; and if ours be the same reason for maiming our words, it will certainly answer the end; for I am sure no other nation will desire to borrow them. Some words are hitherto but fairly split, and therefore only in their way to perfection, as *incog* and *plenipo*: but in a short time it is to be hoped they will be further docked to *inc* and *plen*. This reflection has made me of late years very impatient for a peace, which I believe would save the lives of many brave words, as well as men. The war has introduced abundance of polysyllables[1], which will never be able to live many more campaigns: *speculations*, *operations*, *preliminaries*, *ambassadors*, *pallisadoes*, *com munication*, *circumvallation*, *battalions*: as numerous as they are, if they attack us too frequently in our coffee-houses, we shall certainly put them to flight, and cut off the rear.

"The third refinement observable in the letter I send you consists in the choice of certain words[2], invented by some pretty fellows, such as *banter*, *bamboozle*, *country put* and *kidney*, as it is there applied; some of which are now struggling for the vogue, and others are in possession of it. I have done my utmost for some years past to stop the progress of *mob* and *banter*, but have been plainly borne down by numbers, and betrayed by those who promised to assist me.

"In the last place, you are to take notice of certain

[1] Several of those cited by Swift are used by Shakespeare, Milton, and Dryden.

[2] *Banter*, *bamboozle*, and *put* are of uncertain origin. *Kidney* is used in the same sense by Shakespeare, *Merry Wives of Windsor*, act iii. sc. 5.

choice phrases scattered through the letter, some of them tolerable enough, until they were worn to rags by servile imitators. You might easily find them though they were not in a different print, and therefore I need not disturb them.

"These are the false refinements in our style which you ought to correct: first, by argument and fair means; but if these fail, I think you are to make use of your authority as Censor, and by an annual *Index Expurgatorius* expunge all words and phrases that are offensive to good sense, and condemn those barbarous mutilations of vowels and syllables. In this last point the usual pretence is, that they spell as they speak. A noble standard for language! to depend upon the caprice of every coxcomb who, because words are the clothing of our thoughts, cuts them out and shapes them as he pleases, and changes them oftener than his dress. I believe all reasonable people would be content that such refiners were more sparing in their words, and liberal in their syllables: and upon this head I should be glad you would bestow some advice upon several young readers in our churches, who, coming up from the university full fraught with admiration of our town politeness, will needs correct the style of their prayer-books. In reading the Absolution, they are very careful to say *pardons* and *absolves*: and in the prayer for the royal family, it must be *endue'um, enrich'um, prosper'um,* and *bring'um.* Then in their sermons they use all the modern terms of art, *sham, banter, mob, bubble*[1], *bully, cutting, shuffling,* and *palming*; all which, and many more of the like stamp, as I have heard them often in the pulpit from such young sophisters, so I have read them in some of 'those sermons that have made most noise of late'. The design, it seems, is to avoid the dreadful imputation of pedantry; to show us that they know the

[1] Any one defrauded. So used after the time of the South Sea Bubble.

town, understand men and manners, and have not been
poring upon old unfashionable books in the university.

"I should be glad to see you the instrument of introducing into our style that simplicity which is the best and
truest ornament of most things in life, which the politer
age always aimed at in their building and dress, *simplex
munditiis*, as well as in their productions of wit. It is
manifest that all new affected modes of speech, whether
borrowed from the court, the town, or the theatre, are the
first perishing parts in any language; and, as I could
prove by many hundred instances, have been so in ours.
The writings of Hooker[1], who was a country clergyman,
and of Parsons[2] the Jesuit, both in the reign of Queen
Elizabeth, are in a style that, with very few allowances,
would not offend any present reader, and are much more
clear and intelligible than those of Sir Harry Wotton[3],
Sir Robert Naunton[4], Osborn[5], Daniel[6] the historian,
and several others who *writ* later; but being men of the
court, and affecting the phrases then in fashion, they are
often either not to be understood, or appear perfectly
ridiculous.

"What remedies are to be applied to these evils I have
not room to consider, having, I fear, already taken up

---

[1] 1553–1600. For some years rector of Boscombe, Salisbury. Cf.
Hallam's verdict:—"So little is there of vulgarity in his racy idiom, of
pedantry in his learned phrase, that I know not whether any later writer
has more admirably displayed the capacities of our language".

[2] Robert Parsons (1546–1610), a famous Jesuit agitator in the reign of
Elizabeth.

[3] Sir Henry Wotton (1568–1639). The *Reliquiae Wottonianae* were
edited by Izaak Walton, 1651.

[4] Sir R. Naunton (1563–1635) was author of *Fragmenta Regalia*, an
account of certain Elizabethan celebrities.

[5] Francis Osborn (1589–1658) was author of *Advice to a Son*, concerning which Johnson said, that "were a man to write so now, the boys
would throw stones at him".

[6] Sam. Daniel (1562–1619), a poet and historian. Swift's criticism is
unjust, for Daniel's style has always been praised for its perspicuity.

most of your paper.   Besides, I think it is our office
only to represent abuses, and yours to redress them.   I
am, with great respect, Sir,

"Yours, &c."

XXIII. THE VINDICATION OF ISAAC BICKER-
STAFF.

M R. PARTRIDGE[1] has been lately pleased to treat
me after a very rough manner, in that which is called
his Almanac for the present year: such usage is very in-
decent from one gentleman to another, and does not at all
contribute to the discovery of truth, which ought to be the
great end in all disputes of the learned.   To call a man
a fool and villain, an impudent fellow, only for differing
from him in a point merely speculative, is, in my humble
opinion, a very improper style for a person of his education.   I appeal to the learned world, whether, in last
year's predictions, I gave him the least provocation for
such unworthy treatment.   Philosophers have differed
in all ages; but the discreetest among them have always
differed as became philosophers.   Scurrility and passion,
in a controversy among scholars, is just so much of
nothing to the purpose, and at best a tacit confession

---

[1] The history of the famous joke is briefly this.   In 1708, Swift, in
ridicule of the pretensions of almanac makers, published under the name
of Bickerstaff his sham " Predictions for the year 1708", one of the
predictions being the death of John Partridge on March 29th, 1708.
Partridge was a well-known prophet of the time, whose book was called
"Merlinus Liberatus, by John Partridge, Student in Physick and
Astrology, at the Blue Bell in Salisbury Street, in the Strand, London".
In April Swift published an account of Partridge's death, and many wits
followed this up with numerous epitaphs.   Later appeared "Bickerstaff
Detected, by J. Partridge", an attempt to turn the joke against Swift,
which has been variously attributed to Congreve, Rowe, and Dr. Yalden.
Then, in 1709, Swift vindicated himself in this ironical paper.   Part-
ridge really lived till 1715, and there is an epitaph to him in Mortlake
Churchyard, but he issued no almanac after 1709, for his fame did not
survive his metaphorical death at the hands of Swift.

of a weak cause: my concern is not so much for my own
reputation, as that of the republic of letters, which Mr.
Partridge has endeavoured to wound through my sides.
If men of public spirit must be superciliously treated for
their ingenious attempts, how will true useful knowledge
be ever advanced? I wish Mr. Partridge knew the
thoughts which foreign universities have conceived of his
ungenerous proceedings with me; but I am too tender
of his reputation to publish them to the world. That
spirit of envy and pride, which blasts so many rising
geniuses in our nation, is yet unknown among professors
abroad: the necessity of justifying myself will excuse my
vanity, when I tell the reader, that I have near a hundred
honorary letters from several parts of Europe (some as
far as Muscovy) in praise of my performance, beside
several others which, as I have been credibly informed,
were opened in the post-office, and never sent me. It
is true, the Inquisition[1] in Portugal was pleased to burn
my predictions, and condemn the author and the readers
of them: but I hope, at the same time, it will be considered in how deplorable a state learning lies at present
in that kingdom: and with the profoundest veneration
for crowned heads, I will presume to add, that it a little
concerned his majesty of Portugal to interpose his
authority in behalf of a scholar and a gentleman, the
subject of a nation with which he is now in so strict
an alliance. But the other kingdoms and states of
Europe have treated me with more candour and gener-
osity. If I had leave to print the Latin letters transmitted
to me from foreign parts, they would fill a volume, and
be a full defence against all that Mr. Partridge, or his
accomplices of the Portugal inquisition, will be ever able
to object; who, by the way, are the only enemies my

---

[1] Swift had predicted that the pope would die on the 11th of Sept.,
and it was reported by an ambassador that his book was actually burnt.

predictions have ever met with at home or abroad. But I hope I know better what is due to the honour of a learned correspondence in so tender a point. Yet some of those illustrious persons will perhaps excuse me for transcribing a passage or two[1] in my vindication. The most learned Monsieur Leibnitz thus addresses to me his third letter: "*Illustrissimo Bickerstaffio astrologiæ instauratori*", &c. Monsieur Le Clerc, quoting my predictions in a treatise he published last year, is pleased to say, "*Ita nuperimme Bickerstaffius magnum illud Angliæ sidus*". Another great professor writing of me has these words: "*Bickerstaffius nobilis Anglus, astrologorum hujusce sæculi facile princeps*". Signior Magliabecchi, the great duke's famous library keeper, spends almost his whole letter in compliments and praises. It is true, the renowned professor of astronomy at Utrecht seems to differ from me in one article; but it is after the modest manner that becomes a philosopher; as, *pace tanti viri dixerim*: and page 55, he seems to lay the error upon the printer (as indeed it ought), and says, *vel forsan error typographi, cum alioquin Bickerstaffius vir doctissimus*, &c.

If Mr. Partridge had followed these examples in the controversy between us, he might have spared me the trouble of justifying myself in so public a manner. I believe no man is readier to own his errors than I, or more thankful to those who will please to inform him of them. But it seems, this gentleman, instead of encouraging the progress of his own art, is pleased to look upon all attempts of that kind as an invasion of his province. He has been indeed so wise as to make no objection against the truth of my predictions, except in one single point relating to himself: and to demonstrate how much men are blinded by their own partiality, I do

---

[1] These ludicrous quotations are a burlesque of the style of Swift's old antagonist, Bentley (Nichols).

solemnly assure the reader, that he is the only person, from whom I ever heard that objection offered; which consideration alone, I think, will take off all its weight.

With my utmost endeavours I have not been able to trace above two objections ever made against the truth of my last year's prophecies: the first was of a Frenchman who was pleased to publish to the world "that the Cardinal de Noailles was still alive, notwithstanding the pretended prophecy of Monsieur Biquerstaffe", but how far a Frenchman, a papist, and an enemy is to believed in his own cause, against an English Protestant who is true to the government, I shall leave to the candid and impartial reader.

The other objection is the unhappy occasion of this discourse, and relates to an article in my Predictions, which foretold the death of Mr. Partridge to happen on March 29, 1708.   This he is pleased to contradict absolutely in the almanac he has published for the present year, and in that ungentlemanly manner (pardon the expression) as I have above related.   In that work he very roundly asserts that he "is not only now alive, but was likewise alive upon that very 29th of March, when I had foretold he should die".   This is the subject of the present controversy between us; which I design to handle with all brevity, perspicuity, and calmness. In this dispute, I am sensible the eyes not only of England but of all Europe will be upon us: and the learned in every country will, I doubt not, take part on that side where they find most appearance of reason and truth.

Without entering into criticisms of chronology about the hour of his death, I shall only prove that Mr. Partridge is not alive.   And my first argument is this: about a thousand gentlemen having bought his almanacs for this year merely to find what he said against me, at every line they read, they would lift up their eyes, and cry out, betwixt rage and laughter, "they were sure no man alive ever writ such damned stuff as this". Neither did I ever hear that opinion disputed, so that Mr. Partridge lies under a dilemma, either of disowning his almanac, or allowing himself to be no man alive. Secondly, Death is defined by all philosophers, a separation of the soul and body. Now it is certain, that the poor woman who has best reason to know, has gone about for some time into every alley in the neighbourhood, and sworn to the gossips that her husband had neither life nor soul in him. Therefore, if an uninformed carcase walks still about, and is pleased to call itself Partridge, Mr. Bickerstaff does not think himself any way answerable for that. Neither had the said carcase any right to beat the poor boy who happened to pass by it in the street, crying, "a full and true account of Dr. Partridge's death", &c.

Thirdly, Mr. Partridge pretends to tell fortunes, and recover stolen goods; which all the parish says he must do by conversing with the devil and other evil spirits; and no wise man will ever allow he could converse personally with either till after he was dead.

Fourthly, I will plainly prove him to be dead, out of his own almanac for this year and from the very passage which he produces to make us think him alive. He there says, "he is not only now alive, but was also alive upon that very 29th of March which I foretold he should die on": by this he declares his opinion that a man may be alive now who was not alive a twelve-month ago. And, indeed, there lies the sophistry of his argument. He dares not assert he was alive ever since that 29th of March, but that he "is now alive, and was so on that day". I grant the latter; for he did not die till night, as appears by the printed account of his death in a Letter to a Lord; and whether he be since revived

I leave the world to judge. This indeed is perfect cavilling, and I am ashamed to dwell any longer upon it.

Fifthly, I will appeal to Mr. Partridge himself whether it be probable I could have been so indiscreet to begin my predictions with the only falsehood that ever was pretended to be in them? and this in an affair at home where I had so many opportunities to be exact; and must have given such advantages against me to a person of Mr. Partridge's wit and learning, who, if he could possibly have raised one single objection more against the truth of my prophecies, would hardly have spared me.

And here I must take occasion to reprove the above-mentioned writer of the relation of Mr. Partridge's death in a Letter to a Lord, who was pleased to tax me with a mistake of four whole hours in my calculation of that event. I must confess, this censure, pronounced with an air of certainty, in a matter that so nearly concerned me, and by a grave judicious author, moved me not a little. But though I was at that time out of town, yet several of my friends, whose curiosity had led them to be exactly informed, (for as to my own part, having no doubt at all in the matter, I never once thought of it) assured me I computed to something under half an hour, which (I speak my private opinion) is an error of no very great magnitude that men should raise a clamour about it. I shall only say, it would not be amiss if that author would henceforth be more tender of other men's reputations as well as his own. It is well there were no more mistakes of that kind; if there had, I presume he would have told me of them with as little ceremony.

There is one objection against Mr. Partridge's death which I have sometimes met with, though indeed very slightly offered, that he still continues to write almanacs.

But this is no more than what is common to all of that profession: Gadbury[1], Poor Robin, Dove, Wing, and several
others do yearly publish their almanacs though several
of them have been dead since before the Revolution.
Now the natural reason of this I take to be, that whereas
it is the privilege of authors to live after their death,
almanac-makers are alone excluded, because their dis-
sertations, treating only upon the minutes as they pass,
become useless as those go off.   In consideration of
which, time, whose registers they are, gives them a lease
in reversion, to continue their works after death.

I should not have given the public or myself the
trouble of this vindication if my name had not been
made use of by several persons to whom I never lent it;
one of which, a few days ago, was pleased to father on
me a new set of predictions.   But I think these are
things too serious to be trifled with.   It grieved me to
the heart, when I saw my labours, which had cost me
so much thought and watching, bawled about by the
common hawkers of Grub-street, which I only intended
for the weighty consideration of the gravest persons.
This prejudiced the world so much at first, that several
of my friends had the assurance to ask me whether I
were in jest? to which I only answered coldly, "that the
event would show".   But it is the talent of our age and
nation to turn things of the greatest importance into
ridicule.   When the end of the year had verified all my
predictions, out comes Mr. Partridge's almanac, disputing
the point of his death; so that I am employed, like the
general who was forced to kill his enemies twice over,
whom a necromancer had raised to life.   If Mr. Partridge
have practised the same experiment upon himself, and be

---

[1] A contemporary almanac-maker, whose life was written by Partridge.
Poor Robin's Almanac lasted from 1662 to 1828. The others are adver-
tised in the *Daily Courant* in 1705.

again alive, long may he continue so; that does not the least contradict my veracity: but I think I have clearly proved, by invincible demonstration, that he died, at farthest, within half an hour of the time I foretold, and not four hours sooner, as the above-mentioned author, in his Letter to a Lord, has maliciously suggested, with design to blast my credit, by charging me with so gross a mistake.

HENRY FIELDING.

(1707-1754.)

XXIV. THE COMMONWEALTH OF LETTERS.

Οὐκ ἀγαθὸν πολυκοιρανίη, εἷς κοίρανος ἔστω,
Εἷς Βασιλεὺς, ᾧ ἔδωκε Κρόνου παῖς ἀγκυλυμήτεω
Σκῆπτρόν τ᾽ἠδὲ θέμιστας, ἵνα σφίσιν ἐμβασιλεύῃ.—*Homer.*

> Here is not allowed
> That worst of tyrants, an usurping crowd.
> To one sole monarch Jove commits the sway;
> His are the laws, and him let all obey.—*Pope.*

THOUGH of the three forms of government acknowledged in the schools all have been very warmly opposed and as warmly defended, yet in this point the different advocates will, I believe, very readily agree, that there is not one of the three which is not greatly to be preferred to total anarchy—a state in which there is no subordination, no lawful power, and no settled government, but where every man is at liberty to act in whatever manner it pleaseth him best.

As this is in reality a most deplorable state, I have long lamented, with great anguish of heart, that it is at present the case of a very large body of people in this kingdom —an assertion which, as it may surprise most of my readers, I will make haste to explain, by declaring that I mean the fraternity of the quill, that body of men to whom the public assign the name of authors.

However absurd politicians may have been pleased to represent the *imperium in imperio*, it will here, I doubt not, be found on a strict examination to be extremely necessary, the commonwealth of literature being indeed totally distinct from the greater commonwealth, and no more dependent upon it than the kingdom of England is on that of France. Of this our legislature seems to have been at all times sensible, as they have never attempted any provision for the regulation or correction of this body. In one instance, it is true, there are (I should rather, I believe, say there were) some laws to restrain them; for writers, if I am not mistaken, have been formerly punished for blasphemy against God and libels against the government; nay, I have been told that to slander the reputation of private persons was once thought unlawful here as well as among the Romans, who, as Horace tells us, had a severe law for this purpose.

In promulging these laws (whatever may be the reason of suffering them to grow obsolete) the state seems to have acted very wisely, as such kind of writings are really of most mischievous consequence to the public; but, alas! there are many abuses, many horrid evils, daily springing up in the commonwealth of literature, which appear to affect only that commonwealth, at least immediately, of which none of the political legislators have ever taken any notice, nor hath any civil court of judicature ever pretended to any cognizance of them. Nonsense and dulness are no crimes *in foro civili*; no man can be questioned for bad verses in Westminster Hall; and, amongst the many indictments for battery, not one can be produced for breaking poor Priscian's head[1], though it is done almost every day.

[1] To commit a grammatical error, Priscian being a famous grammarian in the time of Justinian. Cf. *Hudibras*, Pt. II. Can. 2. l. 223.
   " And hold no sin so deeply red,
     As that of breaking Priscian's head."

But though immediately, as I have said, these evils do not affect the greater commonwealth, yet, as they tend tc the utter ruin of the lesser, so they have a remote evil consequence, even on the state itself; which seems, by having left them unprovided for, to have remitted them, for the sake of convenience, to the government of laws and to the superintendence of magistrates of this lesser commonwealth, and never to have foreseen or suspected that dreadful state of anarchy which at present prevails in this lesser empire—an empire which hath formerly made so great a figure in this kingdom, and that, indeed, almost within our own memories.

It may appear strange that none of our English historians have spoken clearly and distinctly of this lesser empire; but this may be well accounted for when we consider that all these histories have been written by two sorts of persons—that is to say, either politicians or lawyers. Now, the former of these have had their imaginations so entirely filled with the affairs of the greater empire that it is no wonder the business of the lesser should have totally escaped their observation. And as to the lawyers, they are well known to have been very little acquainted with the commonwealth of literature, and to have always acted and written in defiance to its laws.

From these reasons it is very difficult to fix, with certainty, the exact period when this commonwealth first began among us. Indeed, if the originals of all the greater empires upon earth, and even of our own, be wrapped in such obscurity that they elude the inquiries of the most diligent sifters of antiquity, we cannot be surprised that this fate should attend our little empire, opposed as it hath been by the pen of the lawyer, overlooked by the eye of the historian, and never once smelt after by the nose of the antiquary.

In the earliest ages the literary state seems to have

been an ecclesiastical democracy, for the clergy are then said to have had all the learning among them; and the great reverence paid at that time to it by the laity appears from hence, that whoever could prove in a court of justice that he belonged to this state, by only reading a single verse in the Testament, was vested with the highest privileges, and might do almost what he pleased, even commit murder with impunity. And this privilege was called the benefit of the clergy.

This commonwealth, however, can scarce be said to have been in any flourishing state of old time even among the clergy themselves; inasmuch as we are told that a rector of a parish, going to law with his parishioners about paving the church, quoted this authority from St. Peter, *Paveant illi, non paveam ego*, which he construed thus: "They are to pave the church, and not I". And this, by a judge who was likewise an ecclesiastic, was allowed to be very good law.

The nobility had clearly no ancient connection with this commonwealth, nor would submit to be bound by any of its laws; witness that provision in an old act of parliament, "That a nobleman shall be entitled to the benefit of his clergy" (the privilege above-mentioned) "even though he cannot read". Nay, the whole body of the laity, though they gave such honours to this commonwealth, appear to have been very few of them under its jurisdiction, as appears by a law cited by Judge Rolls in his Abridgment, with the reason which he gives for it: "The command of the sheriff," says this writer, "to his officer, by word of mouth and without writing, is good; for it may be that neither the sheriff nor his officer can write or read".

But not to dwell on these obscure times, when so very little authentic can be found concerning this commonwealth, let us come at once to the days of Henry the

Eighth, when no less a revolution happened in the lesser than in the greater empire, for the literary government became absolute, together with the political, in the hands of one and the same monarch, who was himself a writer, and dictated, not only law, but common sense too, to all his people, suffering no one to write or speak but according to his will and pleasure.

After this king's demise the literary commonwealth was again separated from the political, for I do not find that his successor on the greater throne succeeded him likewise in the lesser. Nor did either of the two queens, as I can learn, pretend to any authority in this empire, in which the Salique law hath universally prevailed, for though there have been some considerable subjects of the female sex in the literary commonwealth, I never remember to have read of a queen.

It is not easy to say with any great exactness what form of government was preserved in this commonwealth during the reigns of Edward VI., Queen Mary, and Queen Elizabeth, for though there were some great men in those times, none of them seem to have affected the throne of wit; nay, Shakespeare, who flourished in the latter end of the last reign, and who seemed so justly qualified to enjoy this crown, never thought of challenging it.

In the reign of James I. the literary government was an aristocracy, for I do not choose to give it the evil name of oligarchy, though it consisted only of four, namely, Master William Shakespeare, Master Benjamin Jonson, Master John Fletcher, and Master Francis Beaumont. This quadrumvirate, as they introduced a new form of government, thought proper, according to Machiavel's advice, to introduce new names; they therefore called themselves *The Wits*, a name which hath been affected since by the reigning monarchs in this empire.

The last of this quadrumvirate enjoyed the government

alone during his life; after which the troubles that shortly
after ensued involved this lesser commonwealth in all the
confusion and ruin of the greater, nor can anything be
found of it with sufficient certainty till the *Wits*, in the
reign of Charles II., after many struggles among themselves for superiority, at last agreed to elect John Dryden
to be their king.

This King John had a very long reign, though a very
unquiet one; for there were several pretenders to the
throne of wit in his time, who formed very considerable
parties against him, and gave him great uneasiness, of
which his successor hath made mention in the following
lines:—

> Pride, folly, malice, against Dryden rose,
> In various shapes of parsons, critics, beaux.[1]

Besides which, his finances were in such disorder, that
it is affirmed his treasury was more than once entirely
empty.

He died, nevertheless, in a good old age, possessed
of the kingdom of Wit, and was succeeded by King
Alexander, surnamed Pope.

This prince enjoyed the crown many years, and is
thought to have stretched the prerogative much farther
than his predecessor; he is said to have been extremely
jealous of the affections of his subjects, and to have
employed various spies, by whom if he was informed of
the least suggestion against his title, he never failed of
branding the accused person with the word *dunce* on his
forehead in broad letters; after which the unhappy culprit
was obliged to lay by his pen for ever, for no bookseller
would venture to print a word that he wrote.

He did indeed put a total restraint on the liberty of the
press; for no person durst read anything which was writ
without his license and approbation; and this license he

[1] Pope's *Essay on Criticism*, l. 458.

granted only to four during his reign, namely, to the celebrated Dr. Swift, to the ingenious Dr. Young, to Dr.
Arbuthnot, and to one Mr. Gay, four of his principal
courtiers and favourites.

But without diving any deeper into his character, we
must allow that King Alexander had great merit as a
writer, and his title to the kingdom of Wit was better
ounded at least than his enemies have pretended.

After the demise of King Alexander, the literary state
relapsed again into democracy, or rather, indeed, into
downright anarchy; of which, as well as of the conse-
quences, I shall treat in a future paper.

ALEXANDER POPE.

(1688-1744.)

XXV. ON DEDICATIONS.

It matters not how false or forc'd,
So the best things be said o' th' worst,
It goes for nothing when 'tis said,
Only the arrow's drawn to th' head,
Whether it be a swan or goose
They level at: so shepherds use
To set the same mark on the hip
Both of their sound and rotten sheep.
                    —*Hudibras*, Pt. II. Canto i., 627.

THOUGH most things which are wrong in their own
nature are at once confessed and absolved in that
single word Custom; yet there are some which, as they
have a dangerous tendency, a thinking man will the less
excuse on that very account.   Among these I cannot but
reckon the common practice of dedications, which is of
so much the worse consequence, as it is generally used
by the people of politeness, and whom a learned education for the most part ought to have inspired with nobler

and juster sentiments. This prostitution of praise is not
only a deceit upon the gross of mankind, who take their
notion of characters from the learned; but also the better
sort must by this means lose some part at least of that
desire of fame which is the incentive to generous actions,
when they find it promiscuously bestowed on the meri-
torious and undeserving: nay, the author himself, let him
be supposed to have ever so true a value for the patron,
can find no terms to express it, but what have been
already used and rendered suspected by flatterers.   Even
truth itself in a dedication is like an honest man in a
disguise or vizor-mask, and will appear a cheat by being
dressed so like one.   Though the merit of the person is
beyond dispute, I see no reason that because one man is
eminent, therefore another has a right to be impertinent,
and throw praises in his face.   'Tis just the reverse of
the practice of the ancient Romans, when a person was
advanced to triumph for his services.   As they hired
people to rail at him in that circumstance to make him
as humble as they could, we have fellows to flatter him,
and make him as proud as they can. Supposing the writer
not to be mercenary, yet the great man is not more in
reason obliged to thank him for his picture in a dedication, than to thank a painter for that on a sign-post;
except it be a less injury to touch the most sacred part
of him, his character, than to make free with his countenance only.   I should think nothing justified me in this
point but the patron's permission beforehand, that I should
draw him as like as I could; whereas most authors proceed in this affair just as a dauber I have heard of, who,
not being able to draw portraits after the life, was used to
paint faces at random, and look out afterwards for people
whom he might persuade to be like them. To express my
notion of the thing in a word: to say more to a man than
one thinks, with a prospect of interest, is dishonest; and

without it, foolish. And whoever has had success in such an undertaking, must of necessity at once think himself in his heart a knave for having done it, and his patron a fool for having believed it.

I have sometimes been entertained with considering dedications in no very common light. By observing what qualities our writers think it will be most pleasing to others to compliment them with, one may form some judgment which are most so to themselves; and in consequence, what sort of people they are. Without this view one can read very few dedications but will give us cause to wonder how such things came to be said at all, or how they were said to such persons? I have known a hero complimented upon the decent majesty and state he assumed after victory, and a nobleman of a different character applauded for his condescension to inferiors. This would have seemed very strange to me, but that I happened to know the authors. He who made the first compliment was a lofty gentleman, whose air and gait discovered when he had published a new book; and the other tippled every night with the fellows who laboured at the press while his own writings were working off. It is observable of the female poets, and ladies dedicatory, that here (as elsewhere) they far exceed us in any strain or rant. As beauty is the thing that sex are piqued upon, they speak of it generally in a more elevated style than is used by the men. They adore in the same manner as they would be adored. So when the authoress of a famous modern romance begs a young nobleman's permission to pay him her "kneeling adorations", I am far from censuring the expression, as some critics would do, as deficient in grammar or sense; but I reflect, that adorations paid in that posture are what a lady might expect herself, and my wonder immediately ceases. These, when they flatter most, do but as they would be done unto: for, as none are so much concerned at being injured by calumnies as they who are readiest to cast them upon their neighbours, so it is certain none are so guilty of flattery to others as those who most ardently desire it themselves.

What led me into these thoughts was a dedication I happened upon this morning. The reader must understand that I treat the least instances or remains of ingenuity with respect, in what places soever found, or under whatever circumstances of disadvantage. From this love to letters I have been so happy in my searches after knowledge, that I have found unvalued repositories of learning in the lining of band-boxes. I look upon these pasteboard edifices, adorned with the fragments of the ingenious, with the same veneration as antiquaries upon ruined buildings, whose walls preserve divers inscriptions and names, which are nowhere else to be found in the world. This morning, when one of the Lady Lizard's daughters was looking over some hoods and ribands, brought by her tire-woman, with great care and diligence, I employed no less in examining the box which contained them; it was lined with certain scenes of a tragedy, written (as appeared by part of the title there extant) by one of the fair sex. What was most legible was the dedication; which, by reason of the largeness of the characters, was least defaced by those gothic ornaments of flourishes and foliage, wherewith the compilers of these sort of structures do often industriously obscure the works of the learned. As much of it as I could read with any ease, I shall communicate to the reader as follows. . . .

"Though it is a kind of profanation to approach your grace with so poor an offering, yet when I reflect how acceptable a sacrifice of first-fruits was to Heaven, in the earliest and purest ages of religion, that they were honoured with solemn feasts, and consecrated to altars by a divine command, . . . upon that consideration, as an argument of particular zeal, I dedicate. . . . It is impossible to behold you without adoring; yet, dazzled and awed by the glory that surrounds you, men feel a sacred power that refines their flames, and renders them pure as those we ought to offer to the Deity. . . . The shrine is worthy the divinity that inhabits it. In your grace we see what woman was before she fell, how nearly allied to the purity and perfection of angels. And We Adore and Bless the Glorious Work ".

Undoubtedly these and other periods of this most pious dedication could not but convince the duchess of what the eloquent authoress assures her at the end, that she was her servant with most ardent devotion. I think this a pattern of a new sort of style, not yet taken notice of by the critics, which is above the sublime, and may be called the celestial; that is, when the most sacred phrases appropriated to the honour of the Deity are applied to a mortal of good quality. As I am naturally emulous, I cannot but endeavour, in imitation of this lady, to be the inventor, or, at least, the first producer of a kind of dedication, very different from hers and most others, since it has not a word but what the author religiously thinks in it. It may serve for almost any book, either prose or verse, that has been, is, or shall be published, and might run in this manner.

THE AUTHOR TO HIMSELF.

" Most Honoured Sir,

" These labours, upon many considerations, so properly belong to none as to you. First, as it was your most earnest desire alone that could prevail upon me to make them public. Then as I am secure (from that constant indulgence you have ever shown to all which is mine) that no man will so readily take them into protec-

tion, or so zealously defend them.   Moreover, there is
none can so soon discover the beauties; and there are
some parts which, it is possible, few besides yourself are
capable of understanding.   Sir, the honour, affection, and
value I have for you are beyond expression; as great, I
am sure, or greater, than any man else can bear you.   As
for any defects which others may pretend to discover in
you, I do faithfully declare I was never able to perceive
them; and doubt not but those persons are actuated
purely by a spirit of malice or envy, the inseparable
attendants on shining merit and parts, such as I have
always esteemed yours to be.   It may perhaps be looked
upon as a kind of violence to modesty, to say this to you
in public; but you may believe me it is no more than I
have a thousand times thought of you in private.   Might
I follow the impulse of my soul, there is no subject I
could launch into with more pleasure than your panegyric.
But, since something is due to modesty, let me conclude
by telling you, that there is nothing so much I desire as
to know you more thoroughly than I have yet the happiness of doing.   I may then hope to be capable to do you
some real service; but till then can only assure you, that
I shall continue to be, as I am more than any man alive,
Dearest Sir, your affectionate friend, and the greatest of
your admirers."

XXVI. ON EPIC POETRY.

Docebo
Unde parentur opes; quid alat formetque poetam.
—Hor. *Ars Poet.*, 306.
I will teach to write,
Tell what the duty of a poet is,
Wherein his wealth and ornament consist
And how he may be form'd and how improv'd.—*Roscommon.*

IT is no small pleasure to me, who am zealous in the
interests of learning, to think I may have the honour
of leading the town into a very new and uncommon road

of criticism.   As that kind of literature is at present
carried on, it consists only in a knowledge of mechanic
rules which contribute to the structure of different sorts
of poetry; as the receipts of good housewives do to the
making puddings of flour, oranges, plums, or any other
ingredients. It would, methinks, make these my instruc-
tions more easily intelligible to ordinary readers, if I
discoursed of these matters in the style in which ladies
learned in economies dictate to their pupils for the improvement of the kitchen and larder.

I shall begin with epic poetry, because the critics agree
it is the greatest work human nature is capable of.   I
know the French have already laid down many mechanical
rules for compositions of this sort, but at the same time
they cut off almost all undertakers from the possibility of
ever performing them; for the first qualification they
unanimously require in a poet, is a genius.   I shall here
endeavour (for the benefit of my countrymen) to make it
manifest, that epic poems may be made "without a
genius", nay, without learning or much reading.   This
must necessarily be of great use to all those poets who
confess they never read, and of whom the world is convinced they never learn.   What Moliere observes of
making a dinner, that any man can do it with money,
and if a professed cook cannot without, he has his art for
nothing; the same may be said of making a poem, it is
easily brought about by him that has a genius, but the
skill lies in doing it without one.   In pursuance of this
end, I shall present the reader with a plain and certain
receipt, by which even sonneteers and ladies may be
qualified for this grand performance.

I know it will be objected that one of the chief qualifications of an epic poet is to be knowing in all arts and
sciences.   But this ought not to discourage those that
have no learning, as long as indexes and dictionaries may

be had, which are the compendium of all knowledge. Besides, since it is an established rule that none of the terms of those arts and sciences are to be made use of, one may venture to affirm, our poet cannot impertinently offend in this point. The learning which will be more particularly necessary to him, is the ancient geography of towns, mountains, and rivers: for this let him take Cluverius [1], value fourpence.

Another quality required is a complete skill in languages. To this I answer, that it is notorious persons of no genius have been oftentimes great linguists. To instance in the Greek, of which there are two sorts; the original Greek, and that from which our modern authors translate. I should be unwilling to promise impossibilities, but modestly speaking, this may be learned in about an hour's time with ease. I have known one, who became a sudden professor of Greek immediately upon application of the left-hand page of the Cambridge Homer [2] to his eye. It is in these days with authors as with other men, the well-bred are familiarly acquainted with them at first sight; and as it is sufficient for a good general to have surveyed the ground he is to conquer, so it is enough for a good poet to have seen the author he is to be master of. But to proceed to the purpose of this paper.

A RECEIPT TO MAKE AN EPIC POEM.

FOR THE FABLE.

Take out of any old poem, history book, romance, or legend (for instance, Geoffrey of Monmouth, or Don Belianis [3] of Greece), those parts of story which afford

---

[1] The allusion is to the *Germania Antiqua* and *Italia Antiqua* (1624) of Cluverius, works which have been called epoch-making in the history of ancient geography.

[2] The editions of the time had an English version on the left-hand pages.

[3] *The Famous and Delectable History of Don Belianis of Greece* was

most scope for long descriptions.   Put these pieces together, and throw all the adventures you fancy into one
tale.   Then take a hero whom you may choose for the
sound of his name, and put him into the midst of these
adventures.   There let him work for twelve books; at
the end of which you may take him out ready prepared
to conquer, or to marry; it being necessary that the conclusion of an epic poem be fortunate.

To make an Episode.—Take any remaining adventure
of your former collection, in which you could no way
involve your hero; or any unfortunate accident that was
too good to be thrown away; and it will be of use applied
to any other person, who may be lost and evaporate in
the course of the work, without the least damage to the
composition.

For the Moral and Allegory.—These you may extract
out of the fable afterwards, at your leisure.   Be sure you
strain them sufficiently.

FOR THE MANNERS.

For those of the hero, take all the best qualities you
can find in all the celebrated heroes of antiquity; if they
will not be reduced to a consistency, lay them all on a
heap upon him.   But be sure they are qualities which
your patron would be thought to have; and, to prevent
any mistake which the world may be subject to, select
from the alphabet those capital letters that compose his
name, and set them at the head of a dedication before
your poem.   However, do not absolutely observe the
exact quantity of these virtues, it not being determined
whether or no it be necessary for the hero of the poem
to be an honest man.   For the under characters, gather

translated into English in 1598. It was one of the most celebrated
Spanish romances of chivalry, and was reprieved by the curate in *Don
Quixote*, when the barber made a bonfire of the Don's library.

them from Homer and Virgil, and change the names as occasion serves.

Take of deities, male and female, as many as you can use. Separate them into two equal parts, and keep Jupiter in the middle. Let Juno put him in a ferment, and Venus mollify him. Remember on all occasions to make use of volatile Mercury. If you have need of devils, draw them out of Milton's Paradise, and extract your spirits from Tasso. The use of these machines is evident; and since no epic poem can possibly subsist without them, the wisest way is to reserve them for your greatest necessities. When you cannot extricate your hero by any human means, or yourself by your own wits, seek relief from heaven, and the gods will do your business very readily. This is according to the direct prescription of Horace in his *Art of Poetry*:

> *Nec deus intersit, nisi dignus vindice Nodus*
> *Inciderit.*
>
> Never presume to make a God appear,
> But for a business worthy of a God.—*Roscommon.*

That is to say, a poet should never call upon the gods for their assistance but when he is in great perplexity.

For a Tempest. — Take Eurus, Zephyr, Auster, and Boreas, and cast them together in one verse. Add to these of rain, lightning, and of thunder (the loudest you can) *quantum sufficit.* Mix your clouds and billows well together until they foam, and thicken your description here and there with a quicksand. Brew your tempest well in your head, before you set a blowing.

For a Battle. — Pick a large quantity of images and descriptions from Homer's Iliad, with a spice or two of Virgil, and if there remain any overplus you may lay them by for a skirmish.   Season it well with similes, and it will make an excellent battle.

For Burning a Town. — If such a description be necessary, because it is certain there is one in Virgil, Old Troy is ready burnt to your hands.   But if you fear that would be thought borrowed, a chapter or two of the Theory of the Conflagration[1], well circumstanced, and done into verse, will be a good succedaneum.

As for *Similes and Metaphors*, they may be found all over the creation; the most ignorant may gather them, but the danger is in applying them.   For this, advise with your bookseller.

FOR THE LANGUAGE.

(I mean the diction.)   Here it will do well to be an imitator of Milton, for you will find it easier to imitate him in this than anything else.   Hebraisms and Grecisms are to be found in him, without the trouble of learning the languages.   I knew a painter, who (like our poet) had no genius, made his daubings to be thought originals by setting them in the smoke.   You may in the same manner give the venerable air of antiquity to your piece, by darkening it up and down with Old English. With this you may be easily furnished upon any occasion by the dictionary commonly printed at the end of Chaucer.

I must not conclude, without cautioning all writers without genius in one material point, which is never to be afraid of having too much fire in their works.   I should advise rather to take their warmest thoughts, and spread them abroad upon paper; for they are observed to cool before they are read.

[1] A reference to the *Sacred Theory of the Earth*, by Thos. Burnet, D.D., 1689.

GEORGE COLMAN—BONNEL THORNTON.

(1732-1794.)   (1724-1768.)

XXVII. THE OCEAN OF INK.

Suave mari magno, turbantibus æquora ventis,
E terrâ magnum alterius spectare laborem.—Lucret.

When raging winds the ruffled deep deform,
We look at distance, and enjoy the storm;
Toss'd on the waves with pleasure others see,
Nor heed their dangers, while ourselves are free.

WE writers of essays, or (as they are termed) periodical papers, justly claim to ourselves a place among the modern improvers of literature. Neither Bentley nor Burman[1], nor any other equally sagacious commentator, has been able to discover the least traces of any similar productions among the ancients: except we can suppose that the history of Thucydides was retailed weekly in sixpenny numbers; that Seneca dealt out his morality every Saturday, or that Tully wrote speeches and philosophical disquisitions, whilst Virgil and Horace clubbed together to furnish the poetry for a Roman magazine.

There is a word, indeed, by which we are fond of distinguishing our works, and for which we must confess ourselves indebted to the Latin. Myself, and every petty journalist, affect to dignify our hasty performances by styling them Lucubrations; by which we mean, if we mean anything, that as the day is too short for our labours, we are obliged to call in the assistance of the night: not to mention the modest insinuation that our compositions are so correct, that (like the orations of Demosthenes) they may be said to smell of the lamp. We would be understood to follow the directions of the Roman Satirist, "to grow pale by the midnight candle";

[1] Peter Burman (d. 1741), an eminent classical commentator, and professor at Leyden.

though, perhaps, as our own Satirist[1] expresses it, we may be thought

> Sleepless ourselves, to give our readers sleep.

But as a relief from the fatigue of so many restless hours, we have frequently gone to sleep for the benefit of the public: and surely we, whose labours are confined to a sheet and a half, may be indulged in taking a nap now and then, as well as those engaged in longer works; who (according to Horace) are to be excused if a little drowsiness sometimes creeps in upon them.

After this preface, the reader will not be surprised, if I take the liberty to relate a dream of my own. It is usual on these occasions to be lulled to sleep by some book: and most of my brethren pay that compliment to Virgil or Shakespeare: but as I could never discover any opiate qualities in those authors, I chose rather to doze over some modern performance. I must beg to be excused from mentioning particulars, as I would not provoke the resentment of my contemporaries: nobody will imagine that I dipped into any of our modern novels, or took up any of our late tragedies. Let it suffice that I presently fell fast asleep.

I found myself transported in an instant to the shore of an immense sea, covered with innumerable vessels; and though many of them suddenly disappeared every minute, I saw others continually launching forth, and pursuing the same course. The seers of visions and dreamers of dreams have their organs of sight so considerably improved, that they can take in any object, however distant or minute. It is not, therefore, to be wondered at that I could discern everything distinctly, though the waters before me were of the deepest black.

While I stood contemplating this amazing scene, one

[1] Pope, *Dunciad*, i. 94.

of those good-natured genii, who never fail making their appearance to extricate dreamers from their difficulties, rose from the sable stream and planted himself at my elbow. His complexion was of the darkest hue, not unlike that of the demons of a printing-house; his jetty beard shone like the bristles of a blacking brush; on his head he wore a turban of imperial paper; and there hung a calf-skin on his reverend limbs, which was gilt on the back, and faced with robings of morocco, lettered (like a rubric-post) with the names of the most eminent authors. In his left hand he bore a printed scroll, which from the marginal corrections I imagined to be a proof-sheet; and in his right hand he waved the quill of a goose.

He immediately accosted me. "Town[1]," said he, " I am the genius who is destined to conduct you through these turbulent waves. The sea that you now behold is the Ocean of Ink. Those towers, at a great distance, whose bases are founded upon rocks, and whose tops seem lost in the clouds, are situated in the Isle of Fame. Contiguous to these, you may discern by the glittering of its golden sands, is the Coast of Gain, which leads to a fertile and rich country. All the vessels which are yonder sailing with a fair wind on the main sea are making towards one or other of these; but you will observe that on their first setting out they were irresistibly drawn into the eddies of Criticism, where they were obliged to encounter the most dreadful tempests and hurricanes. In these dangerous straits you see with what violence every bark is tossed up and down; some go to the bottom at once; others, after a faint struggle, are beat to pieces; many are much damaged; while a few, by sound planks and tight rigging, are enabled to weather the storm.

At this sight I started back with horror; and the remembrance still dwells so strong upon my fancy, that I

[1] The pseudonym used by the joint editors, Colman and Thornton.

even now imagine the torrent of criticism bursting in upon me, and ready to overwhelm me in an instant.

"Cast a look," resumed my instructor, "on that vast lake divided into two parts, which lead to yonder magnificent structures, erected by the Tragic and Comic Muse. There you may observe many trying to force a passage without chart or compass. Some have been overset by crowding too much sail, and others have foundered by carrying too much ballast. An Arcadian vessel[1] (the master an Irishman) was, through contrary squalls, scarce able to live nine days; but you see that light Italian gondola, *Gli Amanti Gelosi*, skims along pleasantly before the wind, and outstrips the painted frigates of our country, Didone and Artaserse. Observe that triumphant squadron, to whose flag all the others pay homage. Most of them are ships of the first-rate, and were fitted out many years ago. Though somewhat irregular in their make, and but little conformable to the exact rules of art, they will ever continue the pride and glory of these seas; for, as it is remarked by the present Laureate[2], in his prologue to Papal Tyranny,

> ' Shakespeare, whose art no playwright can excel,
> Has launch'd us fleets of plays, and built them well".

The Genius then bade me turn my eye where the water seemed to foam with perpetual agitation. "That," said he, "is the strong current of Politics, often fatal to those who venture on it". I could not but take notice of a poor wretch on the opposite shore, fastened by the ears to a terrible machine. This, the Genius informed me, was the memorable Defoe, set up there as a landmark, to prevent future mariners from splitting on the same rock. To this turbulent prospect succeeded objects of

---

[1] The vessel is a tragedy, *Philoclea*, based on Sidney's *Arcadia*; the gondola refers to an Italian burlesque, and the frigates to two Italian operas (Harrison).   [2] Colley Cibber.

a more placid nature. In a little creek, winding through flowery meads and shady groves, I descried several gilded yachts and pleasure boats, all of them keeping due time with their silver oars, and gliding along the smooth, even, calm, regularly flowing rivulets of Rhyme. Shepherds and shepherdesses played on the banks; the sails were gently swelled with the soft breezes of amorous sighs; and little Loves sported in the silken cordage.

My attention was now called off from these pacific scenes to an obstinate engagement between several ships, distinguished from all others by bearing the Holy Cross for their colours. These, the Genius told me, were employed in the Holy War of Religious Controversy; and he pointed out to me a few corsairs in the service of the infidels, sometimes aiding one party, sometimes siding with the other, as might best contribute to the general confusion. I observed in different parts of the ocean several galleys, which were rowed by slaves. "Those," said the Genius, "are fitted out by very oppressive owners, and are all of them bound to the Coast of Gain. The miserable wretches whom you see chained to the oars are obliged to tug without the least respite; and though the voyage should turn out successful, they have little or no share in the profits. Some few you may observe who rather choose to make a venture on their own bottoms. These work as hard as the galley-slaves, and are frequently cast away; but though they are never so often wrecked, necessity still constrains them to put out to sea again,"

> " *Reficit rates*
> *Quassas, indocilis pauperiem pati.*"—Hor.
> Still must the wretch his shatter'd bark refit,
> For who to starve can patiently submit?

It were needless to enumerate many other particulars that engaged my notice. Among the rest was a large fleet of Annotators, Dutch-built, which sailed very heavy, were often aground, and continually ran foul of each other. The whole ocean, I also found, was infested by pirates, who ransacked every rich vessel that came in their way. Most of these were endeavouring to make the Coast of Gain, by hanging out false colours, or by forging their passports, and pretending to be freighted out by the most reputable traders.

My eyes were at last fixed, I know not how, on a spacious channel running through the midst of a great city. I felt such a secret impulse at this sight that I could not help inquiring particularly about it. "The discovery of that passage," said the Genius, "was first made by one Bickerstaff, in the good ship called *The Tatler*, and who afterwards embarked in the *Spectator* and *Guardian*. These have been followed since by a number of little sloops, skiffs, hoys, and cock-boats, which have been most of them wrecked in the attempt. Thither also must your course be directed."—At this instant the Genius suddenly snatched me up in his arms, and plunged me headlong into the inky flood. While I lay gasping and struggling beneath the waves, methought I heard a familiar voice calling me by name, which awaking me, I with pleasure recollected the features of the Genius in those of my publisher, who was standing by my bedside, and had called upon me for copy.

WILLIAM COWPER.
(1731–1800.)
XXVIII. ON CONVERSATION.

Servata semper lege et ratione loquendi.—Hor.
Your talk to decency and reason suit,
Nor prate like fools or gabble like a brute.

IN the comedy of the *Frenchman in London*, which we were told was acted at Paris with universal applause for several nights together, there is a character of a rough

Englishman, who is represented as quite unskilled in the graces of conversation; and his dialogue consists almost entirely of a repetition of the common salutation of "how do you do?" Our nation has, indeed, been generally supposed to be of a sullen and uncommunicative disposition; while, on the other hand, the loquacious French have been allowed to possess the art of conversing beyond all other people. The Englishman requires to be wound up frequently, and stops as soon as he is down; but the Frenchman runs on in a continual alarum. Yet it must be acknowledged that as the English consist of very different humours, their manner of discourse admits of great variety; but the whole French nation converse alike; and there is no difference in their address between a marquis and a *valet de chambre*. We may frequently see a couple of French barbers accosting each other in the street, and paying their compliments with the same volubility of speech, the same grimace and action, as two courtiers on the Tuilleries.

I shall not attempt to lay down any particular rules for conversation, but rather point out such faults in discourse and behaviour as render the company of half mankind rather tedious than amusing. It is in vain, indeed, to look for conversation where we might expect to find it in the greatest perfection, among persons of fashion; there it is almost annihilated by universal card-playing: insomuch that I have heard it given as a reason why it is impossible for our present writers to succeed in the dialogue of genteel comedy, that our people of quality scarce ever meet but to game. All their discourse turns upon the odd trick and the four honours; and it is no less a maxim with the votaries of whist than with those of Bacchus, that talking spoils company.

Everyone endeavours to make himself as agreeable to society as he can; but it often happens that those who most aim at shining in conversation overshoot their mark. Though a man succeeds, he should not (as is frequently the case) engross the whole talk to himself; for that destroys the very essence of conversation, which is talking together. We should try to keep up conversation like a ball bandied to and fro from one to the other, rather than seize it all to ourselves, and drive it before us like a football. We should likewise be cautious to adapt the matter of our discourse to our company, and not talk Greek before ladies, or of the last new furbelow to a meeting of country justices.

But nothing throws a more ridiculous air over our whole conversation than certain peculiarities easily acquired, but very difficultly conquered and discarded. In order to display these absurdities in a truer light, it is my present purpose to enumerate such of them as are most commonly to be met with; and first to take notice of those buffoons in society, the Attitudinarians and Face-makers. These accompany every word with a peculiar grimace or gesture; they assent with a shrug, and contradict with a twisting of the neck; are angry by a wry mouth, and pleased in a caper or minuet step. They may be considered as speaking harlequins; and their rules of eloquence are taken from the posture-master. These should be condemned to converse only in dumb show with their own persons in the looking-glass; as well as the Smirkers and Smilers, who so prettily set off their faces, together with their words, by a *je-ne-sais-quoi* between a grin and a dimple. With these we may likewise rank the affected tribe of Mimics, who are constantly taking off the peculiar tone of voice or gesture of their acquaintance, though they are such wretched imitators, that (like bad painters) they are frequently forced to write the name under the picture before we can discover any likeness.

Next to these whose elocution is absorbed in action, and who converse chiefly with their arms and legs, we may consider the Professed Speakers. And first, the Emphatical, who squeeze, and press, and ram down every syllable with excessive vehemence and energy. These orators are remarkable for their distinct elocution and force of expression: they dwell on the important particles *of* and *the*, and the significant conjunction *and*, which they seem to hawk up, with much difficulty, out of their own throats, and to cram them, with no less pain, into the ears of their auditors. These should be suffered only to syringe (as it were) the ears of a deaf man, through a hearing-trumpet; though I must confess that I am equally offended with the Whisperers or Low-speakers, who seem to fancy all their acquaintance deaf, and come up so close to you, that they may be said to measure noses with you, and frequently overcome you with the full exhalations of a stinking breath. I would have these oracular gentry obliged to speak at a distance through a speaking-trumpet, or apply their lips to the walls of a whispering-gallery. The Wits, who will not condescend to utter anything but a *bon mot*, and the Whistlers or Tune-hummers, who never articulate at all, may be joined very agreeably together in concert; and to these tinkling cymbals I would also add the sounding brass; the Bawler, who inquires after your health with the bellowing of a town-crier.

The Tatlers, whose pliable pipes are admirably adapted to the "soft parts of conversation", and sweetly "prattling out of fashion", make very pretty music from a beautiful face and a female tongue; but from a rough manly voice and coarse features mere nonsense is as harsh and dissonant as a jig from a hurdy-gurdy. The Swearers I have spoken of in a former paper; but the Half-Swearers, who split, and mince, and fritter their oaths into gad's bud ad's fish, and demme, the Gothic Humbuggers, and those who nickname God's creatures, and call a man a cabbage, a crab, a queer cub, an odd fish, and an unaccountable muskin, should never come into company without an interpreter. But I will not tire my reader's patience by pointing out all the pests of conversation; nor dwell particularly on the Sensibles, who pronounce dogmatically on the most trivial points, and speak in sentences; the Wonderers, who are always wondering what o'clock it is, or wondering whether it will rain or no, or wondering when the moon changes; the Phraseologists, who explain a thing by all that, or enter into particulars, with this and that and t'other; and lastly, the Silent Men, who seem afraid of opening their mouths lest they should catch cold, and literally observe the precept of the Gospel, by letting their conversation be only yea yea, and nay nay.

The rational intercourse kept up by conversation is one of our principal distinctions from brutes. We should therefore endeavour to turn this peculiar talent to our advantage, and consider the organs of speech as the instruments of understanding: we should be very careful not to use them as the weapons of vice, or tools of folly, and do our utmost to unlearn any trivial or ridiculous habits, which tend to lessen the value of such an inestimable prerogative. It is, indeed, imagined by some philosophers, that even birds and beasts (though without the power of articulation) perfectly understand one another by the sounds they utter; and that dogs, cats, &c., have each a particular language to themselves, like different nations. Thus it may be supposed that the nightingales of Italy have as fine an ear for their own native woodnotes as any signor or signora for an Italian air; that the boars of Westphalia gruntle as expressively through the nose as the inhabitants in High German; and that the frogs in the dykes of Holland croak as

intelligibly as the natives jabber their Low-Dutch. However this may be, we may consider those whose tongues
hardly seem to be under the influence of reason, and do
not keep up the proper conversation of human creatures,
as imitating the language of different animals. Thus, for
instance, the affinity between Chatterers and Monkeys,
and Praters and Parrots, is too obvious not to occur at
once; Grunters and Growlers may be justly compared to
Hogs; Snarlers are Curs that continually show their
teeth, but never bite; and the Spitfire passionate are a
sort of wild cats that will not bear stroking, but will purr
when they are pleased. Complainers are Screech-Owls;
and Story-tellers, always repeating the same dull note, are
Cuckoos. Poets that prick up their ears at their own
hideous braying are no better than Asses. Critics in
general are venomous Serpents that delight in hissing,
and some of them who have got by heart a few technical
terms without knowing their meaning are no other than
Magpies. I myself, who have crowed to the whole town
for near three years past, may perhaps put my readers
in mind of a Dunghill Cock; but as I must acquaint
them, that they will hear the last of me on this day fortnight, I hope they will then consider me as a Swan, who is
supposed to sing sweetly at his dying moments.

PHILIP STANHOPE, EARL OF CHESTERFIELD.

(1694-1773.)

XXIX. ON PASSION.

IT is a vulgar notion, and worthy of the vulgar, for it
is both false and absurd, that passionate people are
the best natured people in the world. " They are a little

hasty, it is true; a trifle will put them in a fury; and while they are in that fury, they neither know nor care what they say or do: but then, as soon as it is over, they are extremely sorry and penitent for any injury or mischief they did." This panegyric on these choleric good-natured people, when examined and simplified, amounts in plain common-sense and English to this: that they are good-natured when they are not ill-natured; and that when in their fits of rage they have said or done things that have brought them to the jail or the gallows, they are extremely sorry for it.   It is indeed highly probable that they are; but where is the reparation to those whose reputations, limbs, or lives they have either wounded or destroyed? This concern comes too late, and is only for themselves. Self-love was the cause of the injury, and is the only motive of the repentance.

Had these furious people real good-nature their first offence would be their last, and they would resolve at all events never to relapse.   The moment they felt their choler rising, they would enjoin themselves an absolute silence and inaction, and by that sudden check rather expose themselves to a momentary ridicule (which, by the way, would be followed by universal applause), than run the least risk of being irreparably mischievous.

I know it is said in their behalf, that this impulse to wrath is constitutionally so sudden and so strong that they cannot stifle it, even in its birth; but experience shows us, that this allegation is notoriously false; for we daily observe that these stormy persons both can and do lay those gusts of passion, when awed by respect, restrained by interest, or intimidated by fear.   The most outrageous furioso does not give a loose to his anger in presence of his sovereign, or his mistress; nor the expectant heir in presence of the peevish dotard from whom he hopes for an inheritance.   The soliciting

courtier, though perhaps under the strongest provoca-
tions, from unjust delays and broken promises, calmly
swallows his unavailing wrath, disguises it even under
smiles, and gently waits for more favourable moments;
nor does the criminal fly in a passion at his judge or his
jury.

There is then but one solid excuse to be alleged in
favour of these people; and if they will frankly urge it, I
will candidly admit it, because it points out its own
remedy. I mean, let them fairly confess themselves mad,
as they most unquestionably are; for what plea can those
that are frantic ten times a day bring against shaving,
bleeding, and a dark room, when so many much more
harmless madmen are confined in their cells at Bedlam
for being mad only once in a moon? Nay, I have been
assured by the late ingenious Doctor Monro, that such
of his patients who were really of a good-natured disposition, and who in their lucid intervals were allowed the
liberty of walking about the hospital, would frequently,
when they found the previous symptoms of their returning
madness, voluntarily apply for confinement, conscious of
the mischief which they might possibly do if at liberty.
If those who pretend not to be mad, but who really are
so, had the same fund of good-nature, they would make
the same application to their friends, if they have any.

There is in the Menagiana[1], a very pretty story of one
of these angry gentlemen, which sets their extravagancy
in a very ridiculous light.

Two gentlemen were riding together, one of whom,
who was a choleric one, happened to be mounted on a
high-mettled horse. The horse grew a little troublesome,
at which the rider grew very angry, and whipped and

[1] One of the many popular books of *ana* produced in France in the
17th century, and so named from Menage, poet and grammarian, who
died in Paris, 1692.

spurred him with great fury; to which the horse, almost as wrong-headed as his master, replied with kicking and plunging. The companion, concerned for the danger, and ashamed of the folly of his friend, said to him coolly, " Be quiet, be quiet, and show yourself the wiser of the two ".

This sort of madness, for I will call it by no other name, flows from various causes, of which I shall now enumerate the most general.

Light unballasted heads are very apt to be overset by every gust, or even breeze of passion; they appreciate things wrong, and think everything of importance, but what really is so; hence those frequent and sudden transitions from silly joy to sillier anger, according as the present silly humour is gratified or thwarted. This is the never-failing characteristic of the uneducated vulgar, who often in the same half-hour fight with fury, and shake hands with affection. Such heads give themselves no time to reason; and if you attempt to reason with them they think you rally them, and resent the affront. They are, in short, overgrown children, and continue so in the most advanced age. Far be it from me to insinuate, what some ill-bred authors have bluntly asserted, that this is in general the case of the fairest part of our species, whose great vivacity does not always allow them time to reason consequentially, but hurries them into testiness upon the least opposition to their will; but at the same time, with all the partiality which I have for them, and nobody can have more than I have, I must confess that, in all their debates, I have much more admired the copiousness of their rhetoric than the conclusiveness of their logic.

People of strong animal spirits, warm constitutions, and a cold genius (a most unfortunate and ridiculous, though common compound) are most irascible animals, and very dangerous in their wrath. They are active, puzzling, blundering, and petulantly enterprising and per-severing. They are impatient of the least contradiction, having neither arguments nor words to reply with; and the animal part of their composition bursts out into furious explosions, which have often mischievous conse-quences. Nothing is too outrageous or criminal for them to say or do in these fits; but as the beginning of their frenzy is easily discoverable by their glaring eyes, inflamed countenances, and rapid motions, the company, as con-servators of the peace (which, by the way, every man is, till the authority of a magistrate can be produced), should forcibly seize these madmen, and confine them, in the meantime, in some dark closet, vault, or coal-hole.

Men of nice honour, without one grain of common honesty (for such there are), are wonderfully combustible. The honourable is to support and protect the dishonest part of their character. The consciousness of their guilt makes them both sore and jealous.

There is another very irascible sort of human animals, whose madness proceeds from pride. These are gener-ally the people, who, having just fortunes sufficient to live idle and useless to society, create themselves gentlemen, and are scrupulously tender of the rank and dignity which they have not. They require the more respect, from being conscious that they have no right to any. They construe everything into a slight, ask explanations with heat, and misunderstand them with fury. "Who are you? What are you? Do you know who you speak to? I'll teach you to be insolent to a gentleman," are their daily idioms of speech, which frequently end in assault and battery, to the great emolument of the Round-house and Crown office.

I have known many young fellows, who, at their first setting out in the world, or in the army, have simulated a passion which they did not feel, merely as an indication of spirit, which word is falsely looked upon as synonymous with courage. They dress and look fierce, swear enormously, and rage furiously, seduced by that popular word "spirit". But I beg leave to inform these mistaken young gentlemen, whose error I compassionate, that the true spirit of a rational being consists in cool and steady resolution, which can only be the result of reflection and virtue.

I am very sorry to be obliged to own, that there is not a more irritable part of the species than my brother authors. Criticism, censure, or even the slightest disapprobation of their immortal works excite their most furious indignation. It is true indeed that they express their resentment in a manner less dangerous, both to others and to themselves. Like incensed porcupines, they dart their quills at the objects of their wrath. The wounds given by these shafts are not mortal, and only painful in proportion to the distance from whence they fly. Those which are discharged (as by much the greatest number are) from great heights, such as garrets or four-pair-of-stairs rooms, are puffed away by the wind, and never hit the mark; but those which are let off from a first or second floor, are apt to occasion a little smarting, and sometimes festering, especially if the party wounded be unsound.

Our Great Creator has wisely given us passions to rouse us into action, and to engage our gratitude to him by the pleasures they procure us; but at the same time He has kindly given us reason sufficient, if we will but give that reason fair play, to control those passions; and has delegated authority to say to them, as He said to the waters, "Thus far shall ye go, and no farther". The angry man is his own severest tormentor; his breast knows no peace, while his raging passions are restrained by no sense of either religious or moral duties. What would be his case, if his unforgiving example (if I may use such an expression) were followed by his All-Merciful Maker, whose forgiveness he can only hope for, in proportion as he himself forgives and loves his fellow-creatures?

HORACE WALPOLE, EARL OF ORFORD
(1717-1797.)

xxx. CHANGE OF STYLE.

THE great men who introduced the reformation [1] into these kingdoms were so sensible of the necessity of maintaining devotion in the minds of the vulgar by some external objects, by somewhat of ceremony and form, that they refrained from entirely ripping off all ornament from the drapery of religion. When they were purging the calendar of legions of visionary saints, they took due care to defend the niches of real martyrs from profanation. They preserved the holy festivals, which had been consecrated for many ages to the great luminaries of the church, and at once laid proper observance to the memory of the good, and fell in with the popular humour, which loves to rejoice and mourn at the discretion of the almanac.

In so enlightened an age as the present, I shall perhaps be ridiculed if I hint, as my opinion, that the observation of certain festivals is something more than a mere political institution. I cannot, however, help thinking that even nature itself concurs to confirm my sentiment. Philosophers and freethinkers tell us that a general system was laid down at first, and that no deviations have been made to accommodate it to any subsequent events, or to favour

---

[1] The change of style was introduced by Act of Parliament in 1752. ordaining that the 4th Sept. of that year should be reckoned the 14th.

and authorize any human institutions. When the reformation of the calendar was in agitation, to the great
disgust of many worthy persons, who urged how great
the harmony was in the old establishment between the
holidays and their attributes (if I may call them so), and
what a confusion would follow, if Michaelmas-day, for
instance, was not to be celebrated when stubble-geese are
in their highest perfection; it was replied that such a
propriety was merely imaginary, and would be lost of
itself, even without any alteration of the calendar by
authority: for if the errors in it were suffered to go on,
they would in a certain number of years produce such a
variation, that we should be mourning for good King
Charles on a false thirtieth of January, at a time of year
when our ancestors used to be tumbling over head and
heels in Greenwich-park in honour of Whitsuntide; and
at length, be choosing king and queen for Twelfth-night,
when we ought to be admiring the London Prentice at
Bartholomew Fair[1].

Cogent as these reasons may seem, yet I think I can
confute them from the testimony of a standing miracle,
which, not having submitted to the fallible authority of
an act of parliament, may well be said to put a supernatural negative on the wisdom of this world.   My
readers, no doubt, are already aware that I have in my
eye the wonderful thorn of Glastonbury[2], which, though

---

[1] The fair began every year at Smithfield on Aug. 24.   Originally a
cloth market, it lasted in one form or other from the reign of Henry II.
to 1855.

[2] A famous hawthorn near Glastonbury Abbey in Somersetshire, which
was reputed to blossom on Christmas-day.   Legend said it was the
walking-stick of Joseph of Arimathea.   This essay was doubtless suggested to Walpole by a paragraph in the *Gent's. Mag.*, 1753.   " A vast
concourse of people attended the noted thorn on Christmas day, new
style, but to their great disappointment there was no appearance of its
blowing, which made them watch it narrowly the 5th of January,
Christmas day, old style, when it blowed as usual."

hitherto regarded as a trunk of popish imposture, has notably exerted itself as the most protestant plant in the universe. It is well known that the correction of the calendar was enacted by Pope Gregory the Thirteenth, and that the reformed churches have with a proper spirit of opposition adhered to the old calculation of the emperor Julius Caesar, who was by no means a papist. Near two years ago the popish calendar was brought in (I hope by persons well affected). Certain it is, that the Glastonbury thorn has preserved its inflexibility, and observes its old anniversary. Many thousand spectators visited it on the parliamentary Christmas-day. Not a bud was there to be seen! On the true nativity it was covered with blossoms. One must be an infidel indeed to spurn at such authority. Had I been consulted (and mathematical studies have not been the most inconsiderable of my speculations), instead of turning the calendar topsy-turvy, by fantastic calculations, I should have proposed to regulate the year by the infallible Somersetshire thorn, and to have reckoned the months from Christmas-day, which should always have been kept as the Glastonbury thorn should blow.

Many inconveniences, to be sure, would follow from this system; but as holy things ought to be the first consideration of a religious nation, the inconveniences should be overlooked. The thorn can never blow but on the true Christmas-day; and consequently the apprehension of the year's becoming inverted by sticking to the Julian account can never hold. If the course of the sun varies, astronomers may find out some way to adjust that; but it is preposterous, not to say presumptuous, to be celebrating Christmas-day when the Glastonbury thorn, which certainly must know times and seasons better than an almanac maker, declares it to be heresy.

Nor is Christmas-day the only jubilee which will be

morally disturbed by this innovation.   There is another
anniversary of no less celebrity among Englishmen,
equally marked by a marvellous concomitance of circumstances, and which I venture to prognosticate will not
attend the erroneous calculation of the present system.
The day I mean is the first of April.   The oldest tradition
affirms that such an infatuation attends the first day of
that month, as no foresight can escape, no vigilance can
defeat.   Deceit is successful on that day out of the mouths
of babes and sucklings.   Grave citizens have been bit
upon it; usurers have lent their money on bad security;
experienced matrons have married very disappointing
young fellows; mathematicians have missed the longitude;
alchemists the philosopher's stone; and politicians preferment, on that day.

What confusion will not follow, if the great body of the
nation are disappointed of their peculiar holiday!   This
country was formerly disturbed with very fatal quarrels
about the celebration of Easter; and no wise man will
tell me that it is not as reasonable to fall out for the
observance of April-fool day.   Can any benefits arising
from a regulated calendar make amends for an occasion
of new sects?   How many warm men may resent an
attempt to play them off on a false first of April, who
would have submitted to the custom of being made fools
on the old computation?   If our clergy come to be divided
about Folly's anniversary, we may well expect all the
mischiefs attendant on religious wars; and we shall have
reason to wish that the Glastonbury thorn would declare
as remarkably in favour of the true April-fool day as it
has in behalf of the genuine Christmas.

There are many other inconveniences, which I might
lament very emphatically, but none of weight enough to
be compared with those I have mentioned.   I shall only
hint at a whole system overturned by this revolution in

the calendar, and no provision, that I have heard of, made
by the legislature to remedy it.   Yet in a nation which
bestows such ample rewards on new-year and birthday
odes, it is astonishing that the late act of parliament
should have overlooked that useful branch of our poetry,
which consists of couplets, saws, and proverbs, peculiar
to certain days and seasons.   Why was not a new set of
distichs provided by the late reformers?   Or at least a
clause inserted in the act enjoining the poet-laureate, or
some beneficial genius, to prepare and new-cast the
established rhymes for public use?   Were our astronomers
so ignorant as to think that the old proverbs would serve
for their new-fangled calendar?   Could they imagine that
St. Swithin would accommodate his rainy planet to the
convenience of the calculations?   Who that hears the
following verses but must grieve for the shepherd and
husbandman, who may have all their prognostics con-
founded, and be at a loss to know beforehand the fate of
their markets?   Ancient sages sung,

> If St. Paul be fair and clear,
> Then will betide a happy year;
> But if it either snow or rain,
> Then will be dear all kind of grain:
> And if the wind doth blow aloft,
> Then wars will vex the realm full oft.[1]

I have declared against meddling with politics, and
therefore shall say nothing of the important hints contained in the last lines: yet if certain ill-boding appearances
abroad should have an ugly end, I cannot help saying
that I shall ascribe their evil tendency to our having been
lulled asleep by resting our faith on the calm weather on
the pretended conversion of St. Paul; whereas it was very

[1] It was long believed that the condition of weather on St. Paul's day,
January 25, determined the character of the whole year.   The verses
quoted are one of many translations of four mediæval lines beginning,
" Clara dies Pauli bona tempora denotat anni".

blustering on that festival according to the good old account, as I honestly, though vainly, endeavoured to convince a great minister of state, whom I do not think proper to mention.

But to return to April-fool day; I must beg my readers and admirers to be very particular in their observations on that holiday, both according to the new and old reckoning. And I beg that they will transmit to me or my secretary, Mr. Dodsley, a faithful and attested account of the hap that betides them or their acquaintance on each of those days; how often and in what manner they make or are made fools; how they miscarry in attempts to surprise, or baffle any snares laid for them. I do not doubt but it will be found that the balance of folly lies greatly on the side of the old first of April; nay, I much question whether infatuation will have any force on what I call false April-fool day. I should take it very kind if any of my friends, who may happen to be sharpers, would try their success on the fictitious festival; and if they make fewer dupes than ordinary, I flatter myself that they will unite their endeavours with mine in decrying and exploding a reformation which only tends to discountenance good old practices and venerable superstitions.

SAMUEL JOHNSON.
(1709-1784.)

XXXI. THE ADVANTAGES OF LIVING IN A GARRET.

> The gods they challenge, and affect the skies:
> Heaved on Olympus, tottering Ossa stood;
> On Ossa, Pelion nods with all his wood.—*Pope.*

NOTHING has more retarded the advancement of learning than the disposition of vulgar minds to ridicule and vilify what they cannot comprehend. All industry must be excited by hope; and as the student often proposes no other reward to himself than praise, he is easily discouraged by contempt and insult. He who brings with him into a clamorous multitude the timidity of recluse speculation, and has never hardened his front in public life, or accustomed his passions to the vicissitudes and accidents, the triumphs and defeats of mixed conversation, will blush at the stare of petulant incredulity, and suffer himself to be driven by a burst of laughter from the fortresses of demonstration.   The mechanist will be afraid to assert before hardy contradiction the possibility of tearing down bulwarks with a silkworm's thread; and the astronomer of relating the rapidity of light, the distance of the fixed stars, and the height of the lunar mountains.

If I could by any efforts have shaken off this cowardice I had not sheltered myself under a borrowed name, nor applied to you for the means of communicating to the public the theory of a garret: a subject which, except some slight and transient strictures, has been hitherto neglected by those who were best qualified to adorn it, either for want of leisure to prosecute the various researches in which a nice discussion must engage them, or because it requires such diversity of knowledge, and such extent of curiosity, as is scarcely to be found in any single intellect; or perhaps others foresaw the tumults which would be raised against them, and confined their knowledge to their own breasts, and abandoned prejudice and folly to the direction of chance.

That the professors of literature generally reside in the highest stories has been immemorially observed.   The wisdom of the ancients was well acquainted with the intellectual advantages of an elevated situation: why else were the Muses stationed on Olympus, or Parnassus, by those who could with equal right have raised them bowers in the vale of Tempe, or erected their altars among the flexures of Meander? Why was Jove himself nursed upon a mountain? or why did the goddesses, when the prize of beauty was contested, try the cause upon the top of Ida? Such were the fictions by which the great masters of the earlier ages endeavoured to inculcate to posterity the importance of a garret, which, though they had been long obscured by the negligence and ignorance of succeeding times, were well enforced by the celebrated symbol of Pythagoras,

> " When the wind blows, worship its echo ".

This could not but be understood by his disciples as an inviolable injunction to live in a garret, which I have found frequently visited by the echo and the wind. Nor was the tradition wholly obliterated in the age of Augustus, for Tibullus evidently congratulates himself upon his garret, not without some allusion to the Pythagorean precept:

> " *Quam juvat immites ventos audire cubantem—*
> *Aut, gelidas hibernus aquas cum fuderit auster*
> *Securum somnos, imbre juvante, sequi.*"

> " How sweet in sleep to pass the careless hours,
> Lull'd by the beating winds and dashing showers."

And it is impossible not to discover the fondness of Lucretius, an earlier writer, for a garret, in his description of the lofty towers of serene learning, and of the pleasure with which a wise man looks down upon the confused and erratic state of the world moving below him:

> *Sed nil dulcius est, bene quam munita tenere*
> *Edita doctrina sapientum templa serena;*
> *Despicere unde queas alios, passimque videre*
> *Errare, atque viam palanteis quaerere vitae.*
> 'T is sweet thy labouring steps to guide
> To virtue's heights, with wisdom well supplied,
> And all the magazine of learning fortified:
> From thence to look below on human kind,
> Bewildered in the maze of life, and blind.—*Dryden.*

The institution has, indeed, continued to our own time; the garret is still the usual receptacle of the philosopher and poet; but this, like many ancient customs, is perpetuated only by an accidental imitation, without knowledge of the original reason for which it was established:

Causa latet: res est notissima.
The cause is secret, but th' effect is known.—*Addison.*

Conjectures have, indeed, been advanced concerning these habitations of literature, but without much satisfaction to the judicious inquirer. Some have imagined that the garret is generally chosen by the wits as most easily rented; and concluded that no man rejoices in his aerial abode, but on the days of payment. Others suspect that a garret is chiefly convenient, as it is remoter than any other part of the house from the outer door, which is often observed to be infested by visitants, who talk incessantly of beer, or linen, or a coat, and repeat the same sounds every morning, and sometimes again in the afternoon, without any variation, except that they grow daily more importunate and clamorous, and raise their voices in time from mournful murmurs to raging vociferations. This eternal monotony is always detestable to a man whose chief pleasure is to enlarge his knowledge and vary his ideas. Others talk of freedom from noise, and abstraction from common business or amusements; and some, yet more visionary, tell us that the faculties are enlarged by open prospects, and that the fancy is more at liberty when the eye ranges without confinement.

These conveniences may perhaps all be found in a well-chosen garret; but surely they cannot be supposed sufficiently important to have operated invariably upon different climates, distant ages, and separate nations. Of a universal practice, there must still be presumed a universal cause, which, however recondite and abstruse, may

be perhaps reserved to make me illustrious by its discovery, and you by its promulgation.

It is universally known that the faculties of the mind
are invigorated or weakened by the state of the body,
and that the body is in a great measure regulated by
the various compressions of the ambient element. The
effects of the air in the production or cure of corporeal
maladies have been acknowledged from the time of Hip-
pocrates; but no man has yet sufficiently considered how
far it may influence the operations of the genius, though
every day affords instances of local understanding, of wits
and reasoners, whose faculties are adapted to some single
spot, and who, when they are removed to any other place,
sink at once into silence and stupidity. I have discovered,
by a long series of observations, that invention and
elocution suffer great impediments from dense and impure vapours, and that the tenuity of a defecated air, at a
proper distance from the surface of the earth, accelerates
the fancy, and sets at liberty those intellectual powers
which were before shackled by too strong attraction, and
unable to expand themselves under the pressure of a
gross atmosphere. I have found dulness to quicken into
sentiment in a thin ether, as water, though not very hot,
boils in a receiver partly exhausted; and heads, in appearance empty, have teemed with notions upon rising ground,
as the flaccid sides of a football would have swelled out
into stiffness and extension.

For this reason I never think myself qualified to judge
decisively of any man's faculties whom I have only known
in one degree of elevation; but take some opportunity of
attending him from the cellar to the garret, and try upon
him all the various degrees of rarefaction and condensa-
tion, tension and laxity. If he is neither vivacious aloft,
nor serious below, I then consider him as hopeless; but
as it seldom happens that I do not find the temper to

which the texture of his brain is fitted, I accommodate him
in time with a tube of mercury, first marking the point most
favourable to his intellects, according to rules which I have
long studied, and which I may, perhaps, reveal to mankind in a complete treatise of barometrical pneumatology.

Another cause of the gaiety and sprightliness of the
dwellers in garrets is probably the increase of that ver-
tiginous motion, with which we are carried round by the
diurnal revolution of the earth. The power of agitation
upon the spirits is well known; every man has felt his
heart lightened in a rapid vehicle, or on a galloping horse;
and nothing is plainer, than that he who towers to the
fifth story, is whirled through more space by every cir-
cumrotation than another that grovels upon the ground-
floor. The nations between the tropics are known to be
fiery, inconstant, inventive, and fanciful; because, living
at the utmost length of the earth's diameter, they are
carried about with more swiftness than those whom nature
has placed nearer to the poles; and, therefore, as it becomes a wise man to struggle with the inconveniences of
his country, we must actuate our languor by taking a few
turns round the centre in a garret.

If you imagine that I ascribe to air and motion effects
which they cannot produce, I desire you to consult your
own memory, and consider whether you have never
known a man acquire a reputation in his garret, which,
when fortune or a patron had placed him upon the first
floor, he was unable to maintain; and who never recovered
his former vigour of understanding till he was restored
to his original situation. That a garret will make every
man a wit I am very far from supposing; I know there
are some who would continue blockheads even on the
summit of the Andes or on the peak of Teneriffe. But
let not any man be considered as unimprovable till this
potent remedy has been tried; for perhaps he was formed

to be great only in a garret, as the joiner of Aretæus was
rational in no other place but in his own shop.

I think a frequent removal to various distances from
the centre so necessary to a just estimate of intellectual
abilities, and consequently of so great use in education,
that if I hoped that the public could be persuaded to so
expensive an experiment, I would propose, that there
should be a cavern dug, and a tower erected, like those
which Bacon describes in Solomon's house, for the expansion and concentration of understanding, according
to the exigence of different employments, or constitutions.
Perhaps some that fume away in meditations upon time
and space in the tower might compose tables of interest
at a certain depth; and he that upon level ground stagnates in silence, or creeps in narrative, might, at the
height of half a mile, ferment into merriment, sparkle
with repartee, and froth with declamation.

Addison observes that we may find the heat of Virgil's
climate in some lines of his Georgic; so when I read a
composition I immediately determine the height of the
author's habitation.   As an elaborate performance is commonly said to smell of the lamp, my commendation of a
noble thought, a sprightly sally, or a bold figure, is to
pronounce it fresh from the garret; an expression which
would break from me upon the perusal of most of your
papers, did I not believe that you sometimes quit the
garret, and ascend into the cock-loft.

XXXII. LITERARY COURAGE.

Dum vitant stulti vitia, in contraria currunt.—Hor.

Whilst fools one vice condemn,
They run into the opposite extreme.—*Creech.*

THAT wonder is the effect of ignorance has been often
observed.   The awful stillness of attention with
which the mind is overspread at the first view of an un-

expected effect ceases when we have leisure to disentangle complications and investigate causes. Wonder is a pause of reason, a sudden cessation of the mental progress, which lasts only while the understanding is fixed upon some single idea, and is at an end when it recovers force enough to divide the object into its parts or mark the intermediate gradations from the first agent to the last consequence.

It may be remarked with equal truth that ignorance is often the effect of wonder. It is common for those who have never accustomed themselves to the labour of inquiry, nor invigorated their confidence by conquests over difficulty, to sleep in the gloomy quiescence of astonishment without any effort to animate inquiry or dispel obscurity. What they cannot immediately conceive they consider as too high to be reached, or too extensive to be comprehended; they therefore content themselves with the gaze of folly, forbear to attempt what they have no hope of performing, and resign the pleasure of rational contemplation to more pertinacious study or more active faculties.

Among the productions of mechanic art, many are of a form so different from that of their first materials, and many consist of parts so numerous and so nicely adapted to each other that it is not possible to view them without amazement. But when we enter the shops of artificers, observe the various tools by which every operation is facilitated, and trace the progress of a manufacture through the different hands that, in succession to each other, contribute to its perfection, we soon discover that every single man has an easy task, and that the extremes, however remote, of natural rudeness and artificial elegance are joined by a regular concatenation of effects, of which every one is introduced by that which precedes it, and equally introduces that which is to follow.

The same is the state of intellectual and manual performances. Long calculations or complex diagrams affright the timorous and unexperienced from a second view; but if we have skill sufficient to analyze them into simple principles, it will be discovered that our fear was groundless. *Divide and conquer* is a principle equally just in science as in policy. Complication is a species of confederacy which, while it continues united, bids defiance to the most active and vigorous intellect, but of which every member is separately weak, and which may therefore be quickly subdued, if it can once be broken.

The chief art of learning, as Locke has observed, is to attempt but little at a time. The widest excursions of the mind are made by short flights frequently repeated; the most lofty fabrics of science are formed by the continued accumulation of single propositions.

It often happens, whatever be the cause, that impatience of labour, or dread of miscarriage, seizes those who are most distinguished for quickness of apprehension; and that they who might with greatest reason promise themselves victory are least willing to hazard the encounter. This diffidence, where the attention is not laid asleep by laziness, or dissipated by pleasures, can arise only from confused and general views, such as negligence snatches in haste, or from the disappointment of the first hopes formed by arrogance without reflection. To expect that the intricacies of science will be pierced by a careless glance, or the eminences of fame ascended without labour, is to expect a peculiar privilege, a power denied to the rest of mankind; but to suppose that the maze is inscrutable to diligence or the heights inaccessible to perseverance, is to submit tamely to the tyranny of fancy, and enchain the mind in voluntary shackles.

It is the proper ambition of the heroes of literature to enlarge the boundaries of knowledge by discovering and conquering new regions of the intellectual world. To the success of such undertakings, perhaps, some degree of fortuitous happiness is necessary, which no man can promise or procure to himself; and therefore doubt and irresolution may be forgiven in him that ventures into the unexplored abysses of truth, and attempts to find his way through the fluctuations of uncertainty, and the conflicts of contradiction. But when nothing more is required than to pursue a path already beaten, and to trample obstacles which others have demolished, why should any man so much distrust his own intellect as to imagine himself unequal to the attempt?

It were to be wished that they who devote their lives to study would at once believe nothing too great for their attainment, and consider nothing as too little for their regard; that they would extend their notice alike to science and to life, and unite some knowledge of the present world to their acquaintance with past ages and remote events.

Nothing has so much exposed men of learning to contempt and ridicule as their ignorance of things which are known to all but themselves. Those who have been taught to consider the institutions of the schools as giving the last perfection to human abilities are surprised to see men wrinkled with study, yet wanting to be instructed in the minute circumstances of propriety, or the necessary forms of daily transaction; and quickly shake off their reverence for modes of education, which they find to produce no ability above the rest of mankind.

Books, says Bacon, *can never teach the use of books.* The student must learn by commerce with mankind to reduce his speculations to practice, and accommodate his knowledge to the purposes of life.

It is too common for those who have been bred to scholastic professions, and passed much of their time in academies where nothing but learning confers honours, to disregard every other qualification, and to imagine that they shall find mankind ready to pay homage to their knowledge, and to crowd about them for instruction. They therefore step out from their cells into the open world with all the confidence of authority and dignity of importance; they look round about them at once with ignorance and scorn on a race of beings to whom they are equally unknown and equally contemptible, but whose manners they must imitate, and with whose opinions they must comply, if they desire to pass their time happily among them.

To lessen that disdain with which scholars are inclined to look on the common business of the world, and the unwillingness with which they condescend to learn what is not to be found in any system of philosophy, it may be necessary to consider that, though admiration is excited by abstruse researches and remote discoveries, yet pleasure is not given, nor affection conciliated, but by softer accomplishments, and qualities more easily communicable to those about us. He that can only converse upon questions about which only a small part of mankind has knowledge sufficient to make them curious, must lose his days in unsocial silence, and live in the crowd of life without a companion. He that can only be useful on great occasions may die without exerting his abilities, and stand a helpless spectator of a thousand vexations which fret away happiness, and which nothing is required to remove but a little dexterity of conduct and readiness of expedients.

No degree of knowledge attainable by man is able to set him above the want of hourly assistance, or to extinguish the desire of fond endearments and tender officiousness; and therefore no one should think it unnecessary to learn those arts by which friendship may be gained. Kindness is preserved by a constant reciprocation of benefits or interchange of pleasures; but such benefits only can be bestowed as others are capable to receive, and such pleasures only imparted as others are qualified to enjoy.

By this descent from the pinnacles of art no honour will be lost; for the condescensions of learning are always overpaid by gratitude. An elevated genius employed in little things appears, to use the simile of Longinus, like the sun in his evening declination; he remits his splendour but retains his magnitude, and pleases more though he dazzles less.

XXXIII. DICK MINIM.

CRITICISM is a study by which men grow important and formidable at a very small expense. The power of invention has been conferred by nature upon few, and the labour of learning those sciences which may by mere labour be obtained is too great to be willingly endured; but every man can exert such judgment as he has upon the works of others; and he whom nature has made weak, and idleness keeps ignorant, may yet support his vanity by the name of a Critic.

I hope it will give comfort to great numbers who are passing through the world in obscurity, when I inform them how easily distinction may be obtained. All the other powers of literature are coy and haughty, they must be long courted, and at last are not always gained; but Criticism is a goddess easy of access and forward of advance; who will meet the slow, and encourage the timorous: the want of meaning she supplies with words, and the want of spirit she recompenses with malignity.

This profession has one recommendation peculiar to itself, that it gives vent to malignity without real mischief. No genius was ever blasted by the breath of critics. The poison which, if confined, would have burst the heart, fumes away in empty hisses, and malice is set at ease with very little danger to merit. The critic is the only man whose triumph is without another's pain, and whose greatness does not rise upon another's ruin.

To a study at once so easy and so reputable, so malicious and so harmless, it cannot be necessary to invite my readers by a long or laboured exhortation; it is sufficient, since all would be critics if they could, to show by one eminent example that all can be critics if they will.

Dick Minim, after the common course of puerile studies, in which he was no great proficient, was put an apprentice to a brewer, with whom he had lived two years, when his uncle died in the city, and left him a large fortune in the stocks. Dick had for six months before used the company of the lower players, of whom he had learned to scorn a trade, and, being now at liberty to follow his genius, he resolved to be a man of wit and humour. That he might be properly initiated in his new character, he frequented the coffee - houses near the theatres, where he listened very diligently, day after day, to those who talked of language and sentiments, and unities and catastrophes, till by slow degrees he began to think that he understood something of the stage, and hoped in time to talk himself.

But he did not trust so much to natural sagacity as wholly to neglect the help of books. When the theatres were shut, he retired to Richmond with a few select writers, whose opinions he impressed upon his memory by unwearied diligence; and when he returned with other wits to the town, was able to tell, in very proper phrases, that the chief business of art is to follow nature; that a perfect writer is not to be expected, because genius decays as judgment increases; that the great art is the art of blotting; and that, according to the rule of Horace, every piece should be kept nine years.

Of the great authors he now began to display the

characters, laying down as a universal position that all had beauties and defects. His opinion was that Shake-speare, committing himself wholly to the impulse of nature, wanted that correctness which learning would have given him; and that Jonson, trusting to learning, did not sufficiently cast his eye on nature. He blamed the stanza of Spenser, and could not bear the hexameters of Sidney. Denham and Waller he held the first re-formers of English numbers; and thought that if Waller could have obtained the strength of Denham, or Denham the sweetness of Waller, there had been nothing wanting to complete a poet. He often expressed his commiser-ation of Dryden's poverty, and his indignation at the age which suffered him to write for bread; he repeated with rapture the first lines of *All for Love*[1], but wondered at the corruption of taste which could bear anything so unnatural as rhyming tragedies. In Otway he found uncommon powers of moving the passions, but was dis-gusted by his general negligence, and blamed him for making a conspirator his hero[2]; and never concluded his disquisition without remarking how happily the sound of the clock is made to alarm the audience. Southern[3] would have been his favourite, but that he mixes comic with tragic scenes, intercepts the natural course of the passions, and fills the mind with a wild confusion of mirth and melancholy. The versification of Rowe[4] he thought too melodious for the stage, and too little varied

[1] A tragedy by Dryden, 1678. It is remarkable for possessing one of the best of his celebrated prefaces, for marking the return of the poet to the use of blank verse, and for being an obvious attempt to rival *Antony and Cleopatra.*

[2] The character of Jaffier in Otway's best play, *Venice Preserved*, 1682. The part that excited Minim's praise is in Act v. Sc. 2.

[3] Thos. Southern (1659-1746) was an Irish dramatist of considerable power, who modelled his style on that of Otway. The incongruity alluded to is the fault also of *Venice Preserved.*

[4] Nicholas Rowe (1673-1718), poet laureate, best known as the author of *Jane Shore*, and of an edition of Shakespeare.

in different passions. He made it the great fault of Con greve that all his persons were wits, and that he always wrote with more art than nature. He considered *Cato* rather as a poem than a play, and allowed Addison to be the complete master of allegory and grave humour, but paid no great deference to him as a critic. He thought the chief merit of Prior was in his easy tales and lighter poems, though he allowed that his *Solomon* had many noble sentiments elegantly expressed. In Swift he discovered an inimitable vein of irony, and an easiness which all would hope and few would attain. Pope he was inclined to degrade from a poet to a versifier, and thought his numbers rather luscious than sweet. He often lamented the neglect of *Phaedra and Hippolitus*[1], and wished to see the stage under better regulation.

These assertions passed commonly uncontradicted; and if now and then an opponent started up, he was quickly repressed by the suffrages of the company, and Minim went away from every dispute with elation of heart and increase of confidence.

He now grew conscious of his abilities, and began to talk of the present state of dramatic poetry; wondered what was become of the comic genius which supplied our ancestors with wit and pleasantry, and why no writer could be found that durst now venture beyond a farce. He saw no reason for thinking that the vein of humour was exhausted, since we live in a country where liberty suffers every character to spread itself to its utmost bulk, and which, therefore, produces more originals than all the rest of the world together. Of tragedy he concluded business to be the soul, and yet often hinted that love predominates too much upon the modern stage.

[1] A tragedy produced in 1708 by Edmund Smith (1668–1710). The author's real name was Neale. Johnson included him in his *Lives of the Poets*, and passed an exaggerated encomium on this play.

He was now an acknowledged critic, and had his own seat in a coffee-house, and headed a party in the pit. Minim has more vanity than ill nature, and seldom desires to do much mischief; he will perhaps murmur a little in the ear of him that sits next him, but endeavours to influence the audience to favour, by clapping when an actor exclaims, "Ye gods!" or laments the misery of his country.

By degrees he was admitted to rehearsals; and many of his friends are of opinion that our present poets are indebted to him for their happiest thoughts; by his contrivance the bell was rung twice in *Barbarossa*[1], and by his persuasion the author of *Cleone*[2] concluded his play with a couplet; for what can be more absurd, said Minim, than that part of a play should be rhymed, and part written in blank verse? and by what acquisition of faculties is the speaker, who never could find rhymes before, enabled to rhyme at the conclusion of an act?

He is the great investigator of hidden beauties, and is particularly delighted when he finds *the sound an echo to the sense*. He has read all our poets with particular attention to this delicacy of versification, and wonders at the supineness with which their works have been hitherto perused, so that no man has found the sound of a drum in this distich:

> "When pulpit, drum ecclesiastic,
>   Was beat with fist instead of a stick";

and that the wonderful lines upon honour and a bubble, have hitherto passed without notice:

> "Honour is like the glassy bubble,
>   Which costs philosophers such trouble:
>   Where, one part crack'd, the whole does fly,
>   And wits are crack'd to find out why".

[1] A worthless tragedy by Dr. Brown, a minor poet and dramatist of the time.

[2] A tragedy by Robert Dodsley (1703-1764), editor of the *Collection of Old Plays.*

In these verses, says Minim, we have two striking accommodations of the sound to the sense. It is impossible to utter the two lines emphatically without an act like that which they describe; bubble and trouble causing a momentary inflation of the cheeks by the retention of the breath, which is afterwards forcibly emitted, as in the practice of blowing bubbles. But the greatest excellence is in the third line, which is cracked in the middle to express a crack, and then shivers into monosyllables. Yet hath this diamond lain neglected with common stones, and among the innumerable admirers of Hudibras the observation of this superlative passage has been reserved for the sagacity of Minim.

xxxiv. DICK MINIM.

MR. MINIM had now advanced himself to the zenith of critical reputation; when he was in the pit every eye in the boxes was fixed upon him; when he entered his coffee-house he was surrounded by circles of candidates, who passed their novitiate of literature under his tuition: his opinion was asked by all who had no opinion of their own, and yet loved to debate and decide; and no composition was supposed to pass in safety to posterity, till it had been secured by Minim's approbation.

Minim professes great admiration of the wisdom and munificence by which the academies of the continent were raised; and often wishes for some standard of taste, for some tribunal, to which merit may appeal from caprice, prejudice, and malignity. He has formed a plan for an academy of criticism, where every work of imagination may be read before it is printed, and which shall authoritatively direct the theatres what pieces to receive or reject, to exclude or to revive.

Such an institution would, in Dick's opinion, spread the fame of English literature over Europe, and make London the metropolis of elegance and politeness, the place to which the learned and ingenious of all countries would repair for instruction and improvement, and where nothing would any longer be applauded or endured that was not conformed to the nicest rules, and finished with the highest elegance.

Till some happy conjunction of the planets shall dispose our princes or ministers to make themselves immortal by such an academy, Minim contents himself to preside four nights in a week in a critical society selected by himself, where he is heard without contradiction, and whence his judgment is disseminated through the great vulgar and the small.

When he is placed in the chair of criticism, he declares loudly for the noble simplicity of our ancestors, in opposition to the petty refinements, and ornamental luxuriance. Sometimes he is sunk in despair, and perceives false delicacy daily gaining ground, and sometimes brightens his countenance with a gleam of hope, and predicts the revival of the true sublime. He then fulminates his loudest censures against the monkish barbarity of rhyme; wonders how beings that pretend to reason can be pleased with one line always ending like another; tells how unjustly and unnaturally sense is sacrified to sound; how often the best thoughts are mangled by the necessity of confining or extending them to the dimensions of a couplet; and rejoices that genius has, in our days, shaken off the shackles which had encumbered it so long. Yet he allows that rhyme may sometimes be borne, if the lines be often broken, and the pauses judiciously diversified.

From blank verse he makes an easy transition to Milton, whom he produces as an example of the slow advance of lasting reputation. Milton is the only writer in whose books Minim can read for ever without weariness. What cause is it that exempts this pleasure from satiety he has long and diligently inquired, and believes it to consist in the perpetual variation of the numbers, by which the ear is gratified and the attention awakened. The lines that are commonly thought rugged and unmusical, he conceives to have been written to temper the melodious luxury of the rest, or to express things by a proper cadence: for he scarcely finds a verse that has not this favourite beauty; he declares that he could shiver in a hot-house when he reads that

"the ground
Burns frore, and cold performs the effect of fire";

and that when Milton bewails his blindness, the verse,

"So thick a drop serene has quench'd these orbs",

has, he knows not how, something that strikes him with an obscure sensation like that which he fancies would be felt from the sound of darkness.

Minim is not so confident of his rules of judgment as not very eagerly to catch new light from the name of the author. He is commonly so prudent as to spare those whom he cannot resist, unless, as will sometimes happen, he finds the public combined against them. But a fresh pretender to fame he is strongly inclined to censure, till his own honour requires that he commend him. Till he knows the success of a composition, he intrenches himself in general terms; there are some new thoughts and beautiful passages, but there is likewise much which he would have advised the author to expunge. He has several favourite epithets, of which he has never settled the meaning, but which are very commodiously applied to books which he has not read, or cannot understand. One is manly, another is dry, another stiff, and another flimsy; sometimes he discovers delicacy of style, and sometimes meets with strange expressions.

He is never so great nor so happy as when a youth of promising parts is brought to receive his directions for the prosecution of his studies. He then puts on a very serious air; he advises the pupil to read none but the best authors, and, when he finds one congenial to his own mind, to study his beauties, but avoid his faults, and, when he sits down to write, to consider how his favourite author would think at the present time on the present occasion. He exhorts him to catch those moments when he finds his thoughts expanded and his genius exalted, but to take care lest imagination hurry beyond the bounds of nature. He holds diligence the mother of success; yet enjoins him with great earnestness, not to read more than he can digest, and not to confuse his mind by pursuing studies of contrary tendencies. He tells him, that every man has his genius, and that Cicero could never be a poet. The boy retires illuminated, resolves to follow his genius, and to think how Milton would have thought: and Minim feasts upon his own beneficence till another day brings another pupil.

OLIVER GOLDSMITH.

(1728-1774.)

XXXV. NATIONAL PREJUDICE.

THE English seem as silent as the Japanese, yet vainer than the inhabitants of Siam. Upon my arrival I attributed that reserve to modesty, which I now find has its origin in pride. Condescend to address them first and you are sure of their acquaintance; stoop to flattery and you conciliate their friendship and esteem. They bear hunger, cold, fatigue, and all the miseries of life without shrinking; danger only calls forth their fortitude; they even exult in calamity: but contempt is what they cannot bear. An Englishman fears contempt more than death; he often flies to death as a refuge from its pressure, and dies when he fancies the world has ceased to esteem him.

Pride seems the source not only of their national vices, but of their national virtues also. An Englishman is taught to love the king as his friend, but to acknowledge no other master than the laws which himself has contributed to enact. He despises those nations who, that one may be free, are all content to be slaves; who first lift a tyrant into terror, and then shrink under his power as if delegated from Heaven. Liberty is echoed in all their assemblies; and thousands might be found ready to offer up their lives for the sound, though perhaps not one of all the number understands its meaning. The lowest mechanic, however, looks upon it as his duty to be a watchful guardian of his country's freedom, and often uses a language that might seem haughty even in the mouth of the great emperor who traces his ancestry to the moon.

A few days ago, passing by one of their prisons, I could not avoid stopping, in order to listen to a dialogue which I thought might afford me some entertainment. The conversation was carried on between a debtor through the grate of his prison, a porter, who had stopped to rest his burden, and a soldier at the window. The subject was upon a threatened invasion from France, and each seemed extremely anxious to rescue his country from the impending danger. " For my part," cries the prisoner, "the greatest of my apprehension is for our freedom; if the French should conquer, what would become of English liberty? My dear friends, liberty is the Englishman's prerogative; we must preserve that at the expense of our lives; of that the French shall never deprive us. It is not to be expected that men who are slaves themselves would preserve our freedom should they happen to conquer." "Ay, slaves," cries the porter, "they are al' slaves, fit only to carry burdens, every one of them. Before I would stoop to slavery let this be my poison" (and he held the goblet in his hand), "may this be my poison; but I would sooner list for a soldier."

The soldier, taking the goblet from his friend with much awe, fervently cried out, "It is not so much our liberties as our religion that would suffer by such a change: ay, our religion, my lads. May the devil sink me into flames" (such was the solemnity of his adjuration) "if the French should come over, but our religion would be utterly undone." So saying, instead of a libation, he applied the goblet to his lips, and confirmed his sentiments with a ceremony of the most persevering devotion.

In short, every man here pretends to be a politician; even the fair sex are sometimes found to mix the severity of national altercation with the blandishments of love, and often become conquerors by more weapons of destruction than their eyes.

This universal passion for politics is gratified by daily gazettes, as with us in China. But as in ours the emperor endeavours to instruct his people, in theirs the people endeavour to instruct the administration. You must not, however, imagine that they who compile these papers have any actual knowledge of the politics or the government of a state; they only collect their materials from the oracle of some coffee-house, which oracle has himself gathered them the night before from a beau at a gaming-table, who has pillaged his knowledge from a great man's porter, who has had his information from the great man's gentleman, who has invented the whole story for his own amusement the night preceding.

The English, in general, seem fonder of gaining the

esteem than the love of those they converse with. This gives a formality to their amusements: their gayest conversations have something too wise for innocent relaxation: though in company you are seldom disgusted with the absurdity of a fool, you are seldom lifted into rapture by those strokes of vivacity which give instant though not permanent pleasure.

What they want, however, in gaiety, they make up in politeness. You smile at hearing me praise the English for their politeness—you who have heard very different accounts from the missionaries at Pekin, who have seen such a different behaviour in their merchants and seamen at home. But I must still repeat it, the English seem more polite than any of their neighbours: their great art in this respect lies in endeavouring, while they oblige, to lessen the force of the favour. Other countries are fond of obliging a stranger, but seem desirous that he should be sensible of the obligation. The English confer their kindness with an appearance of indifference, and give away benefits with an air as if they despised them.

Walking, a few days ago, between an English and a French man, into the suburbs of the city, we were overtaken by a heavy shower of rain. I was unprepared; but they had each large coats, which defended them from what seemed to me a perfect inundation. The Englishman, seeing me shrink from the weather, accosted me thus: "Psha, man, what dost shrink at? Here, take this coat; I don't want it; I find it no way useful to me; I had as lief be without it." The Frenchman began to show his politeness in turn. "My dear friend," cries he, "why don't you oblige me by making use of my coat? you see how well it defends me from the rain; I should not choose to part with it to others, but to such a friend as you I could even part with my skin to do him service."

From such minute instances as these, most reverend Fum Hoam, I am sensible your sagacity will collect instruction. The volume of nature is the book of knowledge; and he becomes most wise who makes the most judicious selection.—Farewell.

XXXVI. THE MAN IN BLACK.

THOUGH fond of my acquaintances, I desire an intimacy only with a few. The Man in Black, whom I have often mentioned, is one whose friendship I could wish to acquire, because he possesses my esteem. His manners, it is true, are tinctured with some strange inconsistencies; and he may be justly termed a humorist in a nation of humorists. Though he is generous even to profusion, he affects to be thought a prodigy of parsimony and prudence: though his conversation be replete with the most sordid and selfish maxims, his heart is dilated with the most unbounded love. I have known him profess himself a man-hater, while his cheek was glowing with compassion; and while his looks were softened into pity, I have heard him use the language of the most unbounded ill-nature. Some affect humanity and tenderness, others boast of having such dispositions from nature; but he is the only man I ever knew who seemed ashamed of his natural benevolence. He takes as much pains to hide his feelings as any hypocrite would to conceal his indifference; but on every unguarded moment the mask drops off, and reveals him to the most superficial observer.

In one of our late excursions into the country, happening to discourse upon the provision that was made for the poor in England, he seemed amazed how any of his countrymen could be so foolishly weak as to relieve occasional objects of charity, when the laws had made such ample provision for their support. "In every parish-house," says he, "the poor are supplied with food, clothes, fire, and a bed to lie on; they want no more, I desire no more myself; yet still they seem discontented. I am surprised at the inactivity of our magistrates in not taking up such vagrants, who are only a weight upon the industrious; I am surprised that the people are found to relieve them, when they must be at the same time sensible that it in some measure encourages idleness, extravagance, and imposture.   Were I to advise any man for whom I had the least regard, I would caution him by all means not to be imposed upon by their false pretences: let me assure you, sir, they are impostors, every one of them, and rather merit a prison than relief."

He was proceeding in this strain earnestly to dissuade me from an imprudence of which I am seldom guilty, when an old man, who still had about him the remnants of tattered finery, implored our compassion.   He assured us he was no common beggar, but forced into the shameful profession to support a dying wife and five hungry children.   Being prepossessed against such falsehoods, his story had not the least influence upon me; but it was quite otherwise with the Man in Black: I could see it visibly operate upon his countenance, and effectually interrupt his harangue.   I could easily perceive that his heart burned to relieve the five starving children, but he seemed ashamed to discover his weakness to me.   While he thus hesitated between compassion and pride, I pretended to look another way, and he seized this opportunity of giving the poor petitioner a piece of silver, bidding him at the same time, in order that I should hear, go work for his bread, and not tease passengers with such impertinent falsehoods for the future.

As he had fancied himself quite unperceived, he continued, as we proceeded, to rail against beggars with as much animosity as before: he threw in some episodes on his own amazing prudence and economy, with his pro found skill in discovering impostors; he explained the manner in which he would deal with beggars were he a magistrate, hinted at enlarging some of the prisons for their reception, and told two stories of ladies that were robbed by beggar-men. He was beginning a third to the same purpose, when a sailor with a wooden leg once more crossed our walks, desiring our pity, and blessing our limbs. I was for going on without taking any notice, but my friend, looking wistfully upon the poor petitioner, bid me stop, and he would show with how much ease he could at any time detect an impostor.

He now, therefore, assumed a look of importance, and in an angry tone began to examine the sailor, de manding in what engagement he was thus disabled and rendered unfit for service. The sailor replied, in a tone as angrily as he, that he had been an officer on board a private ship of war, and that he had lost his leg abroad in defence of those who did nothing at home. At this reply, all my friend's importance vanished in a moment; he had not a single question more to ask; he now only studied what method he should adopt to relieve him unobserved. He had, however, no easy part to act, as he was obliged to preserve the appearance of ill-nature before me, and yet relieve himself by relieving the sailor. Casting, therefore, a furious look upon some bundles of chips which the fellow carried in a string at his back, my friend demanded how he sold his matches; but, not waiting for a reply, desired, in a surly tone, to have a shilling's worth. The sailor seemed at first surprised at his demand, but soon recollecting himself, and presenting his whole bundle, "Here, master," says he, "take all my cargo, and a blessing into the bargain".

It is impossible to describe with what an air of triumph my friend marched off with his new purchase: he assure

me that he was firmly of opinion that those fellows must
have stolen their goods, who could thus afford to sell
them for half value. He informed me of several different
uses to which those chips might be applied; he expatiated
largely upon the savings that would result from lighting
candles with a match, instead of thrusting them into the
fire. He averred that he would as soon have parted
with a tooth as his money to those vagabonds unless for
some valuable consideration. I cannot tell how long this
panegyric upon frugality and matches might have con
tinued, had not his attention been called off by another
object more distressing than either of the former. A
woman in rags, with one child in her arms, and another
on her back, was attempting to sing ballads, but with
such a mournful voice that it was difficult to determine
whether she was singing or crying. A wretch, who in
the deepest distress still aimed at good-humour, was an
object my friend was by no means capable of withstand-
ing: his vivacity and his discourse were instantly interrupted; upon this occasion, his very dissimulation had
forsaken him. Even in my presence he immediately
applied his hands to his pockets, in order to relieve her:
but guess his confusion when he found he had already
given away all the money he carried about him to former
objects. The misery painted in the woman's visage was
not half so strongly expressed as the agony in his. He
continued to search for some time, but to no purpose,
till, at length recollecting himself, with a face of ineffable
good-nature, as he had no money, he put into her hands
his shilling's worth of matches.

XXXVII. A CLUB OF AUTHORS.

BY my last advices from Moscow I find the caravan
has not yet departed from China. I still continue
to write, expecting that you may receive a large number

of letters at once. In them you will find rather a minute detail of English peculiarities than a general picture of their manners or dispositions. Happy it were for mankind, if all travellers would thus, instead of characterizing a people in general terms, lead us into a detail of those minute circumstances which first influenced their opinion. The genius of a country should be investigated with a kind of experimental inquiry; by this means we should have more precise and just notions of foreign nations, and detect travellers themselves when they happened to form wrong conclusions.

My friend and I repeated our visit to the club of authors, where, upon our entrance, we found the members all assembled and engaged in a loud debate.

The poet in shabby finery, holding a manuscript in his hand, was earnestly endeavouring to persuade the company to hear him read the first book of an heroic poem which he had composed the day before. But against this all the members very warmly objected. They knew no reason why any member of the club should be indulged with a particular hearing, when many of them had published whole volumes which had never been looked in. They insisted that the law should be observed, where reading in company was expressly noticed. It was in vain that the poet pleaded the peculiar merit of his piece; he spoke to an assembly insensible to all his remonstrances: the book of laws was opened and read by the secretary, where it was expressly enacted, " That whatsoever poet, speech-maker, critic, or historian, should presume to engage the company by reading his own works, he was to lay down sixpence previous to opening the manuscript, and should be charged one shilling an hour while he continued reading, the said shilling to be equally distributed among the company as a recompense for their trouble."

Our poet seemed at first to shrink at the penalty, hesiıating for some time whether he should deposit the fine or shut up the poem; but, looking round, and perceiving two strangers in the room, his love of fame outweighed his prudence, and laying down the sum by law established, he insisted on his prerogative.

A profound silence ensuing, he began by explaining his design. "Gentlemen," says he, "the present piece is not one of your common epic poems which come from the press like paper-kites in summer; there are none of your Turnuses or Didos in it; it is an heroical description of nature. I only beg you'll endeavour to make your souls unison with mine, and hear with the same enthusiasm with which I have written. The poem begins with the description of an author's bedchamber; the picture was sketched in my own apartment; for you must know, gentlemen, that I am myself the hero." Then, putting himself into the attitude of an orator, with all the emphasis of voice and action, he proceeded:—

Where the Red Lion, flaring o'er the way,
Invites each passing stranger that can pay;
Where Calvert's Butt and Parson's black champagne
Regale the drabs and bloods of Drury Lane:
There, in a lonely room, from bailiffs snug,
The Muse found Scroggen stretched beneath a rug.
A window, patched with paper, lent a ray,
That dimly showed the state in which he lay;
The sanded floor, that grits beneath the tread;
The humid wall, with paltry pictures spread;
The royal game of goose was there in view,
And the twelve rules the Royal Martyr drew;
The Seasons, framed with listing, found a place,
And brave Prince William showed his lamp-black face.
The morn was cold; he views with keen desire
The rusty grate, unconscious of a fire;
With beer and milk arrears the frieze was scored,
And five cracked teacups dressed the chimney board,

> A night-cap decked his brows instead of bay;
> A cap by night—a stocking all the day![1]

With this last line he seemed so much elated that he was unable to proceed. "There, gentlemen!" cries he, "there is a description for you; Rabelais' bedchamber is but a fool to it.

> A cap by night—a stocking all the day!

There is sound, and sense, and truth, and nature in the trifling compass of ten little syllables."

He was too much employed in self-admiration to observe the company, who, by nods, winks, shrugs, and stifled laughter, testified every mark of contempt. He turned severally to each for their opinion, and found all, however, ready to applaud. One swore it was inimitable, another said it was damned fine, and a third cried out in a rapture, *Carissimo*. At last, addressing himself to the president, "And pray, Mr. Squint," says he, "let us have your opinion". "Mine," answered the president, taking the manuscript out of the author's hand; "may this glass suffocate me, but I think it equal to anything I have seen; and I fancy," continued he, doubling up the poem and forcing it into the author's pocket, "that you will get great honour when it comes out; *ex ungue Herculem*, we are satisfied, perfectly satisfied." The author made two or three attempts to pull it out a second time, and the president made as many to prevent him. Thus, though with reluctance, he was at last obliged to sit down, contented with the commendations for which he had paid.

When this tempest of poetry and praise was blown over,

---

[1] For the whole description cf. *The Deserted Village*, ll. 225-236. The "game of goose" resembles backgammon; the "twelve rules" ascribed by tradition to Charles I. were such as "Reveal no secrets", "Make no long meals"; "listing" is a frame of useless parings of unpolished wood; "lamp-black face" refers to the cheap silhouettes of William and Mary, sold in large numbers by Elizabeth Pyberg in 1699.

one of the company changed the subject, by wondering
how any man could be so dull as to write poetry at
present, since prose itself would hardly pay. "Would
you think it, gentlemen," continued he, "I have actually
written last week sixteen prayers, twelve ribald jests, and
three sermons, all at the rate of sixpence a piece; and,
what is still more extraordinary, the bookseller had lost
by the bargain? Such sermons would once have gained
me a prebend's stall; but now, alas! we have neither
piety, taste, nor humour among us. Positively, if this
season does not turn out better than it has begun, unless
the ministry commit some blunders to furnish us with a
new topic of abuse, I shall resume my old business of
working at the press, instead of finding it employment."

The whole club seemed to join in condemning the
season as one of the worst that had come for some time:
a gentleman particularly observed that the nobility were
never known to subscribe worse than at present. "I
know not how it happens," said he, "though I follow
them up as close as possible, yet I can hardly get a single
subscription in a week. The houses of the great are as
inaccessible as a frontier garrison at midnight. I never
see a nobleman's door half opened, that some surly porter
or footman does not stand full in the breach. I was
yesterday to wait with a subscription proposal upon my
Lord Squash, the Creolian. I had posted myself at his
door the whole morning, and just as he was getting into
his coach, thrust my proposal snug into his hand, folded
up in the form of a letter from myself. He just glanced
at the superscription, and, not knowing the hand, con-
signed it to his valet-de-chambre; this respectable per-
sonage treated it as his master, and put it into the hands
of the porter; the porter grasped my proposal frowning;
and, measuring my figure from top to toe, put it back in
my own hands unopened."

"To the devil I pitch all the nobility," cries a little man in a peculiar accent; "I am sure they have of late used me most scurvily. You must know, gentlemen, some time ago, upon the arrival of a certain noble duke from his travels, I sat myself down, and vamped up a fine flaunting poetical panegyric, which I had written in such a strain that I fancied it would have even wheedled milk from a mouse. In this I represented the whole kingdom welcoming his grace to his native soil, not forgetting the loss France and Italy would sustain in their arts by his departure. I expected to touch for a bank-bill at least; so, folding up my verses in gilt paper, I gave my last half-crown to a genteel servant to be the bearer. My letter was safely conveyed to his grace, and the servant, after four hours' absence, during which time I led the life of a fiend, returned with a letter four times as big as mine. Guess my ecstasy at the prospect of so fine a return. I eagerly took the packet into my hands that trembled to receive it. I kept it some time unopened before me, brooding over the expected treasure it contained; when opening it, as I hope to be saved, gentlemen, his grace had sent me, in payment for my poem, no bank-bills, but six copies of verses, each longer than mine, addressed to him upon the same occasion."

"A nobleman," cries a member who had hitherto been silent, "is created as much for the confusion of us authors as the catch-pole[1]. I'll tell you a story, gentlemen, which is as true as that this pipe is made of clay:—When I was delivered of my first book, I owed my tailor for a suit of clothes; but that is nothing new, you know, and may be any man's case as well as mine. Well, owing him for a suit of clothes, and hearing that my book took very well, he sent for his money, and insisted upon being paid immediately. Though I was at that time rich in fame—

[1] Sheriff's officer.

for my book ran like wild-fire—yet I was very short in
money, and, being unable to satisfy his demand, prudently
resolved to keep my chamber, preferring a prison of my
own choosing at home to one of my tailor's choosing
abroad. In vain the bailiffs used all their arts to decoy
me from my citadel; in vain they sent to let me know
that a gentleman wanted to speak with me at the next
tavern; in vain they came with an urgent message from
my aunt in the country; in vain I was told that a particular friend was at the point of death and desired to take
his last farewell. I was deaf, insensible, rock, adamant;
the bailiffs could make no impression on my hard heart,
for I effectually kept my liberty by never stirring out of
the room.

"This was very well for a fortnight; when one morning
I received a most splendid message from the Earl of
Doomsday, importing that he had read my book, and was
in raptures with every line of it; he impatiently longed to
see the author, and had some designs which might turn
out greatly to my advantage. I paused upon the contents
of this message, and found there could be no deceit, for
the card was gilt at the edges, and the bearer, I was told,
had quite the looks of a gentleman. Witness, ye powers,
how my heart triumphed at my own importance! I saw
a long perspective of felicity before me; I applauded the
taste of the times which never saw genius forsaken; I had
prepared a set introductory speech for the occasion; five
glaring compliments for his lordship, and two more
modest for myself. The next morning, therefore, in
order to be punctual to my appointment, I took coach,
and ordered the fellow to drive to the street and house
mentioned in his lordship's address. I had the precaution
to pull up the window as I went along, to keep off the
busy part of mankind, and, big with expectation, fancied
the coach never went fast enough. At length, however,

the wished-for moment of its stopping arrived: this for
some time I impatiently expected, and letting down the
window in a transport, in order to take a previous view of
his lordship's magnificent palace and situation, I found—
poison to my sight!—I found myself not in an elegant
street, but a paltry lane, not at a nobleman's door, but the
door of a spunging-house. I found the coachman had all
this while been driving me to jail; and I saw the bailiff,
with a devil's face, coming out to secure me."

To a philosopher no circumstance, however trifling, is
too minute; he finds instruction and entertainment in
occurrences which are passed over by the rest of mankind
as low, trite, and indifferent; it is from the number of
these particulars, which to many appear insignificant, that
he is at last enabled to form general conclusions: this,
therefore, must be my excuse for sending so far as China
accounts of manners and follies, which, though minute in
their own nature, serve more truly to characterize this
people than histories of their public treaties, courts,
ministers, negotiations, and ambassadors.—Adieu.

xxxviii. BEAU TIBBS.

THE people of London are as fond of walking as our
friends at Pekin of riding: one of the principal
entertainments of the citizens here in summer is to repair
about nightfall to a garden[1] not far from town, where
they walk about, show their best clothes, and best faces,
and listen to a concert provided for the occasion.

I accepted an invitation a few evenings ago from my
old friend, the Man in Black, to be one of a party that

[1] Spring-garden, the earlier name of the gardens, was taken from a
pleasure resort near St. James's Park, which contained a "playfully
contrived waterwork, which on being unguardedly pressed by the foot
sprinkled the bystanders". For a charming account of Vauxhall and
its associations, see Mr. Dobson's Essay referred to in the note on
page 184.

was to sup there; and at the appointed hour waited upon him at his lodgings. There I found the company assembled, and expecting my arrival. Our party consisted of my friend, in superlative finery, his stockings rolled, a black velvet waistcoat, which was formerly new, and a gray wig combed down in imitation of hair; a pawnbroker's widow, of whom, by the by, my friend was a professed admirer, dressed out in green damask, with three gold rings on every finger; Mr. Tibbs, the second-rate beau I have formerly described; together with his lady, in flimsy silk, dirty gauze instead of linen, and a hat as big as an umbrella.

Our first difficulty was in settling how we should set out. Mrs. Tibbs had a natural aversion to the water, and the widow, being a little in flesh, as warmly protested against walking; a coach was therefore agreed upon; which being too small to carry five, Mr. Tibbs consented to sit in his wife's lap.

In this manner, therefore, we set forward, being entertained by the way with the bodings of Mr. Tibbs, who assured us he did not expect to see a single creature for the evening above the degree of a cheesemonger; that this was the last night of the gardens, and that consequently we should be pestered with the nobility and gentry from Thames Street and Crooked Lane; with several other prophetic ejaculations, probably inspired by the uneasiness of his situation.

The illuminations began before we arrived, and I must confess, that upon entering the gardens I found every sense overpaid with more than expected pleasure: the lights everywhere glimmering through the scarcely moving trees—the full-bodied concert bursting on the stillness of the night—the natural concert of the birds, in the more retired part of the grove, vying with that which was formed by art—the company gaily dressed, looking satisfaction

—and the tables spread with various delicacies—all con-
spired to fill my imagination with the visionary happiness
of the Arabian lawgiver, and lifted me into an ecstasy of
admiration. " Head of Confucius," cried I to my friend,
"this is fine! this united rural beauty with courtly magnificence! if we except the virgins of immortality, that hang
on every tree, I do not see how this falls short of Mahomet's
Paradise!" "As for that," cries my friend, "if ladies, as
plenty as apples in autumn, can content you, I fancy we
have no need to go to heaven for Paradise."

I was going to second his remarks, when we were
called to a consultation by Mr. Tibbs and the rest of the
company, to know in what manner we were to lay out the
evening to the greatest advantage. Mrs. Tibbs was for
keeping the genteel walk of the garden, where, she
observed, there was always the very best company; the
widow, on the contrary, who came but once a season,
was for securing a good standing place to see the waterworks, which she assured us would begin in less than an
hour at farthest; a dispute therefore began, and as it
was managed between two of very opposite characters,
it threatened to grow more bitter at every reply. Mrs.
Tibbs wondered how people could pretend to know the
polite world, who had received all their rudiments of
breeding behind a counter; to which the other replied,
that though some people sat behind counters, yet they
could sit at the head of their own tables too, and carve
three good dishes of hot meat whenever they thought
proper; which was more than some people could say for
themselves, that hardly knew a rabbit and onions from
a green goose and gooseberries.

It is hard to say where this might have ended, had not
the husband, who probably knew the impetuosity of his
wife's disposition, proposed to end the dispute by ad-
journing to a box, and try if there was anything to be

had for supper that was supportable. To this we all consented; but here a new distress arose: Mr. and Mrs. Tibbs would sit in none but a genteel box—a box where they might see and be seen—one, as they expressed it, in the very focus of public view; but such a box was not easy to be obtained, for though we were perfectly convinced of our own gentility, and the gentility of our appearance, yet we found it a difficult matter to persuade the keepers of the boxes to be of our opinion; they chose to reserve genteel boxes for what they judged more genteel company.

At last, however, we were fixed, though somewhat obscurely, and supplied with the usual entertainment of the place. The widow found the supper excellent, but Mrs. Tibbs thought everything detestable. "Come, come, my dear," cried the husband, by way of consolation, "to be sure we can't find such dressing here as we have at Lord Crump's or Lady Crimp's; but, for Vauxhall dressing, it is pretty good: it is not their victuals, indeed, I find fault with, but their wine; their wine," cries he, drinking off a glass, "indeed, is most abominable."

By this last contradiction the widow was fairly conquered in point of politeness. She perceived now that she had no pretensions in the world to taste; her very senses were vulgar, since she had praised detestable custard, and smacked at wretched wine; she was therefore content to yield the victory, and for the rest of the night to listen and improve. It is true, she would now and then forget herself, and confess she was pleased; but they soon brought her back again to miserable refinement. She once praised the painting of the box in which we were sitting, but was soon convinced that such paltry pieces ought rather to excite horror than satisfaction: she ventured again to commend one of the singers, but Mrs. Tibbs soon let her know, in the style of a connoisseur, that the singer in question had neither ear, voice, nor judgment.

Mr. Tibbs, now willing to prove that his wife's pretensions to music were just, entreated her to favour the company with a song; but to this she gave a positive denial—"For you know very well, my dear," says she, "that I am not in voice to-day, and when one's voice is not equal to one's judgment, what signifies singing? besides, as there is no accompaniment, it would be but spoiling music". All these excuses, however, were overruled by the rest of the company, who, though one would think they already had music enough, joined in the entreaty. But particularly the widow, now willing to convince the company of her breeding, pressed so warmly, that she seemed determined to take no refusal. At last, then, the lady complied, and after humming for some minutes, began with such a voice, and such affectation, as I could perceive gave but little satisfaction to any except her husband. He sat with rapture in his eye, and beat time with his hand on the table.

You must observe, my friend, that it is the custom of this country, when a lady or gentleman happens to sing, for the company to sit as mute and motionless as statues. Every feature, every limb, must seem to correspond in fixed attention; and while the song continues, they are to remain in a state of universal petrifaction. In this mortifying situation we had continued for some time, listening to the song, and looking with tranquillity, when the master of the box came to inform us, that the waterworks[1] were going to begin. At this information I could

[1] "In Goldsmith's day it (the water show) was still in the elementary stage described by Sylvanus Urban in August, 1765, that is to say, it exhibited 'a beautiful landscape in perspective, with a miller's house, a water-mill, and a cascade'. At the proper moment this last presented the exact appearance of water flowing down a declivity, rising up in a foam at the bottom, and then gliding away." (Dobson's *Vignettes*, vol. i. p. 243.)

instantly perceive the widow bounce from her seat; but, correcting herself, she sat down again, repressed by motives of good breeding. Mrs. Tibbs, who had seen the waterworks an hundred times, resolving not to be interrupted, continued her song without any share of mercy, nor had the smallest pity on our impatience. The widow's face, I own, gave me high entertainment; in it I could plainly read the struggle she felt between good breeding and curiosity; she talked of the waterworks the whole evening before, and seemed to have come merely in order to see them; but then she could not bounce out in the very middle of a song, for that would be forfeiting all pretensions to high life, or high-lived company, ever after. Mrs. Tibbs, therefore, kept on singing, and we continued to listen, till at last, when the song was just concluded, the waiter came to inform us that the waterworks were over.

"The waterworks over!" cried the widow; "the waterworks over already! that 's impossible! they can't be over so soon!" "It is not my business," replied the fellow, "to contradict your ladyship; I 'll run again and see." He went, and soon returned with a confirmation of the dismal tidings. No ceremony could now bind my friend's disappointed mistress. She testified her displeasure in the openest manner; in short, she now began to find fault in turn, and at last insisted upon going home, just at the time Mr. and Mrs. Tibbs assured the company that the polite hours were going to begin, and that the ladies would instantaneously be entertained with the horns.—Adieu.

XXXIX. A CITY NIGHT-PIECE.

THE clock just struck two, the expiring taper rises and sinks in the socket, the watchman forgets the hour in slumber, the laborious and the happy are at rest, and nothing wakes but meditation, guilt, revelry, and despair. The drunkard once more fills the destroying bowl, the robber walks his midnight round, and the suicide lifts his guilty arm against his own sacred person.

Let me no longer waste the night over the page of antiquity, or the sallies of contemporary genius, but pursue the solitary walk, where vanity, ever changing, but a few hours past walked before me; where she kept up the pageant, and now, like a froward child, seems hushed with her own importunities.

What a gloom hangs all around! The dying lamp feebly emits a yellow gleam; no sound is heard but of the chiming clock, or the distant watch-dog. All the bustle of human pride is forgotten; an hour like this may well display the emptiness of human vanity.

There will come a time when this temporary solitude may be made continual, and the city itself, like its inhabitants, fade away, and leave a desert in its room.

What cities as great as this have once triumphed in existence, had their victories as great, joy as just, and as unbounded; and, with short-sighted presumption, promised themselves immortality! Posterity can hardly trace the situation of some; the sorrowful traveller wanders over the awful ruins of others; and, as he beholds, he learns wisdom, and feels the transience of every sublunary possession.

"Here," he cries, "stood their citadel, now grown over with weeds; there their senate house, but now the haunt of every noxious reptile; temples and theatres stood here, now only an undistinguished heap of ruin. They are fallen, for luxury and avarice first made them feeble. The rewards of the state were conferred on amusing and not on useful members of society. Their riches and opulence invited the invaders, who, though at first repulsed, returned again, conquered by perseverance, and at last swept the defendants into undistinguished destruction."

How few appear in those streets which but some few hours ago were crowded! and those who appear now no longer wear their daily mask, nor attempt to hide their lewdness or their misery.

But who are those who make the streets their couch, and find a short repose from wretchedness at the doors of the opulent? These are strangers, wanderers, and orphans, whose circumstances are too humble to expect redress, and whose distresses are too great even for pity. Their wretchedness excites rather horror than pity. Some are without the covering even of rags, and others emaciated with disease; the world has disclaimed them; society turns its back upon their distress, and has given them up to nakedness and hunger. These poor shivering females have once seen happier days, and been flattered into beauty. They have been prostituted to the gay luxurious villain, and are now turned out to meet the severity of winter. Perhaps, now lying at the doors of their betrayers, they sue to wretches whose hearts are insensible, to debauchees who may curse, but will not relieve them.

Why, why was I born a man, and yet see the sufferings of wretches I cannot relieve? Poor houseless creatures! the world will give you reproaches, but will not give you relief. The slightest misfortunes of the great, the most imaginary uneasiness of the rich, are aggravated with all the power of eloquence, and held up to engage our attention and sympathetic sorrow. The poor weep unheeded, persecuted by every subordinate species of tyranny; and every law which gives others security becomes an enemy to them.

Why was this heart of mine formed with so much sensibility? or why was not my fortune adapted to its impulse? Tenderness, without a capacity of relieving, only makes the man who feels it more wretched than the object which sues for assistance.—Adieu.

LEIGH HUNT.

(1784-1859.)

XL. A FEW THOUGHTS ON SLEEP.

THIS is an article for the reader to think of when he or she is warm in bed, a little before he goes to sleep, the clothes at his ear, and the wind moaning in some distant crevice.

"Blessings," exclaimed Sancho, "on him that first invented sleep! It wraps a man all round like a cloak." It is a delicious moment certainly—that of being well nestled in bed, and feeling that you shall drop gently to sleep. The good is to come, not past: the limbs have been just tired enough to render the remaining in one posture delightful: the labour of the day is done. A gentle failure of the perceptions comes creeping over one, the spirit of consciousness disengages itself more and more, with slow and hushing degrees, like a mother detaching her hand from that of her sleeping child; the mind seems to have a balmy lid closing over it, like the eye;—'tis closing;—'tis more closing;—'tis closed. The mysterious spirit has gone to take its airy rounds.

It is said that sleep is best before midnight: and Nature herself, with her darkness and chilling dews, informs us so. There is another reason for going to bed betimes; for it is universally acknowledged that lying late in the morning is a great shortener of life. At least, it is never found in company with longevity. It also tends to make people corpulent. But these matters belong rather to the subject of early rising than of sleep.

Sleep at a late hour in the morning is not half so pleasant as the more timely one. It is sometimes, however, excusable, especially to a watchful or overworked head; neither can we deny the seducing merits of "t' other doze", the pleasing wilfulness of nestling in a new posture, when you know you ought to be up, like the rest of the house. But then you cut up the day, and your sleep the next night.

In the course of the day few people think of sleeping, except after dinner; and then it is often rather a hovering and nodding on the borders of sleep than sleep itself. This is a privilege allowable, we think, to none but the old, or the sickly, or the very tired and care-worn; and it should be well understood before it is exercised in company. To escape into slumber from an argument; or to take it as an affair of course, only between you and your biliary duct; or to assent with involuntary nods to all that you have just been disputing, is not so well; much less, to sit nodding and tottering beside a lady; or to be in danger of dropping your head into the fruit-plate or your host's face; or of waking up, and saying "Just so" to the bark of a dog; or "Yes, madam," to the black at your elbow.

Care-worn people, however, might refresh themselves oftener with day-sleep than they do; if their bodily state is such as to dispose them to it. It is a mistake to suppose that all care is wakeful. People sometimes sleep, as well as wake, by reason of their sorrow. The difference seems to depend upon the nature of their temperament; though in the *most* excessive cases, sleep is perhaps Nature's never-failing relief, as swooning is upon the rack. A person with jaundice in his blood shall lie down and go to sleep at noonday, when another of a different complexion shall find his eyes as unclosable as a statue's, though he has had no sleep for nights together. Without meaning to lessen the dignity of suffering, which has quite enough to do with its waking hours, it is this that may often account for the profound sleeps enjoyed the night before hazardous battles, executions, and other demands upon an over-excited spirit.

The most complete and healthy sleep that can be taken in the day is in summer-time, out in a field. There is, perhaps, no solitary sensation so exquisite as that of slumbering on the grass or hay, shaded from the hot sun by a tree, with the consciousness of a fresh but light air running through the wide atmosphere, and the sky stretching far overhead upon all sides. Earth and heaven and a placid humanity seem to have the creation to themselves. There is nothing between the slumberer and the naked and glad innocence of nature.

Next to this, but at a long interval, the most relishing snatch of slumber out of bed is the one which a tired person takes before he retires for the night, while lingering in his sitting-room. The consciousness of being very sleepy, and of having the power to go to bed immediately, gives great zest to the unwillingness to move. Sometimes he sits nodding in his chair; but the sudden and leaden jerks of the head to which a state of great sleepiness renders him liable, are generally too painful for so luxurious a moment; and he gets into a more legitimate posture, sitting sideways with his head on the chair-back, or throwing his legs up at once on another chair, and half reclining. It is curious, however, to find how long an inconvenient posture will be borne for the sake of this foretaste of repose. The worst of it is, that on going to bed the charm sometimes vanishes; perhaps from the colder temperature of the chamber; for a fireside is a great opiate.

Speaking of the painful positions into which a sleepy lounger will get himself, it is amusing to think of the more fantastic attitudes that so often take place in bed. If we could add anything to the numberless things that have been said about sleep by the poets, it would be upon this point. Sleep never shows himself a greater leveller. A man in his waking moments may look as proud and self possessed as he pleases. He may walk proudly, he may sit proudly, he may eat his dinner proudly; he may shave himself with an air of infinite superiority; in a word, he may show himself grand and absurd upon the most trifling occasions. But Sleep plays the petrifying magician. He arrests the proudest lord as well as the humblest clown in the most ridiculous postures: so that if you could draw a grandee from his bed without waking him, no limb-twisting fool in a pantomime should create wilder laughter. The toy with the string between its legs is hardly a posture-master more extravagant. Imagine a despot lifted up to the gaze of his valets, with his eyes shut, his mouth open, his left hand under his right ear, his other twisted and hanging helplessly before him like an idiot's, one knee lifted up, and the other leg stretched out, or both knees huddled up together;—what a scarecrow to lodge majestic power in!

But Sleep is kindly even in his tricks, and the poets have treated him with proper reverence. According to the ancient mythologists he had even one of the Graces to wife. He had a thousand sons, of whom the chief were Morpheus, or the Shaper; Icelos, or the Likely; Phantasus, the Fancy; and Phobetor, the Terror. His dwelling some writers place in a dull and darkling part of the earth; others, with greater compliment, in heaven; and others, with another kind of propriety, by the sea-shore. There is a good description of it in Ovid[1]; but in these abstracted tasks of poetry the moderns outvie the ancients; and there is nobody who has built his bower for him so finely as Spenser. Archimago, in the first book of the *Faerie Queene* (Canto I. st. 39), sends a little spirit down to Morpheus to fetch him a Dream:

[1] *Metam.* xi. 586.

" He, making speedy way through spersed ayre,
　　And through the world of waters, wide and deepe,
　To Morpheus' house doth hastily repaire.
　　Amid the bowels of the earth full steepe
　　And low, where dawning day doth never peepe,
　His dwelling is.　There Tethys his wet bed
　　Doth ever wash; and Cynthia still doth steepe
　In silver dew his ever-drouping head,
　Whiles sad Night over him her mantle black doth spred.

" And more to lull him in his slumber soft
　　A trickling streame from high rocke tumbling downe,
　And ever-drizzling rain upon the loft,
　　Mixed with a murmuring winde, much like the soune
　　Of swarming bees, did cast him in a swoune.
　No other noise, nor people's troublous cryes,
　　As still are wont to annoy the walled towne,
　Might there be heard; but careless Quiet lyes,
　Wrapt in eternall silence, far from enimyes."

Chaucer[1] has drawn the cave of the same god with
greater simplicity; but nothing can have a more deep and
sullen effect than his cliffs and cold running waters.　It
seems as real as an actual solitude, or some quaint old
picture in a book of travels in Tartary.　He is telling
the story of Ceyx and Alcyone in the poem called his
Dream.　Juno tells a messenger to go to Morpheus and
" bid him creep into the body " of the drowned king, to
let his wife know the fatal event by his apparition.

　　　　" This messenger tooke leave, and went
　　　　　Upon his way; and never he stent
　　　　　Till he came to the dark valley,
　　　　　That stant betweene rockes twey.
　　　　　There never yet grew corne, ne gras.
　　　　　Ne tree, ne nought, that aught was.
　　　　　Beast, ne man, ne naught else;
　　　　　Save that there were a few wells
　　　　　Came running fro the cliffs adowne,
　　　　　That made a deadly sleeping soune,
　　　　　And runnen downe right by a cave,
　　　　　That was under a rocky grave,

　　　　　[1] *Book of the Duchess,* 153 *et seq.*

Amid the valley, wonder-deepe.
There these goddis lay asleepe,
Morpheus and Eclympasteire,
That was the god of Sleepis heire,
That slept and did none other worke."

Where the credentials of this new son and heir, Eclympasteire[1], are to be found, we know not; but he acts very
much, it must be allowed, like an heir-presumptive, in
sleeping and doing "none other work".

We dare not trust ourselves with many quotations upon
sleep from the poets; they are so numerous as well as beautiful. We must content ourselves with mentioning that
our two most favourite passages are one in the *Philoctetes*[2]
of Sophocles, admirable for its contrast to a scene of
terrible agony, which it closes; and the other the following address in Beaumont and Fletcher's tragedy of
Valentinian[3], the hero of which is also a sufferer under
bodily torment. He is in a chair, slumbering; and these
most exquisite lines are gently sung with music:

"Care-charming Sleep, thou easer of all woes,
Brother to Death, sweetly thyself dispose
On this afflicted prince. Fall like a cloud
In gentle showers: give nothing that is loud
Or painful to his slumbers: easy, sweet,
And as a purling stream, thou son of Night,
Pass by his troubled senses; sing his pain
Like hollow murmuring wind, or silver rain:
Into this prince, gently, oh gently slide,
And kiss him into slumbers, like a bride."

How earnest and prayer-like are these pauses! How
lightly sprinkled, and yet how deeply settling, like rain,
the fancy! How quiet, affectionate, and perfect the
conclusion!

[1] The derivation is disputed. The name, according to Ten Brink, is
of Chaucer's own invention. Prof. Skeat derives it from *Icelon plastero*
(acc. of πλαϲτήϲ),—the semblance moulder.
[2] Lines 827 *seqq*.   [3] Act v. Sc. ii.

Sleep is most graceful in an infant, soundest in one who has been tired in the open air, completest to the seaman after a hard voyage, most welcome to the mind haunted with one idea, most touching to look at in the parent that has wept, lightest in the playful child, proudest in the bride adored.

XLI. DEATHS OF LITTLE CHILDREN.

A GRECIAN philosopher being asked why he wept for the death of his son, since the sorrow was in vain, replied, "I weep on that account". And his answer became his wisdom. It is only for sophists to contend that we, whose eyes contain the fountains of tears, need never give way to them. It would be unwise not to do so on some occasions. Sorrow unlocks them in her balmy moods. The first bursts may be bitter and overwhelming; but the soil on which they pour would be worse without them. They refresh the fever of the soul—the dry misery which parches the countenance into furrows, and renders us liable to our most terrible "flesh-quakes".

There are sorrows, it is true, so great, that to give them some of the ordinary vents is to run a hazard of being overthrown. These we must rather strengthen ourselves to resist, or bow quietly and drily down, in order to let them pass over us, as the traveller does the wind of the desert. But where we feel that tears would relieve us, it is false philosophy to deny ourselves at least that first refreshment; and it is always false consolation to tell people that because they cannot help a thing, they are not to mind it. The true way is, to let them grapple with the unavoidable sorrow, and try to win it into gentleness by a reasonable yielding. There are griefs so gentle in their very nature that it would be worse than false heroism to refuse them a tear. Of this kind are the deaths of infants. Particular circumstances may render it more or less advisable to indulge in grief for the loss of a little child; but, in general, parents should be no more advised to repress their first tears on such an occasion, than to repress their smiles towards a child surviving, or to indulge in any other sympathy. It is an appeal to the same gentle tenderness; and such appeals are never made in vain. The end of them is an acquittal from the harsher bonds of affliction—from the tying down of the spirit to one melancholy idea.

It is the nature of tears of this kind, however strongly they may gush forth, to run into quiet waters at last. We cannot easily, for the whole course of our lives, think with pain of any good and kind person whom we have lost. It is the divine nature of their qualities to conquer pain and death itself; to turn the memory of them into pleasure; to survive with a placid aspect in our imaginations. We are writing at this moment just opposite a spot which contains the grave of one [1] inexpressibly dear to us. We see from our windows the trees about it, and the church spire. The green fields lie around. The clouds are travelling overhead, alternately taking away the sunshine and restoring it. The vernal winds, piping of the flowery summer-time, are nevertheless calling to mind the far-distant and dangerous ocean, which the heart that lies in that grave had many reasons to think of. And yet the sight of this spot does not give us pain. So far from it, it is the existence of that grave which doubles every charm of the spot; which links the pleasures of our childhood and manhood together; which puts a hushing tenderness in the winds and a patient joy upon the landscape which seems to unite heaven and earth, mortality and immortality, the grass of the tomb and the grass of the green field; and gives a more maternal aspect to the whole kindness of Nature. It does not hinder gaiety itself

[1] The grave of the essayist's mother, at Hampstead.

Happiness was what its tenant, through all her troubles, would have diffused. To diffuse happiness, and to enjoy it, is not only carrying on her wishes, but realizing her hopes; and gaiety, freed from its only pollutions, malignity and want of sympathy, is but a child playing about the knees of its mother.

The remembered innocence and endearments of a child stand us instead of virtues that have died older. Children have not exercised the voluntary offices of friendship; they have not chosen to be kind and good to us; nor stood by us, from conscious will, in the hour of adversity. But they have shared their pleasures and pains with us as well as they could; the interchange of good offices between us has, of necessity, been less mingled with the troubles of the world; the sorrow arising from their death is the only one which we can associate with their memories. These are happy thoughts that cannot die. Our loss may always render them pensive; but they will not always be painful. It is a part of the benignity of Nature that pain does not survive like pleasure, at any time, much less where the cause of it is an innocent one. The smile will remain reflected by memory, as the moon reflects the light upon us when the sun has gone into heaven.

When writers like ourselves quarrel with earthly pain (we mean writers of the same intentions, without implying, of course, anything about abilities or otherwise), they are misunderstood if they are supposed to quarrel with pains of every sort. This would be idle and effeminate. They do not pretend, indeed, that humanity might not wish, if it could, to be entirely free from pain; for it endeavours, at all times, to turn pain into pleasure; or at least to set off the one with the other, to make the former a zest and the latter a refreshment. The most unaffected dignity of suffering does this, and, if wise, acknowledges it. The greatest benevolence towards others, the most unselfish relish of their pleasures, even at its own expense, does but look to increasing the general stock of happiness, though content, if it could, to have its identity swallowed up in that splendid contemplation. We are far from meaning that this is to be called selfishness. We are far, indeed, from thinking so, or of so confounding words. But neither is it to be called pain when most unselfish, if disinterestedness be truly understood. The pain that is in it softens into pleasure, as the darker hue of the rainbow melts into the brighter. Yet even if a harsher line is to be drawn between the pain and pleasure of the most unselfish mind (and ill-health, for instance, may draw it), we should not quarrel with it if it contributes to the general mass of comfort, and were of a nature which general kindliness could not avoid. Made as we are, there are certain pains without which it would be difficult to conceive certain great and overbalancing pleasures. We may conceive it possible for beings to be made entirely happy; but in our composition something of pain seems to be a necessary ingredient, in order that the materials may turn to as fine account as possible, though our clay, in the course of ages and experience, may be refined more and more. We may get rid of the worst earth, though not of earth itself.

Now, the liability to the loss of children—or rather what renders us sensible of it, the occasional loss itself —seems to be one of these necessary bitters thrown into the cup of humanity. We do not mean that every one must lose one of his children in order to enjoy the rest, or that every individual loss afflicts us in the same proportion. We allude to the deaths of infants in general. These might be as few as we could render them. But if none at all ever took place, we should regard every little child as a man or a woman secured; and it will easily be conceived what a world of endearing cares and hopes this security would endanger. The very idea of infancy would lose its continuity with us. Girls and boys would be future men and women, not present children. They would have attained their full growth in our imaginations, and might as well have been men and women at once. On the other hand, those who have lost an infant, are never, as it were, without an infant child. They are the only persons who, in one sense, retain it always, and they furnish their neighbours with the same idea. The other children grow up to manhood and womanhood, and suffer all the changes of mortality. This one alone is rendered an immortal child. Death has arrested it with his kindly harshness, and blessed it into an eternal image of youth and innocence.

Of such as these are the pleasantest shapes that visit our fancy and our hopes. They are the ever-smiling emblems of joy, the prettiest pages that wait upon imagination. Lastly, "Of these is the kingdom of heaven" Wherever there is a province of that benevolent and all-accessible empire, whether on earth or elsewhere, such are the gentle spirits that must inhabit it. To such simplicity, or the resemblance of it, must they come. Such must be the ready confidence of their hearts and creativeness of their fancy. And so ignorant must they be of the "knowledge of good and evil", losing their discernment of that self-created trouble, by enjoying the garden before them, and not being ashamed of what is kindly and innocent.

WILLIAM HAZLITT.

(1778-1830.)

XLII. ON GOING A JOURNEY.

ONE of the pleasantest things in the world is going a journey; but I like to go by myself. I can enjoy society in a room; but out of doors, nature is company enough for me. I am then never less alone than when alone.

> "The fields his study, nature was his book."

I cannot see the wit of walking and talking at the same time. When I am in the country, I wish to vegetate like the country. I am not for criticising hedgerows and black cattle. I go out of town in order to forget the town and all that is in it. There are those who for this purpose go to watering-places, and carry the metropolis with them. I like more elbow-room, and fewer incumbrances. I like solitude, when I give myself up to it, for the sake of solitude; nor do I ask for

> "a friend in my retreat,
> Whom I may whisper, solitude is sweet".

The soul of a journey is liberty, perfect liberty—to think, feel, do, just as one pleases. We go a journey chiefly to be free of all impediments and of all inconveniences; to leave ourselves behind; much more to get rid of others. It is because I want a little breathing-space to muse on indifferent matters, where Contemplation

> "May plume her feathers and let grow her wings,
> That in the various bustle of resort
> Were all too ruffled, and sometimes impair'd",

that I absent myself from the town for a while, without feeling at a loss the moment I am left by myself. Instead of a friend in a post-chaise or in a Tilbury, to exchange good things with and vary the same stale topics over again, for once let me have a truce with impertinence. Give me the clear blue sky over my head, and the green turf beneath my feet, a winding road before me, and a three hours' march to dinner—and then to thinking! It is hard if I cannot start some game on these lone heaths. I laugh, I run, I leap, I sing for joy. From the point of yonder rolling cloud I plunge into my past being, and revel there, as the sunburnt Indian plunges headlong into the wave that wafts him to his native shore. Then long-forgotten things, like "sunken wrack and sumless treasuries", burst upon my eager sight, and I begin to feel, think, and be myself again. Instead of an awkward silence, broken by attempts at wit or dull commonplaces, mine is that undisturbed silence of the heart which alone is perfect eloquence. No one likes puns, alliterations, antitheses, argument, and analysis better than I do; but I sometimes had rather be without them. "Leave, oh, leave me to my repose!" I have just now other business in hand which would seem idle to you, but is with me "very stuff o' the conscience". Is not this wild rose sweet without a comment? Does not this daisy leap to my heart set in its coat of emerald? Yet if I were to explain to you the circumstance that has so endeared it to me, you would only smile. Had I not better then keep it to myself, and let it serve me to brood over from here to yonder craggy point, and from thence onward to the far-distant horizon? I should be but bad company all that way, and therefore prefer being alone. I have heard it said that you may, when the moody fit comes on, walk or ride on by yourself and indulge your reveries. But this looks like a breach of manners, a neglect of others, and you are thinking all the time that you ought to rejoin your party. "Out upon such half-faced fellowship", say I. I like to be either entirely to myself, or entirely at the disposal of others; to talk or be silent, to walk or sit still, to be sociable or solitary. I was pleased with an observation of Mr. Cobbett's, that "he thought it a bad French custom to drink our wine with our meals, and that an Englishman ought to do only one thing at a time". So I cannot talk and think, or indulge in melancholy musing and lively conversation by fits and starts. "Let me have

a companion of my way," says Sterne, "were it but to
remark how the shadows lengthen as the sun declines."
It is beautifully said; but, in my opinion, this continual
comparing of notes interferes with the involuntary impression of things upon the mind, and hurts the sentiment.
If you only hint what you feel in a kind of dumb show,
it is insipid; if you have to explain it, it is making a toil
of a pleasure. You cannot read the book of nature
without being perpetually put to the trouble of trans-
lating it for the benefit of others. I am for this syn-
thetical method on a journey in preference to the
analytical. I am content to lay in a stock of ideas then,
and to examine and anatomize them afterwards. I want
to see my vague notions float like the down of the thistle
before the breeze, and not to have them entangled in the
briars and thorns of controversy. For once, I like to
have it all my own way; and this is impossible unless
you are alone, or in such company as I do not covet.
I have no objection to argue a point with anyone for
twenty miles of measured road, but not for pleasure.
If you remark the scent of a bean-field crossing the road,
perhaps your fellow-traveller has no smell. If you point
to a distant object, perhaps he is short-sighted, and has
to take out his glass to look at it. There is a feeling in
the air, a tone in the colour of a cloud which hits your
fancy, but the effect of which you are unable to account
for. There is, then, no sympathy, but an uneasy craving
after it, and a dissatisfaction which pursues you on the
way, and in the end probably produces ill-humour. Now,
I never quarrel with myself, and take all my own conclusions for granted till I find it necessary to defend
them against objections. It is not merely that you may
not be of accord on the objects and circumstances that
present themselves before you—these may recall a number
of objects, and lead to associations too delicate and

refined to be possibly communicated to others. Yet
these I love to cherish, and sometimes still fondly clutch
them, when I can escape from the throng to do so. To
give way to our feelings before company seems extravagance or affectation; and, on the other hand, to have
to unravel this mystery of our being at every turn, and
to make others take an equal interest in it (otherwise the
end is not answered), is a task to which few are competent.
We must "give it an understanding, but no tongue".
My old friend, Coleridge, however, could do both. He
could go on in the most delightful explanatory way over
hill and dale a summer's day, and convert a landscape
into a didactic poem or a Pindaric ode. "He talked far
above singing." If I could so clothe my ideas in sounding and flowing words, I might perhaps wish to have
someone with me to admire the swelling theme; or I
could be more content, were it possible for me still to hear
his echoing voice in the woods of All-Foxden. They had
"that fine madness in them which our first poets had";
and if they could have been caught by some rare instrument, would have breathed such strains as the following:—

> "Here be woods as green
> As any, air likewise as fresh and sweet
> As when smooth Zephyrus plays on the fleet
> Face of the curled stream, with flow'rs as many
> As the young spring gives, and as choice as any;
> Here be all new delights, cool streams and wells;
> Arbours o'ergrown with woodbines, caves and dells.
> Choose where thou wilt, whilst I sit by and sing,
> Or gather rushes, to make many a ring
> For thy long fingers; tell thee tales of love;
> How the pale Phoebe, hunting in a grove,
> First saw the boy Endymion, from whose eyes
> She took eternal fire that never dies;
> How she conveyed him softly in a sleep,
> His temples bound with poppy, to the steep
> Head of old Latmos, where she stoops each night,
> Gilding the mountain with her brother's light,
> To kiss her sweetest."

Had I words and images at command like these, I would attempt to wake the thoughts that lie slumbering on golden ridges in the evening clouds; but at the sight of nature my fancy, poor as it is, droops and closes up its leaves, like flowers at sunset. I can make nothing out on the spot—I must have time to collect myself.

In general, a good thing spoils out-of-door prospects: it should be reserved for table-talk. Lamb is for this reason, I take it, the worst company in the world out of doors, because he is the best within. I grant there is one subject on which it is pleasant to talk on a journey; and that is, what one shall have for supper when we get to our inn at night. The open air improves this sort of conversation or friendly altercation, by setting a keener edge on appetite. Every mile of the road heightens the flavour of the viands we expect at the end of it. How fine it is to enter some old town, walled and turreted, just at the approach of nightfall, or to come to some straggling village, with the lights streaming through the surrounding gloom, and then, after inquiring for the best entertainment that the place affords, to "take one's ease at one's inn"! These eventful moments in our lives' history are too precious, too full of solid, heartfelt happiness to be frittered and dribbled away in imperfect sympathy. I would have them all to myself, and drain them to the last drop: they will do to talk of or to write about afterwards. What a delicate speculation it is, after drinking whole goblets of tea,

> "The cups that cheer, but not inebriate",

and letting the fumes ascend into the brain, to sit considering what we shall have for supper—eggs and a rasher, a rabbit smothered in onions, or an excellent veal cutlet! Sancho in such a situation once fixed on cow-heel; and his choice, though he could not help it, is not to be disparaged. Then, in the intervals of pictured scenery and Shandean contemplation, to catch the preparation and the stir in the kitchen. *Procul, O procul este profani!* ("Avaunt! avaunt! ye unhallowed.") These hours are sacred to silence and to musing, to be treasured up in the memory, and to feed the course of smiling thoughts hereafter. I would not waste them in idle talk; or if I must have the integrity of fancy broken in upon, I would rather it were by a stranger than a friend. A stranger takes his hue and character from the time and place; he is a part of the furniture and costume of an inn. If he is a Quaker, or from the West Riding of Yorkshire, so much the better. I do not even try to sympathize with him, and he breaks no squares. I associate nothing with my travelling companion but present objects and passing events. In his ignorance of me and my affairs, I in a manner forget myself. But a friend reminds one of other things, rips up old grievances, and destroys the abstraction of the scene. He comes in graciously between us and our imaginary character. Something is dropped in the course of conversation that gives a hint of your profession and pursuits; or from having someone with you that knows the less sublime portions of your history, it seems that other people do. You are no longer a citizen of the world; but your "unhoused free condition is put into circumspection and confine". The *incognito* of an inn is one of its striking privileges—"lord of one's self, un-cumbered with a name". Oh! it is great to shake off the trammels of the world and of public opinion—to lose our importunate, tormenting, everlasting personal identity in the elements of nature, and become the creature of the moment, clear of all ties—to hold to the universe only by a dish of sweetbreads, and to owe nothing but the score of the evening—and no longer seeking for applause and meeting with contempt, to be known by no other title

than *the Gentleman in the parlour*! One may take one's
choice of all characters in this romantic state of uncertainty as to one's real pretensions, and become indefinitely
respectable and negatively right-worshipful. We baffle
prejudice and disappoint conjecture; and from being so
to others, begin to be objects of curiosity and wonder
even to ourselves. We are no more those hackneyed
commonplaces that we appear in the world; an inn re-
stores us to the level of nature, and quits scores with society!
I have certainly spent some enviable hours at inns—sometimes when I have been left entirely to myself, and have
tried to solve some metaphysical problem, as once at
Witham Common, where I found out the proof that likeness is not a case of the association of ideas—at other
times, when there have been pictures in the room, as at
St. Neot's (I think it was), where I first met with Gribelin's
engravings of the Cartoons, into which I entered at once,
and at a little inn on the borders of Wales, where there
happened to be hanging some of Westall's drawings,
which I compared triumphantly (for a theory that I had,
not for the admired artist) with the figure of a girl who
had ferried me over the Severn, standing up in a boat
between me and the twilight—at other times I might
mention luxuriating in books, with a peculiar interest in
this way, as I remember sitting up half the night to read
Paul and Virginia, which I picked up at an inn at
Bridgewater, after being drenched in the rain all day; and
at the same place I got through two volumes of Madame
D'Arblay's *Camilla*. It was on the 10th of April, 1798,
that I sat down to a volume of the *New Eloise*, at the inn
at Llangollen, over a bottle of sherry and a cold chicken.
The letter I chose was that in which St. Preux describes
his feelings as he first caught a glimpse from the heights
of the Jura of the Pays de Vaud, which I had brought
with me as a *bon bouche* to crown the evening with. It

was my birthday, and I had for the first time come from a place in the neighbourhood to visit this delightful spot. The road to Llangollen turns off between Chirk and Wrexham, and on passing a certain point, you come all at once upon the valley, which opens like an amphitheatre, broad, barren hills rising in majestic state on either side, with "green upland swells that echo to the bleat of flocks" below, and the river Dee babbling over its stony bed in the midst of them. The valley at this time "glittered green with sunny showers", and a budding ash-tree dipped its tender branches in the chiding stream. How proud, how glad I was to walk along the highroad that overlooks the delicious prospect, repeating the lines which I have just quoted[1] from Mr. Coleridge's poem! But besides the prospect which opened beneath my feet, another also opened to my inward sight, a heavenly vision, on which were written, in letters large as Hope could make them, these four words, LIBERTY, GENIUS, LOVE, VIRTUE; which have since faded into the light of common day, or mock my idle gaze.

"The beautiful is vanished, and returns not."

Still I would return some time or other to this enchanted spot; but I would return to it alone. What other self could I find to share that influx of thoughts, of regret, and delight, the fragments of which I could hardly conjure up to myself, so much have they been broken and defaced. I could stand on some tall rock, and overlook the precipice of years that separates me from what I then was. I was at that time going shortly to visit the poet whom I have above named. Where is he now? Not only I myself have changed; the world, which was then new to me, has become old and incorrigible. Yet will I turn

---

[1] *Ode to the Departing Year*, stanza vii.

to thee in thought, O sylvan Dee, in joy, in youth and gladness as thou then wert; and thou shalt always be to me the river of Paradise, where I will drink of the waters of life freely !

There is hardly anything that shows the short-sighted-ness or capriciousness of the imagination more than travelling does. With change of place we change our ideas; nay, our opinions and feelings. We can by an effort indeed transport ourselves to old and long-forgotten scenes, and then the picture of the mind revives again; but we forget those that we have just left. It seems that we can think but of one place at a time. The canvas of the fancy is but of a certain extent, and if we paint one set of objects upon it, they immediately efface every other. We cannot enlarge our conceptions, we only shift our point of view. The landscape bares its bosom to the enraptured eye, we take our fill of it, and seem as if we could form no other image of beauty or grandeur. We pass on, and think no more of it; the horizon that shuts it from our sight also blots it from our memory like a dream. In travelling through a wild, barren country, I can form no idea of a woody and cultivated one. It appears to me that all the world must be barren, like what I see of it. In the country we forget the town, and in town we despise the country. "Beyond Hyde Park," says Sir Fopling Flutter[1], "all is a desert." All that part of the map that we do not see before us is blank. The world in our conceit of it is not much bigger than a nutshell. It is not one prospect expanded into another, county joined to county, kingdom to king-dom, land to seas, making an image voluminous and vast; —the mind can form no larger idea of space than the eye can take in at a single glance. The rest is a name written in a map, a calculation of arithmetic. For in-

[1] In Sir George Etherege's *Man of Mode.*

stance, what is the true signification of that immense
mass of territory and population, known by the name of
China, to us? An inch of pasteboard on a wooden globe,
of no more account than a China orange! Things near
us are seen of the size of life: things at a distance are
diminished to the size of the understanding. We measure
the universe by ourselves, and even comprehend the
texture of our own being only piecemeal. In this way,
however, we remember an infinity of things and places.
The mind is like a mechanical instrument that plays a
great variety of tunes, but it must play them in succession.
One idea recalls another, but it at the same time excludes
all others. In trying to renew old recollections, we
cannot, as it were, unfold the whole web of our existence,
we must pick out the single threads. So in coming to a
place where we have formerly lived, and with which we
have intimate associations, everyone must have found
that the feeling grows more vivid the nearer we approach
the spot, from the mere anticipation of the actual impression: we remember circumstances, feelings, persons,
faces, names that we had not thought of for years; but
for the time all the rest of the world is forgotten! To
return to the question I have quitted above.

I have no objections to go to see ruins, aqueducts,
pictures, in company with a friend or party, but rather
the contrary, for the former reason reversed. They are
intelligible matters, and will bear talking about. The
sentiment here is not tacit, but communicable and overt.
Salisbury Plain is barren of criticism, but Stonehenge
will bear a discussion antiquarian, picturesque, and philosophical. In setting out on a party of pleasure, the first
consideration always is where we shall go to: in taking a
solitary ramble, the question is what we shall meet with
by the way. "The mind is its own place"; nor are we
anxious to arrive at the end of our journey. I can

myself do the honours indifferently well to works of art and curiosity. I once took a party to Oxford with no mean *éclat*—showed them that seat of the Muses at a distance,

" With glistering spires and pinnacles adorn'd "—

descanted on the learned air that breathes from the grassy quadrangles and stone walls of halls and colleges —was at home in the Bodleian; and at Blenheim quite superseded the powdered cicerone that attended us, and that pointed in vain with his wand to commonplace beauties in matchless pictures. As another exception to the above reasoning, I should not feel confident in venturing on a journey in a foreign country without a companion. I should want at intervals to hear the sound of my own language. There is an involuntary antipathy in the mind of an Englishman to foreign manners and notions that requires the assistance of social sympathy to carry it off. As the distance from home increases, this relief, which was at first a luxury, becomes a passion and an appetite. A person would almost feel stifled to find himself in the deserts of Arabia without friends and countrymen; there must be allowed to be something in the view of Athens or old Rome that claims the utterance of speech; and I own that the pyramids are too mighty for any single contemplation. In such situations, so opposite to all one's ordinary train of ideas, one seems a species of one's self, a limb torn off from society, unless one can meet with instant fellowship and support. Yet I did not feel this want or craving very pressing once, when I first set my foot on the laughing shores of France. Calais was peopled with novelty and delight. The confused, busy murmur of the place was like oil and wine poured into my ears; nor did the Mariners' Hymn, which was sung from the top of an old crazy vessel in

the harbour, as the sun went down, send an alien sound
into my soul. I only breathed the air of general humanity. I walked over "the vine-covered hills and gay
regions of France", erect and satisfied; for the image of
man was not cast down and chained to the foot of arbitrary thrones: I was at no loss for language, for that of
all the great schools of painting was open to me. The
whole is vanished like a shade. Pictures, heroes, glory,
freedom, all are fled: nothing remains but the Bourbons
and the French people! There is undoubtedly a sensation in travelling into foreign parts that is to be had
nowhere else; but it is more pleasing at the time than
lasting. It is too remote from our habitual associations
to be a common topic of discourse or reference, and, like
a dream or another state or existence, does not piece
into our daily modes of life. It is an animated but a
momentary hallucination. It demands an effort to exchange our actual for our ideal identity; and to feel the
pulse of our old transports revive very keenly, we must
"jump" all our present comforts and connections. Our
romantic and itinerant character is not to be domesticated.
Dr. Johnson remarked how little foreign travel added to
the facilities of conversation in those who had been abroad.
In fact, the time we have spent there is both delightful,
and, in one sense, instructive; but it appears to be cut
out of our substantial, downright existence, and never to
join kindly on to it. We are not the same, but another,
and perhaps more enviable individual, all the time we are
out of our own country. We are lost to ourselves, as
well as our friends. So the poet somewhat quaintly
sings,

"Out of my country and myself I go".

Those who wish to forget painful thoughts, do well to
absent themselves for a while from the ties and objects

that recall them; but we can be said only to fulfil our
destiny in the place that gave us birth. I should on this
account like well enough to spend the whole of my life
in travelling abroad, if I could anywhere borrow another
life to spend afterwards at home!

XLIII. THE SICK CHAMBER.

FROM the crowded theatre to the sick chamber, from
the noise, the glare, the keen delight, to the loneli-
ness, the darkness, the dulness, and the pain, there is but
one step. A breath of air, an overhanging cloud, effects
it; and though the transition is made in an instant, it
seems as if it would last for ever. A sudden illness not
only puts a stop to the career of our triumphs and agreeable sensations, but blots out all recollection of and
desire for them. We lose the relish of enjoyment; we
are effectually cured of our romance. Our bodies are
confined to our beds; nor can our thoughts wantonly
detach themselves and take the road to pleasure, but
turn back with doubt and loathing at the faint evanescent
phantom which has usurped its place. If the folding-
doors of the imagination were thrown open or left ajar, so
that from the disordered couch where we lay, we could
still hail the vista of the past or future, and see the gay
and gorgeous visions floating at a distance, however
denied to our embrace, the contrast, though mortifying,
might have something soothing in it, the mock-splendour
might be the greater for the actual gloom; but the misery
is that we cannot conceive anything beyond or better
than the present evil: we are shut-up and spell-bound in
that, the curtains of the mind are drawn close, we cannot
escape from "the body of this death", our souls are
conquered, dismayed, "cooped and cabined in", and

thrown with the lumber of our corporeal frames in one
corner of a neglected and solitary room. We hate ourselves and everything else; nor does one ray of comfort
"peep through the blanket of the dark" to give us hope.
How should we entertain the image of grace and beauty
when our bodies writhe with pain? To what purpose
invoke the echo of some rich strain of music, when we
ourselves can scarcely breathe? The very attempt is an
impossibility. We give up the vain task of linking delight
to agony, of urging torpor into ecstasy, which makes the
very heart sick. We feel the present pain, and an impatient longing to get rid of it. This were indeed "a consummation devoutly to be wished"; on this we are intent,
in earnest, inexorable, all else is impertinence and folly;
and could we but obtain Ease (that goddess of the infirm
and suffering) at any price, we think we could forswear all
other joys and all other sorrow. *Hoc erat in votis.* All
other things but our disorder and its cure seem less than
nothing and vanity. It assumes a palpable form; it
becomes a demon, a spectre, an incubus hovering over
and oppressing us: we grapple with it; it strikes its fangs
into us, spreads its arms around us, infects us with its
breath, glares upon us with its hideous aspect; we feel it
take possession of every fibre and of every faculty; and
we are at length so absorbed and fascinated by it, that we
cannot divert our reflections from it an instant, for all
other things but pain (and that which we suffer most
acutely) appear to have lost their pith and power to
interest. They are turned to dust and stubble. This is
the reason of the fine resolutions we sometimes form in
such cases, and of the vast superiority of the sick-bed to
the pomps and thrones of the world. We easily renounce
wine when we have nothing but the taste of physic in our
mouths; the rich banquet tempts us not, when " our very
gorge rises " within us. Love and Beauty fly from a bed

twisted into a thousand folds by restless lassitude and tormenting cares, the nerve of pleasure is killed by the pains that shoot through the head or rack the limbs; and indigestion seizes you with its leaden grasp and giant force (down, Ambition!)—you shiver and tremble like a leaf in a fit of the ague. (Avarice, let go your palsied hold!) We then are in mood, without ghostly advice, to betake ourselves to the life of the "hermit poor",

"In pensive place obscure",

and should be glad to prevent the return of a fever raging in the blood by feeding on pulse, and slaking our thirst at the limpid brook. The sudden resolutions, however, or "vows made in pain as violent and void", are generally of short duration: the excess and the sorrow for it are alike selfish; and those repentances which are the most loud and passionate are the surest to end speedily in a relapse; for both originate in the same cause, the being engrossed by the prevailing feeling (whatever it may be), and an utter incapacity to look beyond it.

"The Devil was sick, the Devil a monk would be:
The Devil grew well, the Devil a monk was he!"[1]

It is amazing how little effect physical suffering or local circumstances have upon the mind, except while we are subject to their immediate influence. While the impression lasts they are everything, when it is gone they are nothing. We toss and tumble about in a sick-bed; we lie on our right side, we then change to the left; we stretch ourselves on our backs, we turn on our faces; we wrap ourselves under the clothes to exclude the cold, we throw them off to escape the heat and suffocation; we grasp the pillow in agony, we fling ourselves out of bed, we walk up and down the room with hasty or feeble

[1] Rabelais, Bk. iv. cap. 24.

steps; we return to bed; we are worn out with fatigue
and pain, yet can get no repose for the one nor inter-
mission for the other; we summon all our patience, or
give vent to passion and petty rage; nothing avails; we
seem wedded to our disease, "like life and death in disproportion met"; we make new efforts, try new expedients,
but nothing appears to shake it off, or promise relief from
our grim foe: it infixes its sharp sting into us, or over-
powers us by its sickly and stunning weight; every
moment is as much as we can bear, and yet there seems
no end of our lengthening tortures; we are ready to faint
with exhaustion or work ourselves up to a frenzy: we
"trouble deaf Heaven with our bootless prayers"; we
think our last hour has come, or peevishly wish it were,
to put an end to the scene; we ask questions as to the
origin of evil, and the necessity of pain; we "moralize
our complaints into a thousand similes"; we deny the
use of medicine *in toto*, we have a full persuasion that all
doctors are mad or knaves, that our object is to gain
relief, and theirs (out of the perversity of human nature,
or to seem wiser than we) to prevent it; we catechize the
apothecary, rail at the nurse, and cannot so much as conceive the possibility that this state of things should not
last for ever; we are even angry at those who would give
us encouragement as if they would make dupes or children of us; we might seek a release by poison, a halter,
or the sword, but we have not strength of mind enough—
our nerves are too shaken to attempt even this poor
revenge—when lo! a change comes, the spell falls off,
and the next moment we forget all that has happened to
us. No sooner does our disorder turn its back upon us
than we laugh at it. The state we have been in sounds
like a dream—a fable; health is the order of the day,
strength is ours *de jure* and *de facto*; and we discard all
uncalled-for evidence to the contrary with a smile of con-

temptuous incredulity, just as we throw our physic-bottles
out of the window. I see (as I awake from a short uneasy
doze) a golden light shine through the white window
curtains on the opposite wall—is it the dawn of a new day
or the departing light of evening? I do not well know,
for the opium "they have drugged my posset with " has
made strong havoc with my brain, and I am uncertain
whether time has stood still, or advanced, or gone backward. By "puzzling o'er the doubt" my attention is
drawn a little out of myself to external objects; and I
consider whether it would not administer some relief to
my monotonous languor if I call up a vivid picture of an
evening sky I witnessed a short time before—the white,
fleecy clouds, the azure vault, the verdant fields, and
balmy air! In vain! The wings of fancy refuse to
mount from my bedside. The air without has nothing
in common with the closeness within; the clouds disap-
pear, the sky is instantly overcast and black. I walk out
in this scene soon after I recover; and with those favourite
and well-known objects interposed, can no longer recall
the tumbled pillow, the juleps, or the labels, or the wholesome dungeon in which I was before immured. What is
contrary to our present sensations or settled habits amal-
gamates indifferently with our belief; the imagination
rules over the imaginary themes; the senses and customs
have a narrow sway, and admit but one guest at a time.
It is hardly to be wondered at that we dread physical
calamities so little beforehand; we think no more of
them after they have happened. Out of sight, out of
mind. This will perhaps explain why all actual punishment has so little effect; it is a state contrary to nature,
alien to the will. If it does not touch honour and conscience (and where these are not how can it touch them?)
it goes for nothing; and where these are, it rather sears
and hardens them. The gyves, the cell, the meagre fare,

the hard labour, are abhorrent to the mind of the culprit
on whom they are imposed, who carries the love of liberty
or indulgence to licentiousness, and who throws the
thought of them behind him (the moment he can evade
the penalty) with scorn and laughter,

"Like Samson his green wythes".

So, in travelling, we often meet with great fatigue and in-
convenience from heat or cold, or other accident, and
resolve never to go a journey again; but we are ready to
set off on a new excursion to-morrow. We remember
the landscape, the change of scene, the romantic expectation, and think no more of the heat, the noise, and the
dust. The body forgets its grievances till they recur; but
imagination, passion, pride, have a longer memory and
quicker apprehensions. To the first, the pleasure or pain
is nothing when once over; to the last, it is only then that
they begin to exist. The line in Metastasio,

"The worst of every evil is the fear",

is true only when applied to the latter sort. It is curious
that, on coming out of a sick-room, where one has been
pent up some time, and grown weak and nervous, and
looking at nature for the first time, the objects that present themselves have a very questionable and spectral
appearance; the people in the street resemble flies crawl-
ing about, and seem scarce half alive. It is we who are
just risen from a torpid and unwholesome state, and who
impart our imperfect feelings of existence, health, and
motion to others. Or it may be that the violence and
exertion of the pain we have gone through make common
everyday objects seem unreal and unsubstantial. It is
not till we have established ourselves in form in the
sitting-room, wheeled round the arm-chair to the fire (for
this makes part of our re-introduction to the ordinary

modes of being in all seasons), felt our appetite return, and taken up a book, that we can be considered as at all returned to ourselves. And even then our sensations are rather empirical than positive, as after sleep we stretch out our hands to know whether we are awake. This is the time for reading. Books are then indeed "a world both pure and good", into which we enter with all our hearts, after our revival from illness and respite from the tomb, as with the freshness and novelty of youth. They are not merely acceptable as without too much exertion they pass the time and relieve *ennui*, but from a certain suspension and deadening of the passions, and abstraction of worldly pursuits, they may be said to bring back and be friendly to the guileless and enthusiastic tone of feeling with which we formerly read them. Sickness has weaned us *pro tempore* from contest and cabal; and we are fain to be docile and children again. All strong changes in our present pursuits throw us back upon the past. This is the shortest and most complete emancipation from our late discomfiture. We wonder that anyone who has read the *History of a Foundling*[1] should labour under an indigestion, nor do we comprehend how a perusal of the *Fairy Queen* should not ensure the true believer an uninterrupted succession of halcyon days. Present objects bear a retrospective meaning, and point to "a foregone conclusion". Returning back to life with half-strung nerves and shattered strength, we seem as when we first entered it with uncertain purposes and faltering aims. The machine has received a shock, and it moves on more tremulously than before, and not all at once, in the beaten track. Startled at the approach of death, we are willing to get as far from it as we can by making a proxy of our former selves; and finding the precarious tenure by which we hold existence, and its last sands running out, we

[1] Fielding's *Tom Jones.*

gather up and make the most of the fragments that
memory has stored up for us. Everything is seen through
a medium of reflection and contrast. We hear the sound
of merry voices in the street, and this carries us back to
the recollections of some country town or village group—

> " We see the children sporting on the shore,
>   And hear the mighty waters roaring evermore ".

A cricket chirps on the hearth, and we are reminded of
Christmas gambols long ago. The very cries in the street
seem to be of a former date, and the dry toast eats very
much as it did—twenty years ago. A rose smells doubly
sweet after being stifled with tinctures and essences, and
we enjoy the idea of a journey and an inn the more for
having been bed-rid. But a book is the secret and sure
charm to bring all these implied associations to a focus.
I should prefer an old one, Mr. Lamb's favourite, the
Journey to Lisbon[1], or the Decameron, if I could get it;
but, if a new one, let it be *Paul Clifford*. That book
has the singular advantage of being written by a gentleman, and not about his own class. The characters he
commemorates are every moment at fault between life
and death, hunger and forced loan on the public; and
therefore the interest they take in themselves, and which
we take in them, has no cant or affectation in it, but is
" lively, audible, and full of vent ". A set of well-dressed
gentlemen, picking their teeth with a graceful air after
dinner, and endeavouring to keep their cravats from the
slightest discompose, and saying the most insipid things
in the most insipid manner, do not make a scene. Well,
then, I have got the new paraphrase on the *Beggar's
Opera*, am fairly embarked in it; and at the end of the
first volume, where I am galloping across the heath with
the three highwaymen, while the moon is shining full

[1] Fielding's *Journal of a Voyage to Lisbon.*

upon them, feel my nerves so braced, and my spirits so exhilarated, that, to say truth, I am scarce sorry for the occasion that has thrown me upon the work and the author—have quite forgot my SICK ROOM, and more than ready to recant the doctrine that *Free Admission* [1] to the theatre is

> "The true pathos and sublime
>   Of human life",

for I feel as I read that if the stage shows us the masks of men and the pageant of the world, books let us into their souls and lay open to us the secrets of our own. They are the first and last, the most home-felt, the most heart-felt of all our enjoyments!

CHARLES LAMB.
(1775-1834.)

XLIV. ALL FOOLS' DAY.

THE compliments of the season to my worthy masters, and a merry first of April to us all!

Many happy returns of this day to you—and you and *you*, Sir,—nay, never frown, man, nor put a long face upon the matter. Do not we know one another? what need of ceremony among friends? we have all a touch of *that same*—you understand me—a speck of the motley. Beshrew the man who on such a day as this, the *general festival*, should affect to stand aloof. I am none of those sneakers. I am free of the corporation, and care not who knows it. He that meets me in the forest to-day, shall meet with no wiseacre, I can tell him. *Stultus sum.*

---

[1] The subject of a paper by Hazlitt in *The New Monthly* in the same year as this essay.

Translate me that, and take the meaning of it to yourself
for your pains. What, man! we have four quarters of the
globe on our side, at the least computation.

Fill us a cup of that sparkling gooseberry—we will
drink no wise, melancholy, politic port on this day—and
let us troll the catch of Amiens [1]—*duc ad me—duc ad me*
—how goes it?

> Here shall he see,
> Gross fools as he.

Now would I give a trifle to know, historically and
authentically, who was the greatest fool that ever lived.
I would certainly give him a bumper. Marry, of the
present breed, I think I could without much difficulty
name you the party.

Remove your cap a little further, if you please: it hides
my bauble. And now each man bestride his hobby, and
dust away his bells to what tune he pleases. I will give
you, for my part,

> The crazy old church clock,
> And the bewildered chimes.

Good master Empedocles [2], you are welcome. It is
long since you went a salamander-gathering down Ætna.
Worse than samphire-picking by some odds. 'Tis a mercy
your worship did not singe your mustachios.

Ha, Cleombrotus [3]! and what salads in faith did you
light upon at the bottom of the Mediterranean? You
were founder. I take it, of the disinterested sect of the
Calenturists [4].

Gebir [5], my old freemason, and prince of plasterers at

---

[1] *As You Like It*, ii. 5.

[2] This portion of the essay was apparently suggested by Milton's
account of the Paradise of Fools, *P. L.* iii. 471.

[3] A native of Ambracia, who flung himself into the sea after reading
Plato on Immortality.

[4] Calenture is a tropical fever which sometimes produces in sailors an
hallucination that causes them to leap overboard.

[5] Jabir ibn Haijan, an Arabian alchemist of the eighth century

Babel, bring in your trowel, most Ancient Grand! You have claim to a seat here at my right hand, as patron of the stammerers. You left your work, if I remember Herodotus correctly, at eight hundred million toises[1], or thereabout, above the level of the sea. Bless us, what a long bell-rope you must have pulled, to call your top workmen to their luncheon on the low grounds of Shinar. Or did you send up your garlic and onions by a rocket? I am a rogue if I am not ashamed to show you our Monument on Fish Street Hill, after your altitudes. Yet we think it somewhat.

What, the magnanimous Alexander in tears?—cry, baby, put its finger in its eye, it shall have another globe, round as an orange, pretty moppet!

Mister Adams[2]—'odso, I honour your coat—pray do us the favour to read to us that sermon, which you lent to Mistress Slipslop—the twenty and second in your portmanteau there—on Female Incontinence—the same—it will come in most irrelevantly and impertinently seasonable to the time of day.

Good Master Raymund Lully[3], you look wise. Pray correct that error.

Duns[4], spare your definitions. I must fine you a bumper, or a paradox. We will have nothing said or done syllogistically this day. Remove those logical forms, waiter, that no gentleman break the tender shins of his apprehension stumbling across them.

Landor in his poem *Gebir*, following the example of Clara Reeve's *Progress of Romance*, makes Gebir a character of ancient Egyptian history, and adds the fact that he was punished by heaven for his attempt to build a city. Hence Lamb's association of Gebir with Babel.

[1] A toise=6·395 English feet.

[2] Parson Adams and Mrs. Slipslop are characters in Fielding's *Joseph Andrews*. The former suggested the Vicar of Wakefield.

[3] The "enlightened doctor" (1234–1315), noted for the vanity with which he propounded his fantastic logical doctrines.

[4] Johannes Duns Scotus, Doctor Subtilis (d. 1308), the philosophical opponent of Aquinas.

Master Stephen [1], you are late.—Ha, Cokes, it is you!—
Aguecheek, my dear knight, let me pay my devoir to
you.—Master Shallow, your worship's poor servant to command.—Master Silence, I will use few words with you.—
Slender, it shall go hard if I edge not you in somewhere.
You six will engross all the poor wit of the company
to-day.—I know it, I know it.

Ha! honest R— [2], my fine old Librarian of Ludgate,
time out of mind, art thou here again? Bless thy doublet,
it is not over-new, threadbare as thy stories;—what dost
thou flitting about the world at this rate?—Thy customers
are extinct, defunct, bed-rid, have ceased to read long
ago.—Thou goest still among them, seeing if, peradventure, thou canst hawk a volume or two.—Good Granville
S— [3], thy last patron is flown.

> King Pandion, he is dead,
> All thy friends are lapt in lead [4].

Nevertheless, noble R—, come in, and take your seat
here between Armado [5] and Quisada; for in true courtesy,
in gravity, in fantastic smiling to thyself, in courteous
smiling upon others, in the goodly ornature of well-
apparelled speech, and the commendation of wise
sentences, thou art nothing inferior to those accomplished
Dons of Spain. The spirit of chivalry forsake me for
ever, when I forget thy singing the song of Macheath [6],
which declares that he might be *happy with either*, situated
between those two ancient spinsters—when I forget the

---

[1] Stephen is a character in Jonson's *Every Man in his Humour*, Cokes
in Jonson's *Bartholomew Fair*, Aguecheek in *Twelfth Night*, and Shallow
and Silence in *2 K. Henry IV.*

[2] Ramsay, Keeper of the London Library.

[3] Sharp, a well-known abolitionist (1735–1813).

[4] By Rich. Barnfield.

[5] A Spaniard in *Love's Labour's Lost.* Quisada is another form of Don
Quixote.

[6] The highwayman in Gay's *Beggar's Opera.*

inimitable formal love which thou didst make, turning now to the one, and now to the other, with that Malvolian smile—as if Cervantes, not Gay, had written it for his hero; and as if thousands of periods must revolve, before the mirror of courtesy could have given his invidious preference between a pair of so goodly-propertied and meritorious-equal damsels.

To descend from these altitudes, and not to protract our Fools' Banquet beyond its appropriate day, for I fear the second of April is not many hours' distant—in sober verity I will confess a truth to thee, reader. I love a *Fool*—as naturally as if I were of kith and kin to him. When a child, with child-like apprehensions, that dived not below the surface of the matter, I read those Parables —not guessing at the involved wisdom—I had more yearnings towards that simple architect, that built his house upon the sand, than I entertained for his more cautious neighbour: I grudged at the hard censure pronounced upon the quiet soul that kept his talent; and— prizing their simplicity beyond the more provident, and, to my apprehension, somewhat *unfeminine* wariness of their competitors—I felt a kindliness, that almost amounted to a *tendre*, for those five thoughtless virgins.—I have never made an acquaintance since, that lasted, or a friendship that answered with any that had not some tincture of the absurd in their characters. I venerate an honest obliquity of understanding. The more laughable blunders a man shall commit in your company, the more tests he giveth you that he will not betray or overreach you. I love the safety which a palpable hallucination warrants; the security, which a word out of reason ratifies. And take my word for this, reader, and say a fool told it you, if you please, that he who hath not a dram of folly in his mixture, hath pounds of much worse matter in his composition. It is observed that "the foolisher the fowl or

fish,—woodcocks,—dotterels—cods' heads, &c., the finer
the flesh thereof", and what are commonly the world's
received fools but such whereof the world is not worthy?
and what have been some of the kindliest patterns of our
species, but so many darlings of absurdity, minions of the
goddess, and her white boys?—Reader, if you wrest my
words beyond their fair construction, it is you, and not I,
that are the *April Fool*.

XLV. MRS. BATTLE'S OPINIONS ON WHIST.

A CLEAR fire, a clean hearth,[1] and the rigour of the
game." This was the celebrated *wish* of old Sarah
Battle (now with God), who, next to her devotions, loved
a good game of whist. She was none of your lukewarm
gamesters, your half-and-half players, who have no objection to take a hand, if you want one to make up a rubber;
who affirm that they have no pleasure in winning; that
they like to win one game and lose another; that they
can while away an hour very agreeably at a card-table,
but are indifferent whether they play or no; and will
desire an adversary, who has slipped a wrong card, to
take it up and play another.[2] These insufferable triflers
are the curse of a table. One of these flies will spoil a
whole pot. Of such it may be said that they do not play
at cards, but only play at playing at them.

Sarah Battle was none of that breed. She detested
them, as I do, from her heart and soul, and would not,
save upon a striking emergency, willingly seat herself at
the same table with them. She loved a thorough-paced
partner, a determined enemy. She took, and gave, no
concessions. She hated favours. She never made a

[1 This was before the introduction of rugs, reader. You must remember the intolerable crash of the unswept cinders betwixt your foot
and the marble.]

[2 As if a sportsman should tell you he liked to kill a fox one day and
lose him the next.]

revoke, nor ever passed it over in her adversary without exacting the utmost forfeiture. She fought a good fight: cut and thrust. She held not her good sword (her cards) "like a dancer". She sate bolt upright; and neither showed you her cards, nor desired to see yours. All people have their blind side—their superstitions; and I have heard her declare, under the rose, that Hearts was her favourite suit.

I never in my life—and I knew Sarah Battle many of the best years of it—saw her take out her snuff-box when it was her turn to play; or snuff a candle in the middle of a game; or ring for a servant, till it was fairly over. She never introduced, or connived at, miscellaneous conversation during its process. As she emphatically observed, cards were cards; and if I ever saw unmingled distaste in her fine last-century countenance, it was at the airs of a young gentleman of a literary turn, who had been with difficulty persuaded to take a hand; and who, in his excess of candour, declared, that he thought there was no harm in unbending the mind now and then, after serious studies, in recreations of that kind! She could not bear to have her noble occupation, to which she wound up her faculties, considered in that light. It was her business, her duty, the thing she came into the world to do—and she did it. She unbent her mind afterwards—over a book.

Pope was her favourite author: his Rape of the Lock her favourite work. She once did me the favour to play over with me (with the cards) his celebrated game of Ombre in that poem; and to explain to me how far it agreed with, and in what points it would be found to differ from, tradrille. Her illustrations were apposite and poignant; and I had the pleasure of sending the substance of them to Mr. Bowles[1]; but I suppose they came too

---

[1] William Lisle Bowles (1762–1850), published an edition of Pope in 1807.

late to be inserted among his ingenious notes upon that author.

Quadrille, she has often told me, was her first love; but whist had engaged her maturer esteem. The former, she said, was showy and specious, and likely to allure young persons. The uncertainty and quick shifting of partners—a thing which the constancy of whist abhors; the dazzling supremacy and regal investiture of Spadille [1] —absurd, as she justly observed, in the pure aristocracy of whist, where his crown and garter give him no proper power above his brother-nobility of the Aces:—the giddy vanity, so taking to the inexperienced, of playing alone; above all, the overpowering attractions of a *Sans Prendre Vole* [2]—to the triumph of which there is certainly nothing parallel or approaching in the contingencies of whist;— all these, she would say, make quadrille a game of capti- vation to the young and enthusiastic. But whist was the *solider* game; that was her word. It was a long meal; not like quadrille, a feast of snatches. One or two rub- bers might co-extend in duration with an evening. They gave time to form rooted friendships, to cultivate steady enmities. She despised the chance-started, capricious, and ever fluctuating alliances of the other. The skir- mishes of quadrille, she would say, reminded her of the petty ephemeral embroilments of the little Italian states, depicted by Machiavel; perpetually changing postures and connections ; kissing and scratching in a breath :—but the wars of whist were comparable to the long, steady, deep- rooted, rational antipathies of the great French and Eng- lish nations.

A grave simplicity was what she chiefly admired in her favourite game. There was nothing silly in it, like the

---

[1] The ace of spades.
[2] A technical phrase in the game of Ombre, meaning to win all the possible stakes on the board.

nob in cribbage—nothing superfluous. No *flushes*—that most irrational of all pleas that a reasonable being can set up:—that anyone should claim four by virtue of holding cards of the same mark and colour, without reference to the playing of the game, or the individual worth or pretensions of the cards themselves! She held this to be a solecism; as pitiful an ambition at cards as alliteration is in authorship. She despised superficiality, and looked deeper than the colours of things. Suits were soldiers, she would say, and must have an uniformity of array to distinguish them: but what should we say to a foolish squire, who should claim a merit from dressing up his tenantry in red jackets, that never were to be marshalled—never to take the field? She even wished that whist were more simple than it is; and, in my mind, would have stripped it of some appendages, which, in the state of human frailty, may be venially, and even commendably, allowed of. She saw no reason for the deciding of the trump by the turn of the card. Why not one suit always trumps? Why two colours, when the mark of the suit would have sufficiently distinguished them without it?

"But the eye, my dear madam, is agreeably refreshed with the variety. Man is not a creature of pure reason— he must have his senses delightfully appealed to. We see it in Roman Catholic countries, where the music and the paintings draw in many to worship, whom your Quaker spirit of unsensualizing would have kept out. You yourself have a pretty collection of paintings—but confess to me, whether, walking in your gallery at Sandham, among those clear Vandykes, or among the Paul Potters in the ante-room, you ever felt your bosom glow with an elegant delight, at all comparable to *that* you have it in your power to experience most evenings over a well-arranged assortment of the court-cards?—the pretty antic habits, like heralds in a procession—the gay triumph-assuring scarlets—the contrasting deadly-killing sables—the 'hoary majesty of spades'—Pam [1] in all his glory!

"All these might be dispensed with; and with their naked names upon the drab pasteboard, the game might go on very well, pictureless. But the *beauty* of cards would be extinguished for ever. Stripped of all that is imaginative in them, they must degenerate into mere gambling. Imagine a dull deal board, or drum head, to spread them on, instead of that nice verdant carpet (next to nature's), fittest arena for those courtly combatants to play their gallant jousts and tourneys in! Exchange those delicately-turned ivory markers—(work of Chinese artist, unconscious of their symbol,—or as profanely slighting their true application as the arrantest Ephesian journeyman that turned out those little shrines for the goddess)—exchange them for little bits of leather (our ancestors' money), or chalk and a slate!"

The old lady, with a smile, confessed the soundness of my logic; and to her approbation of my arguments on her favourite topic that evening, I have always fancied myself indebted for the legacy of a curious cribbage-board, made of the finest Sienna marble, which her maternal uncle (old Walter Plumer, whom I have elsewhere celebrated) brought with him from Florence:—this, and a trifle of five hundred pounds, came to me at her death.

The former bequest (which I do not least value) I have kept with religious care; though she herself, to confess a truth, was never greatly taken with cribbage. It was an essentially vulgar game, I have heard her say,—disputing with her uncle, who was very partial to it. She would never heartily bring her mouth to pronounce "*Go*",

---

[1] A term for the knave of clubs in the game of Loo.

or " *That's a go* ". She called it an ungrammatical game.
The pegging teased her. I once knew her to forfeit a
rubber (a five-dollar stake) because she would not take
advantage of the turn-up knave, which would have given
it her, but which she must have claimed by the disgrace-
ful tenure of declaring " *two for his heels* ". There is
something extremely genteel in this sort of self-denial.
Sarah Battle was a gentlewoman born.

Piquet she held the best game at the cards for two
persons, though she would ridicule the pedantry of the
terms—such as pique—repique—the capot—they savoured
(she thought) of affectation. But games for two, or even
three, she never greatly cared for. She loved the quadrate
or square. She would argue thus:—Cards are warfare:
the ends are gain, with glory. But cards are war, in disguise of a sport: when single adversaries encounter, the
ends proposed are too palpable. By themselves, it is too
close a fight; with spectators, it is not much bettered.
No looker-on can be interested, except for a bet, and
then it is a mere affair of money; he cares not for your
luck *sympathetically*, or for your play. Three are still
worse; a mere naked war of every man against every man,
as in cribbage, without league or alliance; or a rotation
of petty and contradictory interests, a succession of heartless leagues, and not much more hearty infractions of
them, as in tradrille. But in square games (*she meant
whist*), all that is possible to be attained in card-playing
is accomplished. There are the incentives of profit with
honour, common to every species—though the *latter* can
be but very imperfectly enjoyed in those other games,
where the spectator is only feebly a participator. But
the parties in whist are spectators and principals too.
They are a theatre to themselves, and a looker-on is not
wanted. He is rather worse than nothing, and an impertinence. Whist abhors neutrality, or interests beyond

its sphere. You glory in some surprising stroke of skill
or fortune, not because a cold—or even an interested—
bystander witnesses it, but because your *partner* sympa-
thizes in the contingency. You win for two, you triumph
for two. Two are exalted. Two again are mortified;
which divides their disgrace, as the conjunction doubles
(by taking off the invidiousness) your glories. Two losing
to two are better reconciled, than one to one in that
close butchery. The hostile feeling is weakened by
multiplying the channels. War becomes a civil game.
By such reasonings as these the old lady was accustomed
to defend her favourite pastime.

No inducement could ever prevail upon her to play at
any game, where chance entered into the composition,
for nothing. Chance, she would argue—and here, again,
admire the subtlety of her conclusion;—chance is nothing,
but where something else depends upon it. It is obvious
that cannot be *glory.* What rational cause of exultation
could it give to a man to turn up size ace a hundred
times together by himself, or before spectators, where no
stake was depending? Make a lottery of a hundred
thousand tickets with but one fortunate number, and what
possible principle of our nature, except stupid wonder-
ment, could it gratify to gain that number as many times
successively without a prize? Therefore she disliked the
mixture of chance in backgammon, where it was not played
for money. She called it foolish, and those people idiots,
who were taken with a lucky hit under such circumstances.
Games of pure skill were as little to her fancy. Played
for a stake, they were a mere system of over-reaching.
Played for glory, they were a mere setting of one man's
wit—his memory, or combination-faculty rather—against
another's; like a mock-engagement at a review, bloodless
and profitless. She could not conceive a game wanting
the spritely infusion of chance, the handsome excuses of

good fortune. Two people playing at chess in a corner of a room, whilst whist was stirring in the centre, would inspire her with insufferable horror and ennui. Those well-cut similitudes of Castles and Knights, the *imagery* of the board, she would argue (and I think in this case justly), were entirely misplaced and senseless. Those hard-head contests can in no instance ally with the fancy. They reject form and colour. A pencil and dry slate (she used to say) were the proper arena for such combatants.

To those puny objectors against cards, as nurturing the bad passions, she would retort, that man is a gaming animal. He must be always trying to get the better in something or other—that this passion can scarcely be more safely expended than upon a game at cards: that cards are a temporary illusion; in truth, a mere drama; for we do but *play* at being mightily concerned, where a few idle shillings are at stake, yet, during the illusion, we are as mightily concerned as those whose stake is crowns and kingdoms. They are a sort of dream-fighting; much ado; great battling, and little bloodshed; mighty means for disproportioned ends: quite as diverting, and a great deal more innoxious, than many of those more serious *games* of life, which men play without esteeming them to be such.

With great deference to the old lady's judgment in these matters, I think I have experienced some moments in my life, when playing at cards *for nothing* has even been agreeable. When I am in sickness, or not in the best spirits, I sometimes call for the cards, and play a game at piquet *for love* with my cousin Bridget—Bridget Elia[1].

I grant there is something sneaking in it; but with a toothache, or a sprained ankle—when you are subdued and humble,—you are glad to put up with an inferior spring of action.

The essayist's sister, Mary Lamb.

There is such a thing in nature, I am convinced, as *sick whist.*

I grant it is not the highest style of man—I deprecate the manes of Sarah Battle—she lives not, alas! to whom I should apologize.

At such times, those terms which my old friend objected to, come in as something admissible. I love to get a tierce or a quatorze, though they mean nothing. I am subdued to an inferior interest. Those shadows of winning amuse me.

That last game I had with my sweet cousin (I capotted her)—(dare I tell thee how foolish I am?)—I wished it might have lasted for ever, though we gained nothing, and lost nothing, though it was a mere shade of play: I would be content to go on in that idle folly for ever. The pipkin should be ever boiling, that was to prepare the gentle lenitive to my foot, which Bridget was doomed to apply after the game was over; and, as I do not much relish appliances, there it should ever bubble. Bridget and I should be ever playing.

XLVI. DREAM CHILDREN: A REVERIE.

CHILDREN love to listen to stories about their elders, when *they* were children; to stretch their imagination to the conception of a traditionary great-uncle, or grandame, whom they never saw. It was in this spirit that my little ones crept about me the other evening to hear about their great-grandmother Field[1], who lived in a great house in Norfolk (a hundred times bigger than that in which they and papa lived), which had been the scene—so at least it was generally believed in that part of the country —of the tragic incidents which they had lately become familiar with from the ballad of the Children in the Wood.

[1] Mary Field, the essayist's grandmother.

Certain it is that the whole story of the children and their cruel uncle was to be seen fairly carved out in wood upon the chimney-piece of the great hall, the whole story down to the Robin Redbreasts; till a foolish rich person pulled it down to set up a marble one of modern invention in its stead, with no story upon it. Here Alice put out one of her dear mother's looks, too tender to be called upbraiding. Then I went on to say how religious and how good their great-grandmother Field was, how beloved and respected by everybody, though she was not indeed the mistress of this great house, but had only the charge of it (and yet in some respects she might be said to be the mistress of it too) committed to her by the owner, who preferred living in a newer and more fashionable mansion which he had purchased somewhere in the adjoining county; but still she lived in it in a manner as if it had been her own, and kept up the dignity of the great house in a sort while she lived, which afterwards came to decay, and was nearly pulled down, and all its old ornaments stripped and carried away to the owner's other house, where they were set up, and looked as awkward as if someone were to carry away the old tombs they had seen lately at the Abbey, and stick them up in Lady C.'s tawdry gilt drawing-room. Here John smiled, as much as to say, "that would be foolish indeed". And then I told how, when she came to die, her funeral was attended by a concourse of all the poor, and some of the gentry too, of the neighbourhood for many miles round, to show their respect for her memory, because she had been such a good and religious woman; so good, indeed, that she knew all the Psaltery by heart, ay, and a great part of the Testament besides. Here little Alice spread her hands. Then I told what a tall, upright, graceful person their great-grandmother Field once was; and how in her youth she was esteemed the best dancer—here Alice's little right foot

played an involuntary movement, till, upon my looking
grave, it desisted—the best dancer, I was saying, in the
county, till a cruel disease, called a cancer, came, and
bowed her down with pain; but it could never bend her
good spirits, or make them stoop, but they were still upright, because she was so good and religious.   Then I
told how she was used to sleep by herself in a lone chamber of the great lone house; and how she believed that
an apparition of two infants was to be seen at midnight
gliding up and down the great staircase near where she
slept, but she said, "those innocents would do her no
harm"; and how frightened I used to be, though in those
days I had my maid to sleep with me, because I was never
half so good or religious as she—and yet I never saw the
infants.   Here John expanded all his eyebrows and tried
to look courageous.   Then I told how good she was to
all her grandchildren, having us to the great house in the
holidays, where I in particular used to spend many hours
by myself, in gazing upon the old busts of the twelve
Cæsars, that had been Emperors of Rome, till the old
marble heads would seem to live again, or I to be turned
into marble with them; how I never could be tired with
roaming about that huge mansion, with its vast empty
rooms, with their worn-out hangings, fluttering tapestry,
and carved oaken panels, with the gilding almost rubbed
out—sometimes in the spacious old-fashioned gardens,
which I had almost to myself, unless when now and then
a solitary gardening man would cross me—and how the
nectarines and peaches hung upon the walls, without my
ever offering to pluck them—and because I had more
pleasure in strolling about among the old melancholy-
looking yew-trees, or the firs, and picking up the red
berries, and the fir-apples, which were good for nothing
but to look at—or in lying about on the fresh grass with
all the fine garden smells around me—or basking in the

orangery, till I could almost fancy myself ripening too
along with the oranges and the limes in that grateful
warmth—or in watching the dace that darted to and fro
in the fish-pond, at the bottom of the garden, with here
and there a great sulky pike hanging midway down the
water in silent state, as if it mocked at their impertinent
friskings,—I had more pleasure in those busy-idle diversions than in all the sweet flavours of peaches, nectarines,
oranges, and such-like common baits of children. Here
John slily deposited back upon the plate a bunch of
grapes, which, not unobserved by Alice, he had meditated
dividing with her, and both seemed willing to relinquish
them for the present as irrelevant. Then, in somewhat
a more heightened tone, I told how, though their great-
grandmother Field loved all her grandchildren, yet in an
especial manner she might be said to love their uncle,
John L——[1], because he was so handsome and spirited a
youth, and a king to the rest of us; and instead of moping
about in solitary corners, like some of us, he would mount
the most mettlesome horse he could get, when but an imp
no bigger than themselves, and make him carry him half
over the county in a morning, and join the hunters when
there were any out—and yet he loved the old great house
and gardens too, but had too much spirit to be always
pent up within their boundaries—and how their uncle
grew up to man's estate as brave as he was handsome,
to the admiration of everybody, but of their great-grandmother Field most especially; and how he used to carry
me upon his back when I was a lame-footed boy—for he
was a good bit older than me—many a mile when I could
not walk for pain;—and how in after-life he became lame-
footed too, and I did not always (I fear) make allowances
enough for him when he was impatient and in pain, nor

---

[1] Elia's brother, who died in 1821, the year before the publication of
this essay in the *London Magazine*.

remember sufficiently how considerate he had been to me
when I was lame-footed, and how when he died, though
he had not been dead an hour, it seemed as if he had
died a great while ago, such a distance there is betwixt
life and death; and how I bore his death as I thought
pretty well at first, but afterwards it haunted and haunted
me; and though I did not cry or take it to heart as some
do, and as I think he would have done if I had died, yet
I missed him all day long, and knew not till then how
much I had loved him. I missed his kindness, and I
missed his crossness, and wished him to be alive again,
to be quarrelling with him (for we quarrelled sometimes),
rather than not have him again, and was as uneasy without
him, as he, their poor uncle, must have been when the
doctor took off his limb. Here the children fell a-crying,
and asked if their little mourning which they had on was
not for uncle John, and they looked up, and prayed me not
to go on about their uncle, but to tell them some stories
about their pretty dead mother. Then I told how for
seven long years, in hope sometimes, sometimes in despair,
yet persisting ever, I courted the fair Alice W--n[1]; and
as much as children could understand, I explained to
them what coyness, and difficulty, and denial, meant in
maidens—when suddenly turning to Alice, the soul of the
first Alice looked out at her eyes with such a reality of
representment, that I became in doubt which of them
stood there before me, or whose that bright hair was; and
while I stood gazing, both the children gradually grew
fainter to my view, receding, and still receding, till nothing
at last but two mournful features were seen in the utter-
most distance, which, without speech, strangely impressed
upon me the effects of speech: "We are not of Alice, nor
of thee, nor are we children at all. The children of Alice

---

[1] Alice Winterton, the name under which Lamb alludes in his essays
to his first love, Ann Simmons.

call Bartrum[1] father. We are nothing; less than nothing,
and dreams. We are only what might have been, and
must wait upon the tedious shores of Lethe millions of
ages before we have existence, and a name"—and immediately awaking, I found myself quietly seated in my
bachelor arm-chair, where I had fallen asleep, with the
faithful Bridget unchanged by my side—but John L——
(or James Elia) was gone for ever.

XLVII. THE CONVALESCENT.

A PRETTY severe fit of indisposition which, under the
name of a nervous fever, has made a prisoner of me
for some weeks past, and is but slowly leaving me, has
reduced me to an incapacity of reflecting upon any topic
foreign to itself. Expect no healthy conclusions from me
this month, reader; I can offer you only sick men's
dreams.

And truly the whole state of sickness is such; for what
else is it but a magnificent dream for a man to lie a-bed,
and draw daylight curtains about him; and, shutting out
the sun, to induce a total oblivion of all the works which
are going on under it? To become insensible to all
the operations of life, except the beatings of one feeble
pulse?

If there be a regal solitude, it is a sick-bed. How the
patient lords it there; what caprices he acts without control! how king-like he sways his pillow—tumbling, and
tossing, and shifting, and lowering, and thumping, and
flatting, and moulding it, to the ever-varying requisitions
of his throbbing temples!

He changes sides oftener than a politician. Now he
lies full length, then half length, obliquely, transversely,
head and feet quite across the bed; and none accuses

---

[1] Bartrum was the real name of the husband of "Alice W—n".

him of tergiversation. Within the four curtains he is absolute. They are his Mare Clausum.

How sickness enlarges the dimensions of a man's self to himself! He is his own exclusive object. Supreme selfishness is inculcated upon him as his only duty. 'Tis the Two Tables of the Law to him. He has nothing to think of but how to get well. What passes out of doors, or within them, so he hear not the jarring of them, affects him not.

A little while ago he was greatly concerned in the event of a lawsuit, which was to be the making or the marring of his dearest friend. He was to be seen trudging about upon this man's errand to fifty quarters of the town at once, jogging this witness, refreshing that solicitor. The cause was to come on yesterday. He is absolutely as indifferent to the decision as if it were a question to be tried at Pekin. Peradventure from some whispering, going on about the house, not intended for his hearing, he picks up enough to make him understand that things went cross-grained in the court yesterday, and his friend is ruined. But the word "friend", and the word "ruin", disturb him no more than so much jargon. He is not to think of anything but how to get better.

What a world of foreign cares are merged in that absorbing consideration!

He has put on the strong armour of sickness, he is wrapped in the callous hide of suffering; he keeps his sympathy, like some curious vintage, under trusty lock and key, for his own use only.

He lies pitying himself, honing and moaning to himself; he yearneth over himself; his bowels are even melted within him, to think what he suffers; he is not ashamed to weep over himself.

He is for ever plotting how to do some good to himself; studying little stratagems and artificial alleviations.

He makes the most of himself; dividing himself, by an allowable fiction, into as many distinct individuals as he hath sore and sorrowing members. Sometimes he meditates—as of a thing apart from him—upon his poor aching head, and that dull pain which, dozing or waking, lay in it all the past night like a log, or palpable substance of pain, not to be removed without opening the very skull, as it seemed, to take it thence. Or he pities his long, clammy, attenuated fingers. He compassionates himself all over; and his bed is a very discipline of humanity, and tender heart.

He is his own sympathizer; and instinctively feels that none can so well perform that office for him. He cares for few spectators to his tragedy. Only that punctual face of the old nurse pleases him, that announces his broths and his cordials. He likes it because it is so unmoved, and because he can pour forth his feverish ejaculations before it as unreservedly as to his bed-post.

To the world's business he is dead. He understands not what the callings and occupations of mortals are; only he has a glimmering conceit of some such thing, when the doctor makes his daily call; and even in the lines on that busy face he reads no multiplicity of patients, but solely conceives of himself as *the sick man*. To what other uneasy couch the good man is hastening, when he slips out of his chamber, folding up his thin douceur so carefully, for fear of rustling—is no speculation which he can at present entertain. He thinks only of the regular return of the same phenomenon at the same hour to-morrow.

Household rumours touch him not. Some faint murmur, indicative of life going on within the house, soothes him, while he knows not distinctly what it is. He is not to know anything, not to think of anything. Servants gliding up or down the distant staircase, treading as

upon velvet, gently keep his ear awake, so long as he
troubles not himself further than with some feeble guess
at their errands.   Exacter knowledge would be a burthen
to him; he can just endure the pressure of conjecture.
He opens his eye faintly at the dull stroke of the
muffled knocker, and closes it again without asking
"Who was it?"   He is flattered by a general notion
that inquiries are making after him, but he cares not to
know the name of the inquirer.   In the general stillness,
and awful hush of the house, he lies in state, and feels
his sovereignty.

To be sick is to enjoy monarchal prerogatives.   Compare the silent tread and quiet ministry, almost by the
eye only, with which he is served—with the careless de-
meanour, the unceremonious goings in and out (slapping
of doors, or leaving them open) of the very same attendants, when he is getting a little better—and you will
confess that from the bed of sickness (throne let me
rather call it) to the elbow-chair of convalescence, is a fall
from dignity, amounting to a deposition.

How convalescence shrinks a man back to his pristine
stature!   Where is now the space, which he occupied so
lately, in his own, in the family's eye?

The scene of his regalities, his sick-room, which was
his presence chamber, where he lay and acted his despotic
fancies—how is it reduced to a common bed-room!   The
trimness of the very bed has something petty and un-
meaning of it.   It is *made* every day.   How unlike to
that wavy, many-furrowed, oceanic surface, which it presented so short a time since, when to *make* it was a service
not to be thought of at oftener than three or four day
revolutions, when the patient was with pain and grief to
be lifted for a little while out of it, to submit to the en-
croachments of unwelcome neatness, and decencies which
his shaken frame deprecated; then to be lifted into it

again, for another three or four days' respite, to flounder
it out of shape again, while every fresh furrow was an
historical record of some shifting posture, some uneasy
turning, some seeking for a little ease; and the shrunken
skin scarce told a truer story than the crumpled cover-
lid.

Hushed are those mysterious sighs—those groans—
so much more awful, while we knew not from what
caverns of vast hidden suffering they proceeded. The
Lernean pangs are quenched. The riddle of sickness
is solved; and Philoctetes is become an ordinary per-
sonage.

Perhaps some relic of the sick man's dream of greatness
survives in the still lingering visitations of the medical
attendant. But how is he, too, changed with everything
else? Can this be he—this man of news—of chat—of
anecdote—of everything but physic—can this be he, who
so lately came between the patient and his cruel enemy,
as on some solemn embassy from Nature, erecting himself into a high meditating party?—Pshaw! 'tis some old
woman.

Farewell with him all that made sickness pompous—the
spell that hushed the household—the desert-like stillness,
felt throughout its inmost chambers—the mute attendance
—the inquiry by looks—the still softer delicacies of self-
attention—the sole and single eye of distemper alonely
fixed upon itself—world-thoughts excluded—the man a
world unto himself—his own theatre—

What a speck is he dwindled into!

In this flat swamp of convalescence, left by the ebb of
sickness, yet far enough from the terra-firma of established
health, your note, dear Editor, reached me, requesting—
an article. In Articulo Mortis, thought I; but it is something hard—and the quibble, wretched as it was, relieved

me. The summons, unseasonable as it appeared, seemed
to link me on again to the petty businesses of life, which
I had lost sight of; a gentle call to activity, however
trivial; a wholesome weaning from that preposterous
dream of self-absorption—the puffy state of sickness—in
which I confess to have lain so long, insensible to the
magazines and monarchies of the world alike; to its laws,
and to its literature. The hypochondriac flatus is sub-
siding; the acres, which in imagination I had spread over
—for the sick man swells in the sole contemplation of
his single sufferings, till he becomes a Tityus to himself—
are wasting to a span, and for the giant of self-importance,
which I was so lately, you have me once again in my
natural pretensions—the lean and meagre figure of your
insignificant Essayist.

XLVIII. DETACHED THOUGHTS ON BOOKS AND READING.

To mind the inside of a book is to entertain one's self with the forced
product of another man's brain. Now, I think a man of quality and
breeding may be much amused with the natural sprouts of his own.—
Lord Foppington, in " The Relapse". [1]

AN ingenious acquaintance of my own was so much
struck with this bright sally of his Lordship, that he
has left off reading altogether, to the great improvement
of his originality. At the hazard of losing some credit
on this head, I must confess that I dedicate no inconsiderable portion of my time to other people's thoughts. I
dream away my life in others' speculations. I love to
lose myself in other men's minds. When I am not walking, I am reading; I cannot sit and think. Books think
for me.

I have no repugnances. Shaftesbury is not too genteel
for me, nor Jonathan Wild too low. I can read any-

[1] A play by Sir John Vanbrugh, 1697.

thing which I call *a book*. There are things in that shape which I cannot allow for such.

In this catalogue of *books which are no books*—biblia a-biblia—I reckon Court Calendars, Directories, Pocket Books, Draught Boards, bound and lettered on the back, Scientific Treatises, Almanacs, Statutes at Large: the works of Hume, Gibbon, Robertson, Beattie, Soame Jenyns [1], and generally, all those volumes which "no gentleman's library should be without": the Histories of Flavius Josephus (that learned Jew), and Paley's Moral Philosophy. With these exceptions, I can read almost anything. I bless my stars for a taste so catholic, so unexcluding.

I confess that it moves my spleen to see these *things in books' clothing* perched upon shelves, like false saints, usurpers of true shrines, intruders into the sanctuary, thrusting out the legitimate occupants. To reach down a well-bound semblance of a volume, and hope it some kind-hearted play-book, then, opening what "seem its leaves", to come bolt upon a withering Population Essay. To expect a Steele or a Farquhar, and find—Adam Smith. To view a well-arranged assortment of blockheaded Encyclopædias (Anglicanas or Metropolitanas) set out in an array of russia, or morocco, when a tithe of that good leather would comfortably re-clothe my shivering folios, would renovate Paracelsus himself, and enable old Raymund Lully to look like himself again in the world. I never see these impostors, but I long to strip them, to warm my ragged veterans in their spoils.

To be strong-backed and neat-bound is the desideratum of a volume. Magnificence comes after. This, when it can be afforded, is not to be lavished upon all kinds of books indiscriminately. I would not dress a set of

---

[1] 1704–1787. Author of *A Free Inquiry into the Nature and Origin of Evil.*

magazines, for instance, in full suit. The dishabille, or
half binding (with russia backs ever) is *our* costume. A
Shakespeare or a Milton (unless the first editions), it
were mere foppery to trick out in gay apparel. The
possession of them confers no distinction. The exterior
of them (the things themselves being so common), strange
to say, raises no sweet emotions, no tickling sense of
property in the owner. Thomson's Seasons, again, looks
best (I maintain it) a little torn and dog's-eared. How
beautiful to a genuine lover of reading are the sullied
leaves, and worn-out appearance, nay, the very odour
(beyond russia) if we would not forget kind feelings in
fastidiousness, of an old "Circulating Library" Tom
Jones, or Vicar of Wakefield! How they speak of the
thousand thumbs that have turned over their pages with
delight!—of the lone sempstress, whom they may have
cheered (milliner, or hard-working mantua-maker) after
her long day's needle-toil, running far into midnight, when
she has snatched an hour, ill spared from sleep, to steep
her cares, as in some Lethean cup, in spelling out their
enchanting contents! Who would have them a whit less
soiled? What better condition could we desire to see
them in?

In some respects the better a book is, the less it demands from binding. Fielding, Smollett, Sterne, and
all that class of perpetually self-reproductive volumes—
Great Nature's Stereotypes—we see them individually
perish with less regret, because we know the copies of
them to be "eterne". But whère a book is at once both
good and rare—where the individual is almost the species,
and when *that* perishes,

> We know not where is that Promethean torch
> That can its light relumine,—

such a book, for instance, as the Life of the Duke of

Newcastle, by his Duchess—no casket is rich enough, no
casing sufficiently durable, to honour and keep safe such
a jewel.

Not only rare volumes of this description, which seem
hopeless ever to be reprinted, but old editions of writers,
such as Sir Philip Sidney, Bishop Taylor, Milton in his
prose works, Fuller—of whom we *have* reprints, yet the
books themselves, though they go about, and are talked
of here and there, we know have not endenizened themselves (nor possibly ever will) in the national heart, so as
to become stock books—it is good to possess these in
good and costly covers.   I do not care for a First Folio
of Shakespeare.   (You cannot make a *pet* book of an
author whom everybody reads.)   I rather prefer the
common editions of Rowe and Tonson, without notes,
and with *plates*, which, being so execrably bad, serve as
maps or modest remembrancers, to the text; and, without
pretending to any supposable emulation with it, are so
much better than the Shakespeare gallery engravings
which *did*.   I have a community of feeling with my
countrymen about his Plays, and I like those editions of
him best which have been oftenest tumbled about and
handled.   On the contrary I cannot read Beaumont and
Fletcher but in Folio.   The Octavo editions are painful
to look at, I have no sympathy with them.   If they were
as much read as the current editions of the other poet,
I should prefer them in that shape to the older one.   I
do not know a more heartless sight than the reprint of
the Anatomy of Melancholy.   What need was there of
unearthing the bones of that fantastic old great man, to
expose them in a winding-sheet of the newest fashion to
modern censure? what hapless stationer could dream of
Burton ever becoming popular?   The wretched Malone
could not do worse, when he bribed the sexton of Strat-
ford Church to let him whitewash the painted effigy of old

Shakespeare, which stood there, in rude but lively fashion
depicted, to the very colour of the cheek, the eye, the
eyebrow, hair, the very dress he used to wear—the only
authentic testimony we had, however imperfect, of these
curious parts and parcels of him. They covered him
over with a coat of white paint. By —, if I had been
a justice of peace for Warwickshire, I would have clapt
both commentator and sexton fast in the stocks, for a pair
of meddling sacrilegious varlets.

I think I see them at their work—these sapient trouble-
tombs.

Shall I be thought fantastical if I confess that the names
of some of our poets sound sweeter, and have a finer
relish to the ear—to mine, at least—than that of Milton
or of Shakespeare? It may be that the latter are more
staled and rung upon in common discourse. The sweet-
est names, and which carry a perfume in the mention, are
Kit Marlowe, Drayton, Drummond of Hawthornden, and
Cowley.

Much depends upon *when* and *where* you read a book.
In the five or six impatient minutes, before the dinner is
quite ready, who would think of taking up the Fairy
Queen for a stop-gap, or a volume of Bishop Andrewes'[1]
sermons?

Milton almost requires a solemn service of music to be
played before you enter upon him. But he brings his
music, to which, who listens, had need bring docile
thoughts, and purged ears.

Winter evenings,—the world shut out—with less of
ceremony the gentle Shakespeare enters. At such a
season the Tempest, or his own Winter's Tale.

These two poets you cannot avoid reading aloud—to
yourself, or (as it chances) to some single person listening.
More than one—and it degenerates into an audience.

---

[1] Bishop of Winchester. His Sermons were published in 1628.

Books of quick interest, that hurry on for incidents, are for the eye to glide over only. It will not do to read them out. I could never listen to even the better kind of modern novels without extreme irksomeness.

A newspaper, read out, is intolerable. In some of the Bank offices it is the custom (to save so much individual time) for one of the clerks—who is the best scholar—to commence upon the *Times* or the *Chronicle* and recite its entire contents aloud, *pro bono publico*. With every advantage of lungs and elocution, the effect is singularly vapid. In barbers' shops and public-houses, a fellow will get up and spell out a paragraph, which he communicates as some discovery. Another follows, with *his* selection. So the entire journal transpires at length by piecemeal. Seldom-readers are slow readers, and without this expedient, no one in the company would probably ever travel through the contents of a whole paper.

Newspapers always excite curiosity. No one ever lays one down without a feeling of disappointment.

What an eternal time that gentleman in black, at Nando's[1], keeps the paper! I am sick of hearing the waiter bawling out incessantly, "The *Chronicle* is in hand, Sir".

(As in these little diurnals I generally skip the Foreign News, the Debates and the Politics, I find the *Morning Herald* by far the most entertaining of them. It is an agreeable miscellany rather than a newspaper.)

Coming into an inn at night—having ordered your supper—what can be more delightful than to find lying in the window-seat, left there time out of mind by the carelessness of some former guest—two or three numbers of the old Town and Country Magazine, with its amusing *tête-à-tête* pictures—"The Royal Lover and Lady G—", "The Melting Platonic and the old Beau",—and such·

---

[1] A coffee-house at 17 Fleet Street.

like antiquated scandal? Would you exchange it—at that time, and in that place—for a better book?

Poor Tobin[1], who latterly fell blind, did not regret it so much for the weightier kinds of reading—the Paradise Lost, or Comus, he could have *read* to him—but he missed the pleasure of skimming over with his own eye a magazine, or a light pamphlet.

I should not care to be caught in the serious avenues of some cathedral alone, and reading *Candide*.

I do not remember a more whimsical surprise than having been once detected—by a familiar damsel—reclined at my ease upon the grass, on Primrose Hill (her Cythera), reading—*Pamela*. There was nothing in the book to make a man seriously ashamed at the exposure; but as she seated herself down by me, and seemed determined to read in company, I could have wished it had been—any other book. We read on very sociably for a few pages; and, not finding the author much to her taste, she got up, and—went away. Gentle casuist, I leave it to thee to conjecture, whether the blush (for there was one between us) was the property of the nymph or the swain in this dilemma. From me you shall never get the secret.

I am not much of a friend to out-of-doors reading. I cannot settle my spirits to it. I knew a Unitarian minister, who was generally to be seen upon Snow Hill (as yet Skinner's Street *was not*), between the hours of ten and eleven in the morning, studying a volume of Lardner[2]. I own this to have been a strain of abstraction beyond my reach. I used to admire how he sidled along, keeping clear of secular contacts. An illiterate encounter with a porter's knot, or a bread-basket, would have quickly put to flight all the theology I am master of, and have left me worse than indifferent to the five points

---

[1] John Tobin, a dramatist (1770–1804).
[2] A theological writer (1684–1768).

(I was once amused—there is a pleasure in affecting affectation—at the indignation of a crowd that was jostling in with me at the pit-door of Covent Garden Theatre, to have a sight of Master Betty—then at once in his dawn and his meridian—in *Hamlet.* I had been invited, quite unexpectedly, to join a party, whom I met near the door of the playhouse, and I happened to have in my hand a large octavo of Johnson and Steevens's *Shakespeare,* which, the time not admitting of my carrying it home, of course went with me to the theatre. Just in the very heat and pressure of the doors opening—the *rush,* as they term it —I deliberately held the volume over my head, open at the scene in which the young Roscius had been most cried up, and quietly read by the lamp-light. The clamour became universal. "The affectation of the fellow," cried one. "Look at that gentleman *reading,* Papa," squeaked a young lady, who, in her admiration of the novelty, almost forgot her fears. I read on. "He ought to have his book knocked out of his hand," exclaimed a pursy cit, whose arms were too fast pinioned to his side to suffer him to execute his kind intention. Still I read on—and, till the time came to pay my money, kept as unmoved as Saint Anthony at his holy offices, with the satyrs, apes, and hobgoblins mopping and making mouths at him, in the picture, while the good man sits as undisturbed at the sight as if he were the sole tenant of the desert. The individual rabble (I recognized more than one of their ugly faces) had damned a slight piece of mine a few nights before, and I was determined the culprits should not a second time put me out of countenance.)

There is a class of street readers, whom I can never contemplate without affection—the poor gentry, who, not having wherewithal to buy or hire a book, filch a little learning at the open stalls—the owner, with his hard eye, casting envious looks at them all the while, and thinking

when they will have done. Venturing tenderly, page after
page, expecting every moment when he shall interpose his
interdict, and yet unable to deny themselves the gratifica-
tion, they "snatch a fearful joy". Martin B—[1] in this
way, by daily fragments, got through two volumes of
Clarissa, when the stall-keeper damped his laudable ambition, by asking him (it was in his younger days) whether
he meant to purchase the work. M. declares that under
no circumstance in his life did he ever peruse a book
with half the satisfaction which he took in those uneasy
snatches. A quaint poetess[2] of our day has moralized
upon this subject in two very touching but homely
stanzas:

> I saw a boy with eager eye
> Open a book upon a stall,
> And read, as he'd devour it all;
> Which, when the stall-man did espy,
> Soon to the boy I heard him call,
> "You, sir, you never buy a book,
> Therefore in one you shall not look".
> The boy pass'd slowly on, and with a sigh
> He wish'd he never had been taught to read,
> Then of the old churl's books he should have had no need.
>
> Of sufferings the poor have many,
> Which never can the rich annoy.
> I soon perceived another boy,
> Who look'd as if he had not any
> Food, for that day at least,—enjoy
> The sight of cold meat in a tavern larder.
> This boy's case, then thought I, is surely harder,
> Thus hungry, longing, thus without a penny,
> Beholding choice of dainty-dressed meat:
> No wonder if he wished he ne'er had learn'd to eat.

[1] The son of Admiral Burney, an intimate friend of Lamb.
[2] Mary Lamb.

XLIX. REJOICINGS UPON THE NEW YEAR'S COMING OF AGE.

THE *Old Year* being dead, and the *New Year* coming of age, which he does, by Calendar Law, as soon as the breath is out of the old gentleman's body, nothing would serve the young spark but he must give a dinner upon the occasion, to which all the *Days* in the year were invited. The *Festivals*, whom he deputed as his stewards, were mightily taken with the notion. They had been engaged time out of mind, they said, in providing mirth and good cheer for mortals below; and it was time they should have a taste of their own bounty. It was stiffly debated among them whether the *Fasts* should be admitted. Some said the appearance of such lean, starved guests, with their mortified faces, would pervert the ends of the meeting. But the objection was overruled by *Christmas Day*, who had a design upon *Ash Wednesday* (as you shall hear), and a mighty desire to see how the old Domine would behave himself in his cups. Only the *Vigils* were requested to come with their lanterns, to light the gentlefolks home at night.

All the *Days* came to their day. Covers were provided for three hundred and sixty-five guests at the principal table, with an occasional knife and fork at the side-board for the *Twenty-Ninth of February*.

I should have told you that cards of invitation had been issued. The carriers were the *Hours*: twelve little, merry, whirligig foot-pages, as you should desire to see, that went all round, and found out the persons invited well enough, with the exception of *Easter Day, Shrove Tuesday*, and a few such *Movables*, who had lately shifted their quarters.

Well, they all met at last—foul *Days*, fine *Days*, all sorts of *Days*, and a rare din they made of it. There was nothing but, Hail! fellow *Day*, well met—brother *Day*—sister *Day*—only *Lady Day* kept a little on the aloof, and seemed somewhat scornful. Yet some said *Twelfth Day* cut her out and out, for she came in a tiffany suit, white and gold, like a queen on a frostcake, all royal, glittering, and *Epiphanous*. The rest came, some in green, some in white—but old *Lent and his family* were not yet out of mourning. Rainy *Days* came in, dripping; and sunshiny *Days* helped them to change their stockings. *Wedding Day* was there in his marriage finery, a little the worse for wear. *Pay Day* came late, as he always does; and *Doomsday* sent word—he might be expected.

April Fool (as my young lord's jester) took upon himself to marshal the guests, and wild work he made with it. It would have posed old Erra Pater[1] to have found out any given *Day* in the year to erect a scheme upon —good *Days*, bad *Days*, were so shuffled together, to the confounding of all sober horoscopy.

He had stuck the *Twenty-First of June* next to the *Twenty-Second of December*, and the former looked like a Maypole siding a marrow-bone. *Ash Wednesday* got wedged in (as was concerted) betwixt *Christmas* and *Lord Mayor's Day*. Lord! how he laid about him! Nothing but barons of beef and turkeys would go down with him.—to the great greasing and detriment of his new sackcloth bib and tucker. And still *Christmas Day* was at his elbow, plying with him the wassail-bowl, till he roared and hiccupp'd, and protested there was no faith in dried ling, but commended it to the devil for a sour, windy, acrimonious, censorious, hy-po-crit-crit — critical mess, and no dish for a gentleman. Then he dipt his fist into the middle of the great custard that stood before his *left-hand neighbour*, and daubed his hungry beard all over

---

[1] A proverbial name for an almanac, cf. *Hudibras*, Pt. I. Can. i. l. 120.

with it, till you would have taken him for the *Last Day in December*, it so hung in icicles.

At another part of the table *Shrove Tuesday* was helping the *Second of September* to some cock broth, which courtesy the latter returned with the delicate thigh of a hen pheasant—so there was no love lost for that matter. The *Last of Lent* was spunging upon *Shrove-tide's* pancakes; which *April Fool* perceiving, told him that he did well, for pancakes were proper to a *good fry-day*.

In another part, a hubbub arose about the *Thirtieth of January*, who, it seems, being a sour, puritanic character, that thought nobody's meat good or sanctified enough for him, had smuggled into the room a calf's head[1], which he had had cooked at home for that purpose, thinking to feast thereon incontinently; but as it lay in the dish, *March Manyweathers*, who is a very fine lady, and subject to the meagrims, screamed out there was a " 'human head' in the platter ", and raved about Herodias' daughter to that degree that the obnoxious viand was obliged to be removed, nor did she recover her stomach till she had gulped down a *Restorative*, confected of *Oak Apple*, which the merry *Twenty-Ninth of May* always carries about with him for that purpose.

The King's Health being called for after this, a notable dispute arose between the *Twelfth of August*[2] (a zealous old Whig gentlewoman) and the *Twenty-Third of April*[3] (a new-fangled woman of the Tory stamp), as to which of them should have the honour to propose it. *August* grew hot upon the matter, affirming time out of mind the prescriptive right to have lain with her, till her rival had basely supplanted her; whom she represented as little

---

[1] An allusion to the Calves' Head Club, which celebrated the anniversary of Charles's execution by dining on this dish.

[2] The birthday of George IV.

[3] The festival of St. George.

better than a *kept* mistress who went about in *fine clothes*, while she (the legitimate Birthday) had scarcely a rag, &c.

April Fool, being made mediator, confirmed the right, in the strongest form of words, to the appellant, but decided for peace' sake that the exercise of it should remain with the present possessor. At the same time, he slyly rounded the first lady in the ear, that an action might lie against the Crown for *bi-geny*.

It beginning to grow a little duskish, *Candlemas* lustily bawled out for lights, which was opposed by all the *Days*, who protested against burning daylight. Then fair water was handed round in silver ewers, and the *same lady* was observed to take an unusual time in *Washing* herself.

May Day, with that sweetness which is peculiar to her, in a neat speech proposing the health of the founder, crowned her goblet (and by her example the rest of the company) with garlands. This being done, the lordly *New Year*, from the upper end of the table, in a cordial but somewhat lofty tone, returned thanks. He felt proud on an occasion of meeting so many of his worthy father's late tenants, promised to improve their farms, and at the same time to abate (if anything was found unreasonable) in their rents.

At the mention of this, the four *Quarter Days* involuntarily looked at each other, and smiled; *April Fool* whistled to an old tune of "New Brooms"; and a surly old rebel at the farther end of the table (who was discovered to be no other than the *Fifth of November*) muttered out, distinctly enough to be heard by the whole company, words to this effect—that "when the old one is gone, he is a fool that looks for a better". Which rudeness of his, the guests resenting, unanimously voted his expulsion; and the malcontent was thrust out neck and heels into the cellar, as the properest place for such a *boutefeu* and firebrand as he had shown himself to be.

Order being restored, the young lord (who, to say truth, had been a little ruffled, and put beside his oratory) in as few and yet as obliging words as possible, assured them of entire welcome; and, with a graceful turn, singling out poor *Twenty-Ninth of February*, that had sate all this while mumchance at the sideboard, begged to couple his health with that of the good company before him, which he drank accordingly; observing that he had not seen his honest face any time these four years, with a number of endearing expressions besides. At the same time removing the solitary *Day* from the forlorn seat which had been assigned him, he stationed him at his own board, somewhere between the *Greek Calends* and *Latter Lammas*.

Ash Wednesday, being now called upon for a song, with his eyes fast stuck in his head, and as well as the Canary he had swallowed would give him leave, struck up a Carol, which *Christmas Day* had taught him for the nonce; and was followed by the latter, who gave "Miserere" in fine style, hitting off the mumping notes and lengthened drawl of *Old Mortification* with infinite humour. *April Fool* swore they had exchanged conditions; but *Good Friday* was observed to look extremely grave, and *Sunday* held her fan before her face that she might not be seen to smile.

Shrove-tide, Lord Mayor's Day, and *April Fool* next joined in a glee—

Which is the properest day to drink?[1]

in which all the Days chiming in, made a merry burden.

They next fell to quibbles and conundrums. The question being proposed, who had the greatest number of followers? The *Quarter Days* said there could be no

[1] The first line of an old Ranelagh catch.

question as to that; for they had all the creditors in the world dogging their heels. But *April Fool* gave it in favour of the *Forty Days before Easter*; because the debtors in all cases outnumbered the creditors, and they kept *Lent* all the year.

All this while *Valentine's Day* kept courting pretty *May*, who sate next him, slipping amorous *billets-doux* under the table, till the *Dog Days* (who are naturally of a warm constitution) began to be jealous, and to bark and rage exceedingly. *April Fool*, who likes a bit of sport above measure, and had some pretensions to the lady besides, as being but a cousin once removed, clapped and halloo'd them on; and as fast as their indignation cooled, those mad wags, the *Ember Days*, were at it with their bellows, to blow it into a flame; and all was in a ferment, till old Madam *Septuagesima* (who boasts herself the *Mother of the Days*) wisely diverted the conversation with a tedious tale of the lovers which she could reckon when she was young, and of one, Master *Rogation Day*, in particular, who was for ever putting the *question* to her; but she kept him at a distance, as the chronicle would tell, by which I apprehend she meant the Almanac. Then she rambled on to the *Days that were gone*, the *good old Days*, and so to the *Days before the Flood*—which plainly showed her old head to be little better than crazed and doited.

Day being ended, the *Days* called for their cloaks and greatcoats, and took their leave. *Lord Mayor's Day* went off in a mist as usual; *Shortest Day* in a deep black fog, that wrapt the little gentleman all round like a hedgehog. Two *Vigils*—so watchmen are called in heaven— saw *Christmas Day* safe home—they had been used to the business before. Another *Vigil*—a stout, sturdy patrole, called the *Eve of St. Christopher*—seeing *Ash Wednesday* in a condition little better than he should be,

e'en whipt him over his shoulders, pick-a-back fashion:
and *Old Mortification* went floating home singing:

On the bat's back I do fly,

and a number of old snatches besides, between drunk
and sober; but very few Aves or Penitentiaries (you may
believe me) were among them. *Longest Day* set off west-
ward in beautiful crimson and gold; the rest, some in one
fashion, some in another; but *Valentine* and pretty *May*
took their departure together in one of the prettiest
silvery twilights a Lover's Day could wish to set in.